ZEN MASTER TALES

ZEN MASTER TALES

Stories from the Lives of

TAIGU, SENGAI, HAKUIN, AND RYŌKAN

PETER HASKEL

SHAMBHALA

Shambhala Publications, Inc.
2129 13th Street
Boulder, Colorado 80302
www.shambhala.com

Cover art: Matsumoto Hoji
Cover design: Daniel Urban-Brown
Interior design: Claudine Mansour Design

9 8 7 6 5 4 3 2 1

First Edition
Printed in the United States of America

∞ This edition is printed on acid-free paper that meets
the American National Standards Institute Z39.48 Standard.

♻ This book is printed on 30% postconsumer recycled paper.
For more information please visit www.shambhala.com.

Shambhala Publications is distributed worldwide by
Penguin Random House, Inc., and its subsidiaries.

Library of Congress Cataloging-in-Publication Data

Names: Haskel, Peter, author.
Title: Zen master tales: stories from the lives of Taigu, Sengai, Hakuin, and Ryōkan /
Peter Haskel.
Description: Boulder: Shambhala, 2022. | Includes bibliographical references and index.
Identifiers: LCCN 2021025328 | ISBN 9781611809602 (trade paperback)
Subjects: LCSH: Zen Buddhism—Anecdotes. | Zen stories.
Classification: LCC BQ9265.6 .H375 2022 | DDC 294.3/927—dc23
LC record available at https://lccn.loc.gov/2021025328

For Hannah

Ye men of gloom and austerity, who paint the face
of Infinite Benevolence with an eternal frown;
read in the Everlasting Book, wide open to your view,
the lesson it would teach. Its pictures are not in black
and somber hues, but bright and glowing tints;
its music—save when you drown it—is not in sighs
and groans, but songs and cheerful sounds.
Listen to the million voices in the summer air, and
find one dismal as your own. Remember if ye can,
the sense of hope and pleasure which every glad return of
day awakens in the breast of all your kind who have
not changed their nature; and learn some wisdom . . .
when their hearts are lifted up they know not why
by all the mirth and happiness it brings.

—CHARLES DICKENS,
Barnaby Rudge, 1841

Meaning comes not from systems of thought
but from stories.

—LORD JONATHAN SACKS

CONTENTS

INTRODUCTION

When I was pursuing my graduate studies at Columbia, the university's specialist in Chinese and Japanese Zen was Philip B. Yampolsky, a formidable and exacting scholar of Zen history who also served as the director of the East Asian Library. With his curling mustache, sideburns, and perpetual scowl, he had the intimidating appearance of an antebellum riverboat gambler or, for some of his Japanese subordinates, a *sengoku daimyo*, one of the samurai warlords whose perpetual feuding terrified late fifteenth- and sixteenth-century Japan.

My dissertation, many years in the making, dealt with Bankei Yōtaku (1622–1693) and certain of his Zen contemporaries, all eccentric and colorful individuals, like Bankei himself, and the subjects of many anecdotes and legends. I submitted the draft to Professor Yampolsky in his office, a cozy aerie overlooking the old wood-paneled library. Chewing on a well-worn cigar, he paged carefully through my offering, starting, as always, with the endnotes. As he proceeded through the text, his face gradually flushed a bright red. Finally he looked up from beneath beetling brows and riveted me with an accusing stare.

"But these are just stories!" he protested. "They're not history . . ."

Of course he was right. Crestfallen, I slunk back to the library and began the task of reworking my paper along strictly academic lines, a sobering but invaluable learning experience. In a lighter vein, and perhaps to buoy my flagging spirits, Professor Yampolsky phoned me the next day to suggest that I might retain these portions for the future, something I could pick up again "after my dissertation," and I have always promised myself to do just that.

Even now, at a remove of some forty years, I confess that such stories—as that is to varying degrees what they are—still charm me. Indeed I plead guilty to finding more "Zen" in them by and large than in the more factual—or at least historically verifiable—records of Zen in premodern Japan. Casual readers who share these feelings are quite welcome to skip the following introduction and the individual biographies for each section and simply go right to the stories themselves, which are, after all, the core of the book.

In my defense, Zen, from its still misty beginnings in China, where it is read "Chan," has been deeply intertwined with its myths, its tales and "stories." Indeed, it is the preservation and celebration of these that have imparted to the teaching much of its distinctiveness and appeal. Put another way, it is stories and their enduring fascination that lie at the heart of so much that has come to be associated with Zen and its development.

Among Chan's most familiar myths are the stories surrounding Bodhidharma (d. 528?), the semilegendary South Indian monk and putative First Patriarch of Chinese Chan. Carrying the teaching from India to China, crossing the Yangtze River on a single slender reed, he is said to have spent nine years meditating before the wall of a cliff. There, he is approached by an aspiring pupil, the monk Huike (487–593), later Chan's Second Patriarch, who stands in the snow ignored by the Indian master till Huike cuts off an arm to demonstrate his sincerity.[1]

Other such stories lie at the heart of what might be called Chan's founding scripture, the *Platform Sutra*. Despite the many references to celebrated texts from the Buddhist canon, certain elements make the *Platform Sutra* distinct and distinctively Chinese. Notably, this is the only sutra dealing specifically with a

Chan school, and the only sutra that purports to convey not the teachings of Shakyamuni, the historical Buddha, or another Indian buddha or bodhisattva, but those of an ordinary Chinese individual, a "living buddha" present in a particular time and place. In the text, set in the early Tang dynasty (618–907), Huineng, an illiterate layman peddling firewood in the market, is suddenly enlightened on hearing a line from the *Diamond Sutra*: "Manifest the mind that does not attach anywhere." He then goes to the temple of the Fifth Patriarch, Hongren (600–674), where he is relegated to work as a kind of human treadmill hulling the monastery rice.[2] One day Hongren challenges his students to compose a verse expressing their understanding of Chan. The temple's senior monk, Shenxiu (605–706), brushes his submission on a public wall, and seeing it, Huineng begs a lettered monk to read it to him and then inscribe his reply. The upshot is that Hongren secretly summons Huineng in the dark of night and picks him from among the eminent monks of his assembly to become the sixth (and last numbered) Chinese patriarch, his successor in Chan. Huineng, fleeing his jealous brethren, secludes himself in the forest among a band of hunters, ultimately emerging to champion the mind-to-mind transmission of sudden enlightenment passed on from Bodhidharma himself.[3]

This direct and mysterious transmission from teacher to disciple is the central theme of the collections of Chan biographies that appear in China in the tenth and early eleventh centuries. These deploy dramatic stories that frequently feature the lightning give-and-take of encounter dialogues between various protagonists. The earliest of these compendia, the *Patriarchs' Hall Collection* (*Zutang ji*, 952),[4] appeared in the closing years of the Five Dynasties period (907–942), a brief but, for Chan, critical time of social and political upheaval between the collapse of the Tang dynasty and the founding of the Song dynasty (960–1279). Called "the oldest extant history of Chan,"[5] the *Patriarchs' Hall* was followed by collections of Chan biographies that purport to chronicle the "transmission of the lamp" of intuitive wisdom from master to disciple, most notably the *Jingde Transmission of the Lamp* (*Jingde chuandeng lu*) of 1004 and its 1036 successor *Extensive Tiensheng Transmission of the Lamp* (*Tiensheng guangdeng lu*).[6] The latter collection, the *Guangdeng lu*, aims to make the case for the superiority of not just Chan among other schools of Chinese Buddhism but of a particular line, that of Mazu Daoyi (709–788), with whom Chan as we know it is sometimes said to begin and whose methods for teaching might include beating students with a stick, shouting at them, and pulling them violently by their noses.[7]

The seemingly gratuitous displays of violence and abuse in the records of Mazu and his descendants may at first glance seem shocking or offensive. They were intended to be so. Such forceful words and acts have been regarded by generations of East Asian readers not as instances of random aggression but as prods to awakening. They are thought of as a means of dramatically short-circuiting the delusive framework that separates us from reality, a sort of intervention to startle students awake. The roughhousing is closer in spirit to the Marx Brothers or Laurel and Hardy than to the blind violence and invective of a street brawl. Zen's "barnyard" quality, as one scholar terms it, was especially appealing to the well-bred and highly educated members of China's bureaucratic elite. Indeed, this roughness is itself part of Zen's distinct urgency and charm, hard-hitting and direct, but hardly an endorsement of or invitation to brutality for its own sake.

In the *Guangdeng lu*, Mazu is hailed as the spiritual descendent of Bodhidharma and the Sixth Patriarch, Huineng, as well as the spiritual progenitor of Linji Yixuan (d. 866), revered as the most illustrious representative of the Mazu line. The inclusion of a preface by the Song emperor Renzong (r. 1022–1063) lends the collection and its particular view of Linji Chan as the school's single orthodox teaching something of an official imprimatur.[8]

Such transmission accounts (*deng lu*), whose depictions of Chan teachers and their interactions with students and with one another grow increasingly more outré, lead in turn to works devoted to the teachings of a single Tang- or Five Dynasties–era Chan master. Known as *yu lu* (J. *goroku*), records of words or sayings (though including a variety of wordless responses), the prime example of these texts is the record of Linji Yixuan, for whom the Linji (J. Rinzai) school, which ultimately dominated Song Chan, is named.[9] Linji's record, the *Linji lu*, is notable for elements of the "madcap" Chan frequently associated in the popular imagination with the later Tang and Five Dynasties masters. An example is the following account of the death of Linji's obstreperous colleague Puhua (d. 860), who was known for wandering the streets and ringing a small bell:

> One day Puhua went about the streets asking people he met for a one-piece gown [a typical sewn Chinese monk's outfit]. They all offered him one, but he declined them all. Linji had the steward of the temple buy a coffin, and when Puhua came back, the Master said, "I've fixed up a one-piece gown for you."
>
> Puhua put the coffin on his shoulders and went around the streets calling out, "Linji fixed me up a one-piece gown. I'm going to the East Gate to depart this life." All the townspeople scrambled after him to watch.
>
> "No, not today," said Puhua, "but tomorrow I'll go to the South Gate to depart this life." [Again,] all the townspeople scrambled after him to watch.
>
> After Puhua had done the same thing for three days, no one believed him anymore. On the fourth

day, not a single person followed him to watch. He
went outside the town walls all by himself, got into
the coffin, and asked a passerby to nail it up. The news
immediately got about. The townspeople all came
scrambling; upon opening the coffin, they saw he had
vanished, body and all. Only the sound of his bell
could be heard in the sky, receding away: tinkle . . .
tinkle . . . tinkle . . .[10]

Familiar as they are to students of Chan, many of the episodes
described in the Chan classics and noted above are patently fiction, not fact. Even the moving story of Huineng in the *Platform
Sutra* has been characterized as "a brilliant and religiously mean-
ingful bit of fiction."[11] Yet some intangible quality about these
stories has captured the imagination of generations of Zen adepts, and continues to do so. Inherent in all these texts is the
notion that the transmission and what is transmitted must be
living, direct, constantly functioning, like a ball tossed spontaneously back and forth among players. As Iriya Yoshitaka, the
late scholar of Chinese language and Zen, observes in speaking of
Mazu, Chan insists on the manifestation in daily activity of one's
concrete experience of reality.[12] As such, the "words and deeds,"
the tales of the old masters, however seemingly exaggerated or
farfetched, are viewed as revelations, testimony to the ancients'
profound understanding of things as they are.

As with so many of the figures from the "golden age of Chan"
in the Tang and Five Dynasties periods, our specific knowledge
of Mazu's and Linji's often brash words and unorthodox teaching methods derives exclusively from later, primarily Song dynasty sources. Recent scholarship in both East Asia and the West
has begun to upend the accepted, frequently sectarian picture
of Chan as descending directly from the masters depicted in
classics such as the *Record of Linji*. Albert Welter, for example,

makes a strong argument that Mazu, Linji, and the whole cast of "hero Chan masters" from Chan's golden age are for the most part "myths," created retrospectively by chroniclers in early Song China.[13] The chroniclers' purpose was to offer a fresh, dynamic, and at times raw and outspoken teaching that would appeal to the cultural and political power brokers of the new age, inaugurating a new Chan orthodoxy, that of the Linji line. By deftly inserting this revolutionary picture of Tang Chan into the framework of a dimly remembered past, the new teaching was endowed with both a history and a pedigree, however specious and contrived.

The Linji record, as we have it, Welter contends, is "not a reflection of Linji the man and his teachings" but "a carefully drawn formulation at the hands of later storytellers." In part, this development was culturally determined, attributable to a "Chinese penchant for fictionalization in history and biography, coupled with the importance of stories."[14]

At present, all that can be said with certainty is that the records of the eighth- and ninth-century Chan masters, with their arsenal of impulsive antics and wild words, exist in written form from at least the cusp of the Song dynasty. But whether these narratives, and the vivid world they conjure up, predate their tenth- and eleventh-century chronicles, and if so, by how much, remains a vexing and possibly unanswerable question.

The koan (gong'an) method, which has dominated much of Zen since the Song dynasty, centers also on narratives of uncertain authenticity: the responses, spoken or otherwise, of the revered teachers of the past, particularly the masters of the preceding Tang and Five Dynasties periods, recorded in classic Chinese koan collections such as the *Blue Cliff Record* (*Biyan lu*, 1128) and *Gateless Gate* (*Wumen guan*, 1229).[15] These collections include brief interlinear comments (*hsialu*) that introduce a new idiom to the literature of Chan, a distinctive and deliberately jarring juxtaposition of Buddhist terminology with elements drawn from literary and popular Chinese culture, including proverbs, imprecations, and other expressions heavily imbued with the slang of the period. ("You don't know the smell of your own shit!" "Washing a dirt clod in mud." "Dragging each other into a fire pit.")[16]

The *Blue Cliff Record* opens with the koan "Zhaozhou's '*Wu!*,'" which, with the Linji master Dahui Zonggao (1089–1163), revered as the koan method's foremost proponent in Song China, became a principal entrance for koan study and remains so today.[17]

> Zhaozhou was asked by a monk "Does a dog have
> buddha nature or doesn't it?"
> Zhaozhou said, "*Wu!*" (J. *Mu!*; literally, "no," "it
> doesn't," etc.).[18]

Dahui urged his students to focus unremittingly in their meditation practice on the *huatou*, the "nub," "crux," or "essence" of the koan (here, for example, Zhaozhou's answer, "*Wu!*").[19] This, Dahui held, led in turn to "great doubt" (*dayi*), an all-consuming existential struggle with the koan, culminating in "great satori" (*dawu*), an ecstatic spiritual breakthrough into the original nature of things that overturns all the student's prior experiences of reality. "You may be assailed by doubts," Dahui wrote to one of his students, "doubts by the thousands, the tens of thousands; but all these will [resolve into] a single doubt. Just break through the doubt surrounding your huatou and instantly you'll shatter *all* your doubts. . . . Just take up the case 'A dog has no buddha nature. . . .' If you can penetrate this '*Wu!*' penetrate it immediately through and through, you won't need to go questioning others, asking about the Buddha's words, the patriarchs' words, the words of reverend masters everywhere, but will be forevermore enlightened about being and non-being."[20] While seated meditation, *zuoshan* (J. *zazen*), was crucial to this endeavor, most effective of all in sundering the barrier of the huatou, Dahui maintained, was uninterrupted practice amid one's daily activity.[21]

Like the fanciful episodes surrounding Bodhidharma, the Sixth Patriarch, and Puhua, the koan collections are most often stories of the past recalled, recorded, perhaps even contrived in later generations for the edification of Chan students. For such adepts, they are true, not in a literal but in a more compelling sense: they reveal in a quirky, enigmatic, and at times deliberately jolting fashion something about the human mind and its place in the universe that cannot be conveyed by mere words. It is this something, inherent in such stories, that has sustained the teaching in all its manifestations in East Asia over a millennium, first in China, then Korea, and lastly in Japan.

～

It is not the continent but Japan of the Edo period (1600–1867/68) that is the source of the materials presented here. Although also a premodern setting, it is one far distant in time and culture from the Tang and Song masters who formulated what we today know as Zen. But Iriya Yoshitaka's observation about Chinese Chan still holds true: Japanese Zen likewise established its "focus on the individual's ordinary activity as the function, the manifestation of the absolute."[22] Most of these Japanese stories, however unabashedly humorous and at times crude, impart something of the character of the Zen masters involved, whose attainment must be plainly manifest in even the most humble and unlikely of situations.

The new age inaugurated in 1600 by Tokugawa rule, though like its medieval precursors essentially a feudal society governed by a military elite, was to prove a period of unprecedented peace and prosperity for Japan. The Zen school, which had flourished during the preceding age of internecine warfare dubbed the

"Warring States" or Sengoku period (approximately 1467–1568), continued to receive the patronage of both the leading samurai clans, the emperor and imperial court, and the rising merchant class, whose chōnin, or townspeople, culture quickly came to dominate cities such as Edo (now Tokyo) and Osaka.

Zen and the other sects of Buddhism, however, found themselves under assault by a Confucian establishment that in many respects provided the ideological framework for the Tokugawa regime and its many powerful vassals. These included the daimyo, or hereditary clan chieftains, whose domains straddled the nation's seventy-two traditional provinces. Many Confucians carped that a teaching such as Zen, conducted largely in the isolation of temple precincts, had little to offer to the Japanese masses—the farmers and artisans who performed the actual productive functions that sustained Tokugawa society. As in Marxism, the merchant class was reviled by most Edo-era Confucians as little more than a parasite on the national body, and as such was relegated to the bottom rungs of the social order, together with the Buddhist priesthood.[23]

While nominally subscribing to the Confucian ethic that in theory underpinned Tokugawa society, Buddhism, including Zen—a particular object of Confucian ire—rarely rose to a spirited defense of its own teachings. Yet the frequent encounters in this period's Zen stories between Zen masters and ordinary men and women of all classes of Japanese society, and their preservation in written form by monks and laypersons, testify to a new integration of Zen with the world outside the temples and hermitages. The stories seem to attest, in a kind of implicit rebuttal to the Confucians, that if Zen is to function, it must function everywhere. If it is to work, it must work for everyone, from prostitutes and professional entertainers to daimyo, from the bartender to the rice farmer. Sengai carouses with the town drunk. Ryōkan spends his days playing ball with the village children and joins the locals in their all-night dances costumed as a flirtatious maiden. And Hakuin interacts freely with the common folk of his native Shizuoka, handing out koan and bringing his neighbors to satori, according to his testimony, with the aid of their own pungent dialect and slang.[24] Indeed, Hakuin celebrates in his art and writing the villagers' labors and pastimes, enthusing in the humor and raucousness that fill the rural society around him.

As my other Columbia advisor, Yoshito Hakeda, loved to point out, the protagonists of the Chinese Chan stories—even the untrammeled Mazu and the vituperative Linji—though memorably and dramatically presented in their records, remain somehow remote, semihagiographic figures. By contrast, the Zen masters who enliven many of the anecdotes culled from Edo Japan present themselves, seemingly at firsthand, warts and all. They appear as true-life personalities interacting within a vivid environment that stands forth in its own right in full color and detail. Additionally, one can't help remarking that the vast number of episodes in the classic Chinese records, apart from those few that record interactions with local commanders or officials, show the Tang and Song teachers primarily confronting other Chan monks and masters. By contrast, the tales surrounding Ryōkan, Sengai, and Hakuin, while offering many vignettes involving their priestly followers and disciples, are conspicuous for the number of ordinary villagers and townspeople, sometimes anonymous but often identified by their given names, who are a regular feature of such anecdotes. Only Taigu Sōchiku is probably an exception in this respect, being something of a misanthropist and dedicated loner.

Like many of their early Chinese counterparts, the Edo teachers assembled here tended to remain in provincial temples throughout most of their lives as Zen masters—Hakuin and Ryōkan in the vicinity of, respectively, their native Hara and Izumozaki, and Sengai in Hakata. Yet at least as depicted in the stories about them, all stayed in close contact with the local population, unlike the Chinese masters. (Again, Taigu is the exception, being reclusive in later life, and prior to that having spent time in Kyoto serving as abbot of Myōshinji and involved in the politics central to the life of the great Rinzai headquarters temple.)

Many of these features may reflect the "democratization" of Zen in Edo-period Japan. This was a development spurred in part by Confucian critiques of the teaching's lack of practical application to this-worldly concerns in the still largely agrarian society favored by Confucian scholars.[25] But it was also driven by the vigor of the emergent townspeople culture. It was this chōnin culture—emanating from the bustling cities of Edo and Osaka, from the metropolises' busy markets and trading houses and colorful entertainment districts—that came to dominate much of the distinctive, and distinctively Japanese, popular art forms that characterize the period of Tokugawa rule. These include haiku; Kabuki; *bunraku* (puppet dramas accompanied by music and narration); and *ukiyo-e*, the prints (and paintings) of the "floating world" of professional actors, sumo champions, courtesans, and the like who occupied a cult status among urbanites of the day.

One surprising aspect of some of the Japanese Zen stories in this period is the role played by women, who figure as serious Zen students in a land that was, and in many respects remains, a "man's world" (*otoko shakai*). Though generally relegated to the background, women in premodern Japan were not infrequently key figures in their families' business enterprises in the cities and towns. In the countryside they were crucial to many aspects of farming and crafts work. Even in typical warrior households, the samurai wife was indispensable to her husband's economic survival. Though we hear of few, if any, celebrated female Zen masters, prominent male teachers such as Bankei and Hakuin openly testify to the full ability of women, both lay and religious, to realize the deepest truths of Zen enlightenment.

During the Middle Ages, Zen, particularly Rinzai Zen, had been a form of Buddhism associated with the ruling elite in the capitals of Kamakura and Kyoto, a teaching carrying enormous "snob appeal." Only gradually in the fifteenth and sixteenth centuries, and largely because of its aristocratic associations, did Rinzai Zen begin to attract the patronage of provincial warlords and the rising merchant class in commercial centers such as Sakai. In the new age of Tokugawa rule, certain teachers seemed to sense that, as with literary and artistic culture, the time had arrived for Zen to be accessible to the common people, even in rural Japan. The essentials of zazen, koan study, and enlightenment, such masters affirmed, could be conveyed to all members of Japanese society, presented directly not in the classical Chinese-inflected language written and read by the temple monks but in the speech of ordinary Japanese, including even comic verse and work songs.

While this involved a certain recasting of the teaching, the aim was not a watered-down, accommodationist version of Zen practice and enlightenment simply incorporating familiar devotional beliefs that had persisted since the Middle Ages, such as the worship of redeeming buddhas and bodhisattvas like Amida (Amitabha) and Kannon (Avalokitesvara). While such popular accommodations were not wholly rejected, what was required, many masters maintained, was "the thing itself," the Zen mind, transmitted through generations of buddhas and patriarchs. Some sought to reinvent Zen practice as something for everyone, whatever their circumstances. Bankei Yōtaku, who attracted overflow crowds to his public lectures, famously dispensed with the koan as an artificial device and insisted on direct experience of the "Unborn Buddha Mind, brightly illuminating." Suzuki Shōsan (1579–1655), a former samurai whose warrior training imbues his teachings, sought to spread Zen among the different classes of Japanese society, not by vitiating it but by stripping it of what he viewed as extraneous elements. In the process, he concocted a teaching very much of its time and place—that is, Japan in the premodern period.

Hakuin Ekaku (1685–1769) too sought to make Zen available to men and women of every class, not by reinventing the teaching but by resurrecting it through a revival of the dynamic koan Zen of the Song masters such as Dahui and Xutang Zhiyu (1185–1269).[26] Presented by Hakuin in a popular format, Dahui-style koan study leading to sudden enlightenment was now the prerogative of Japanese from every station of life and no longer the preserve of priests, warlords, social-climbing commoners, and the like. Hence, Hakuin's later adoption of his own "Sound of One Hand" koan, in place of "*Wu!*"(*Mu!*). Hence, too, his multitude of vernacular works presented in popular contemporary format, embracing even supernatural elements such as possession by native deities. The same is true of Hakuin's humorous, fanciful brush paintings of religious and mundane subjects. The two at times combined, so that Kannon, the bodhisattva of mercy, is given the face of one of Hakuin's country neighbors,[27] while various other buddhas, bodhisattvas, Zen patriarchs, and even the stock Edo comic figure "Grandma" bear a suspicious resemblance to Hakuin himself in the master's occasional self-portraits.[28]

It is not hard to see how such creative and colorful personalities could lead to folk traditions surrounding Zen teachers with links to the common people of premodern Japan. Figures such as Hakuin, Taigu Ryōkan (1758–1831), and Sengai Gibon (1750–1837) came to be regarded as both Zen masters and beloved local characters about whom humorous, even outrageous accounts were soon circulating. Such tales hearken back to the late medieval Zen master and poet Ikkyū Sōjun (1394–1481), an unconventional figure crucial to the restoration of the great Kyoto headquarters temple Daitokuji. Ikkyū's at times outrageous behavior, including his open affair with a blind female courtesan, became the stuff of legend even in his lifetime, and during the Edo period, stories, often comic ones, surrounding the Zen master were published for popular consumption under the rubric *Ikkyūbanashi* (Ikkyū tales).[29]

Even in this relatively recent period of Zen's development, then, "stories" seem to have retained a certain importance, answering an unarticulated need on the part of both monks and laypeople. Hakuin, revered as Japanese Rinzai Zen's "second founder," shared in this as well, freely embroidering his many autobiographical writings with episodes that often strain belief. An example is Hakuin's well-known description of seeking out the anchorite Hakuyūshi in 1710 at Hakuyūshi's cave in the mountains of Shirakawa, east of Kyoto. Finding the young Zen monk physically and mentally depleted from his arduous koan practice, Hakuyūshi instructs Hakuin in a series of Taoist-inspired revitalizing meditation techniques, which enable Hakuin to persist in his quest and reputedly continue to sustain him through his long and exacting subsequent career.[30] Hakuin's account of his meeting with the mysterious Hakuyūshi, however, is now acknowledged by Japanese scholars to be an invention, devised by Hakuin to lend color to his narration, Hakuyūshi having fallen to his death from a cliff a year before the master claims to have visited him in his cave.[31]

Perhaps of more consequence, Hakuin's Dharma descendants, who by and large constitute what is today the Japanese Rinzai school, base their sect's lineage on yet another story, Hakuin's sanction and acknowledgment as heir by another of his teachers, the Zen master Shōju Rojin (Dōkyō Etan, 1642–1721), whom Hakuin met in 1708. The story is detailed in Hakuin's "authorized" biography, *Chronological Biography of the Zen Teacher Hakuin* (*Hakuin oshō nenpu*), by his Dharma heir Tōrei Enji (1721–1792), an undated text on which Hakuin is known to have closely collaborated. The work tells how the young Hakuin, following years of grueling practice on the "*Mu!*" koan under a succession of teachers, finally believes he has realized satori when, after ten days and nights of single-minded meditation, he happens to hear the evening gong of a nearby temple.[32] Having learned of Shōju's reputation, he then travels to present his hard-won realization to the old master at his temple in Iiyama, a village in the province of Shinano (now Nagano Prefecture). Shōju promptly disabuses him of the idea that he has attained satori and instead delivers a drubbing to the astonished Hakuin, who is knocked off the temple verandah and lands on the ground unconscious, to Shōju's loud laughter. Devastated, Hakuin nonetheless remains to study with Shōju and plods on with his koan practice.

After ten consecutive days and nights struggling with the "*Mu!*" koan, Hakuin is begging in the local village and positions himself before a particular house, whose elderly landlady, in no mood to provide alms, shouts at him to move along. But so preoccupied is Hakuin with his koan that he remains frozen to the spot, dazed and insensible to the old lady's abuse. Annoyed, she smacks the monk with a bamboo broom and at that moment Hakuin suddenly experiences satori. He rushes to Shōju, who instantly recognizes his attainment, acknowledging his enlightenment experience.[33]

Although he spent his entire teaching life in Shinano as an obscure country priest and became known to posterity primarily by way of Hakuin's writings, Shōju boasted an illustrious lineage through a branch of the Kyoto headquarters temple Myōshinji, a lineage tracing itself directly to the founders of the so-called Ōtōkan. This composite term refers to the three celebrated medieval teachers from whom the Rinzai school derives the authenticity of its transmission: Daiō, who carried from Song China the koan Zen of his teacher Xutang; Daiō's leading heir, Daitō (Shūhō Myōchō, 1282–1337), founder of the celebrated Kyoto headquarters temple Daitokuji; and Daitō's heir Kanzan Egen (1277–1360), founder of Myōshinji. Hakuin believed himself to be a reincarnation of Xutang and saw his mission as revitalizing the particular strain of Song koan Zen propagated by Daiō and his line, a strain that Hakuin regarded as the only authentic transmission of Zen brought to Japan from the continent.

In his writings, Hakuin vividly describes his eventual enlightenment under Shōju and the master's recognition of his realization, continually referring to Shōju as his principal teacher and praising Xutang and the celebrated Japanese members of Xutang's lineage. The latter include Shojū's teacher Shidō Mu'nan (or Bu'nan, 1603–1676),[34] an early popularizer of Zen, and Mu'nan's illustrious teacher Gudō Tōshoku (1579–1661), who had opposed the entry of Pure Land–inflected Ming Zen at Myōshinji and was close to the retired emperor Gomizuno'o (1596–1680), an important patron of Zen in seventeenth-century Japan.[35]

Again, however, modern scholarship has found no evidence that Shōju actually gave Hakuin *inka* (literally, "seal of approval"), a Zen master's formal written sanction of enlightenment. In Japanese Rinzai Zen, inka constitutes proof of a student's attainment and spiritual connection with a particular master, whose signature appears on the document along with the name of the student. Indeed, by his own admission, the young Hakuin stayed with Shōju a mere eight months before moving on to study with a variety of other Zen teachers in an effort to resolve his lingering spiritual doubts. And while Hakuin's writings quote admiringly from Shōju's teachings, Hakuin never again returned to see Shōju. In 1718, when Hakuin became a Zen master in the Myōshinji line, it was not as Shōju's heir but as heir to the heir of the local Zen monk who had first ordained the thirteen-year-old Hakuin—a succession practice common in Zen temples in premodern Japan.[36]

In spite of this, those within Hakuin's teaching lineage—one that embraces not only Hakuin's heirs and their immediate progeny but nearly all present-day Rinzai Zen masters—implicitly accept the notion that Hakuin received Shōju's sanction and was heir to his teaching of Zen. This claim cannot be documented, although it appears on any standard lineage chart of the Rinzai school. This lineage—traced back from the present day through Hakuin, Shōju, and the leading members of the Ōtōkan to Xutang, Linji, and the Sixth Patriarch—is recited routinely as part of the liturgy at Rinzai temples. As has often been noted, Rinzai Zen in Japan is Hakuin Zen. But while present-day Rinzai Zen's descent from Hakuin and his heirs is clearly delineated, Hakuin's own succession from his teacher is not. The modern Rinzai sect, which prides itself on indisputable evidence of succession from a given master to his disciple, seems to have suspended its normal standards of evidence for Hakuin's "story." This story, promulgated in Hakuin's later writings, substitutes for the usual proofs of Dharma succession a kind of retrospective spiritual identification with Shōju, emphasizing Hakuin's commitment to the revival of Xutang's brand of koan Zen, which Hakuin believed to be embodied by Shōju and his line.[37]

It should be noted that Hakuin's inventing, dramatizing, or distorting the details of his life in autobiographical works would have been considered in no way reprehensible in the Zen world of Edo Japan. Hakuin's purpose in the bulk of his many writings, his autobiographical works included, was not documentary, to clarify or nail down facts. It was rather to propagate Dahui's style of koan study, to urge the effectiveness of all-out submersion in the koan in order to spur numbers of men and women, lay and religious, to satori and to then exhort them to assist others and to extend their efforts so as to experience a lifetime of satoris large and small.

Hakuin seems to have delighted in formulating and even publishing many of his own tales. Most of the Zen stories translated here, however, were assembled by third parties, masters' disciples and their priestly descendants, or lay enthusiasts in the particular localities with which figures such as Sengai and Ryōkan were identified. As in the more formal Chinese records, the object of these often homespun Japanese narratives is to put on display the masters' manifestations of Zen in daily life. Unlike in China, though, there is a conspicuous emphasis on the Japanese Zen teachers' encounters with not merely students in a monastic setting but people of every stripe—the ordinary men and women, young and old, who populated the world outside the temples. It is precisely for this reason that such stories, however homely at times, were dear to those who remembered, retold, and recorded them: they constituted testimony to what was viewed as the enlightened nature of their colorful protagonists. Whether fact, legend, or a blending of both, such Zen stories were preserved in Japan because they suggest a special kind of dramatic synthesis. They narrate the perfect interpenetration of the worlds of enlightenment and common human experience, which the Zen teacher, by tradition, is expected to demonstrate in even his most humble activities and interactions.

This is also apparent in another aspect of many of the Zen stories that follow—namely, the element of humor. This particular facet of Zen can probably be traced back to its Chinese roots and in particular to the influence of philosophical Taoism and texts such as the *Zhuangzi* (fourth century B.C.E.), with its madcap dialogue and cast of deliberately outrageous eccentrics. But it is also a familiar feature of many of the tales surrounding figures such as Sengai and Ryōkan. The mind awakened to reality itself is frequently associated in the Zen records, and even the popular imagination, with a quirky hilarity—with "getting the joke." This cast of mind can be seen to pervade Sengai's and Hakuin's brush paintings, most especially in their depictions of Zen figures such as the First Patriarch, Bodhidharma, and the "laughing Buddha" Hotei (Ch. Budai, d. 916), with his ragged appearance and the huge cloth sack (*hotei*) from which he takes his name. The image of the sage as a preposterous old man convulsed with delight, a common idiom in both Taoism and Zen, is quite foreign to the dignified demeanor and occasional pathos expressive of holiness in most Eastern and Western religious traditions. Indeed, Zen may be the only religion in which carefree laughter and the expression of wisdom are so seamlessly intertwined.

⌣

My choice of stories to include in this volume was subjective, predicated on those I personally found to be most engaging while best lending themselves to translation. I have, for example, omitted many stories that were based on the punning and other wordplay so beloved of the Japanese, materials whose humor is often lost amid a welter of tiresome notes and explanations. I have also tried to avoid repeating text found in my earlier books. Hence the absence of any stories concerning Takuan and Tōsui and of materials from Itsuzan Sonin's *Dharma Words of Zen Master Bankei* (*Bankei zenji hōgo*) and Kera Yoshishige's *Curious Accounts of Zen Master Ryōkan* (*Ryōkan zenji kiwa*)—both rich firsthand sources for these beguiling figures but ones I've translated elsewhere.

In addition, the capsule biographies that precede the sections for each of the four Zen masters are not intended as exhaustive reviews of their lives and teachings. Rather, these are thumbnail sketches highlighting the salient aspects of the masters' careers and approaches to Zen, especially those that may help in appreciating the image of the masters presented in the accounts that have come to surround them. The treatment of Hakuin, in this respect, is somewhat more extensive, given his pivotal role in the subsequent history of Japanese Zen, as well as the abundance of (albeit often unverified) autobiographical material in his writings. Ryōkan's life is similarly treated at greater length due to the wide recognition the master received in Japan during the twentieth century and the plethora of studies and other works that accompanied this revival of interest.

For reasons of space and continuity in a work essentially devoted to stories, I have also deliberately passed over a number of subjects touched on in my previous books and exhaustively dealt with by Japanese scholars. Among these are the institutional development of Japanese Zen in the Kamakura, Muromachi, and Edo periods; the founding of the first Zen temples by émigré Chinese masters and Japanese monks returning from the continent; the tensions between the official Gozan, or "Five Mountains," temples and those Rinzai and Sōtō headquarters temples, such as Daitokuji and Myōshinji, Eiheiji and Sōjiji, which were largely outside the system and all of which became dominant in the Zen world of late medieval and Edo Japan; and changes in the Song koan Zen introduced by the temples' Chinese and Japanese founders, which in many cases came to resemble an Esoteric Buddhist–style secret oral transmission that continued into the Edo period itself. I've likewise omitted any discussion of the temple system of the Tokugawa *bakufu*, or military government, which sought to control the Buddhist sects, including Zen, while deploying the parish temples as enforcers in its ongoing persecution of Christianity in Japan. Zen masters, even eccentric ones such as Sengai, were not exempt from participation in the bakufu's "religious census" (sometimes referred to as *shūmon aratame*) and other measures aimed at rooting out hidden Christians.[38]

The book uses "Edo," the new capital of the Tokugawa shogunate and the site of present-day Tokyo, as a shorthand for "Edo period," as is often done with other important place names used to designate periods of Japanese history, including religious and cultural history. Examples are Kamakura and Muromachi—the former, the military capital of Japan from 1192 to 1333; the latter, a district of Kyoto that gave its name to the period of the Ashikaga shogunate, which ruled (though often in name only) from 1333 to 1573.

While this is a book on Japanese Zen personalities, I've opted by and large to use Chan when the context is plainly Chinese. *Master* is capitalized in the translations when referring to the particular Zen priest who is the subject at hand—that is, Taigu, Sengai, Hakuin, or Ryōkan. Otherwise it is lowercase.

This book involved the efforts of many organizations and persons. The First Zen Institute of America in New York City graciously made available to me its library and computer facilities. Maria Collora, Michael Hotz—my high school sidekick and now president of the First Zen Institute—John Storm, and Peeter Lamp all read the manuscript at various stages and offered countless valuable suggestions, as did my friend Dan Stevenson, professor of religion at the University of Kansas, who lent valuable perspective on the Chinese portions of the material. Ikuyo Nakagawa offered her help in untangling difficulties in certain of the Japanese texts, while the institute's Ian R. Chandler, Milan Nikolic, and Melissa Lebruin were always ready to augment my rudimentary computer skills. Matt Zepelin, Shambala's editor extraordinaire, assisted in skillfully shepherding the book from acquisition to publication. Thomas Y. Kirchner, a longtime Rinzai monk attached to Kyoto's Hanazono University International Research Institute for Zen Buddhism, kindly assisted me in assembling many of the Japanese materials. He and Jeff Shore, another distinguished member of Hanazono's faculty and a lay Zen master in the Rinzai school, made available the research facilities at the university's handsome library. But this book is really a tribute to the Zen priest and scholar Nōnin Kōdō, also a faculty member at Hanazono, who over the past years has performed a remarkable task of assembling, editing, and seeing to publication a mass of stories surrounding leading Edo-period Zen masters, including all those assembled here. This volume is a direct result of Nōnin's valuable and extensive work, from which I and others have greatly benefited.

—PETER HASKEL
New York City, Summer 2021

TAIGU
TALES

Springtime arrives in the human world
bestowing innumerable blessings
Each and every flower an offering,
a thus-come buddha!
Unexpectedly, the lingering snow
has melted away
And everything in the vast universe
beams with delight.

—TAIGU SŌCHIKU,
Taigu oshō gyōjoitsu, Taigu oshō goroku, 197

Taigu (also read Daigu, 1584–1669) is generally ranked among the leading figures of seventeenth-century Rinzai Zen. Like nearly all celebrated Rinzai masters of the early Edo period, with the notable exception of Takuan Sōhō (1573–1645), he was a prominent member of the Myōshinji line, Myōshinji being the powerful Kyoto temple whose masters would come to dominate Japanese Zen.

In his 1703 collection of Japanese Buddhist biographies *Honchō kōsōden*, the Myōshinji scholar priest Mangen Shipan laments that the authentic Zen transmission failed to survive beyond the first five or six generations of teachers, having languished till its revival by a handful of early-Edo Myōshinji masters, including Taigu, Gudō Tōshoku, and Ungo Kiyō (1582–1659).[1] Taigu was a close colleague of Gudō and Ungo, both of whom he accompanied for a time on a renowned 1607 *angya*, or Zen pilgrimage, and, like them, was sought out by the retired emperor and Zen enthusiast Gomizuno'o.

Many of the details of Taigu's biography are lacking.[2] He was born in 1584 in the town of Sano in the old province of Mino (now Gifu Prefecture) to a family named Takefu (also read Mutō). Mino had been a leading center of the Myōshinji line's expansion during the preceding Muromachi period, and at age ten, Taigu entered the nearby Zen temple, where he became a monk under the Myōshinji-line teacher Jōgen Sōkō (d. 1610), receiving the religious name Sōchiku. In 1615 he reportedly received Dharma transmission from Jōgen's heir Chimon Genso (d. 1630), along with the second Buddhist name Taigu, "Great Fool." Subsequently he is said to have served a term as abbot of Myōshinji, receiving the imperially conferred purple robe. In 1626 Taigu became abbot of Nansenji, a Myōshinji branch temple in Edo, but in 1630 was expelled from Myōshinji (an event described in one of the stories) and was not allowed to return to the temple until 1636. In the interim, in 1634, he founded Enkyōji in what is now Shiga Prefecture, and that year at the temple he experienced his first great enlightenment. Between 1657 and 1660, under the patronage of Matsudaira Mitsumichi (1636–1674), daimyo of Fukui (present-day Fukui Prefecture), Taigu founded Daianji, in what is now Fukui City. In 1664, the aging Taigu received the honorary title Shosō Hisō Zenji (Zen Master All Forms Are without Form) from the emperor Reigen (r. 1683–1687) and five years later passed away at Daianji at age eighty-five.

As apparent in the episodes that follow, Taigu could be an abrasive and cantankerous teacher. But he remains honored as one of the pillars of Myōshinji Zen during this formative and at times troubled period in the temple's history, when the shogunate was clamping down on the major Zen temples' autonomy and the temples themselves were divided internally over the arrival in Japan of a new generation of Chinese Zen masters, the most important of whom was Yinyuan Longqi (1592–1673).

Within Myōshinji in the late 1650s, opposition to the newly arrived Chinese teachers was spearheaded by Gudō and Taigu, who viewed the syncretic Ming Zen they espoused, freely incorporating Pure Land and even some Taoist elements, as alien and degenerate. At the same time, a steady stream of enthusiastic Myōshinji monks and teachers continued to flock to the Nagasaki temples where the Chinese masters had established themselves. Some of these Japanese monks became the Ming masters' disciples, and there was even an attempt, led by one of the temple's distinguished masters, Ryōkei Shōsen (1606–1670), to make Yinyuan the abbot at Myōshinji. This movement was adamantly opposed by Gudō, Taigu, and other temple "conservatives" who reputedly sought to restore what they regarded as the founder Kanzan's original Song-style Zen, with its unalloyed emphasis on koan practice and the classic Song koan collection the *Blue Cliff Record*. The resulting acrimony ultimately led Ryōkei to abandon Myōshinji in 1664 to become Yinyuan's first Japanese Dharma heir. Ryōkei's name was consequently stricken from the temple register the following year, together with those of other Myōshinji priests who had become followers of the immigrant masters, the founders of what became the Rinzai Ōbaku school.

〜〜

The Taigu oshō gyōjitsu, *from which the following anecdotes are taken, was originally compiled in 1768 at Nansenji.[3] The text, including Taigu's goroku, or collected poems and other inscriptions for particular formal religious occasions, was published in 2012 by Hanazono University's Institute for Zen Studies. The volume, edited by Nōnin Kōdō, is entitled* Taigu oshō goroku, shūi, gyōjitsu

(Formal record, gleanings, and biographical accounts of Master Taigu).

In the fifth year of Keichō (1600), the Master found himself caught up in the warfare engulfing Gifu.[4] The Master fled, shouldering his book satchel (*kyū*) and taking his elderly teacher Jōgen.[5]

A renegade warrior brandishing a sword attempted to make off with the Master's book satchel, but the Master grabbed the thief's arm, pursuing him and shouting loudly, "These are the personal records of my Dharma transmission and I'm not letting you get away with them—even if it costs me my life!" And so saying, the Master snatched back the satchel from the bandit's hand. The bandit, fearing the Master's strength, let go the satchel and fled.

Having routed the renegade warrior, Taigu bid farewell to Jōgen and traveled on pilgrimage to the Atsuta shrine in Owari, where he offered fervent prayers that he might realize the great matter of enlightenment. After this, the Master traveled to study under various Zen teachers, dwelling alone in forests and fields, and never forgetful of his purpose for even a single day.

After the passing of Jōgen, the Master became Dharma heir to Chimon.[6] Early in the Genna era (1615–1623), the Master resided in Edo and served as abbot of Nansenji, of which he was recognized as the temple's second founder.

⌒

There was a certain Korean Zen master named Myōkan, who lived in Yoshino, in Yamato Province.[7] Myōkan was a practitioner of exceptional endowments, who had meditated deeply on this matter [of Zen].

One day Myōkan asked a monk, "You have traveled widely on Zen pilgrimage, interviewing teachers. Who among them have you found to be a man of transcendent insight?"

The monk replied, "In all Japan there are no real Zen masters apart from one man called Taigu. His behavior is coarse, and he loves to drink, so that he goes about half drunk and half sober, cursing everyone, with no restraint over what comes out of his mouth. Yet for all that, one cannot fathom his spiritual depths."

Myōkan, delighted, exclaimed, "That is my true friend and master! I won't take up drinking myself, and I won't adopt his coarse behavior, but I'll just follow his teaching."

And that very day, Myōkan packed for his journey.

After going some one hundred *ri*, Myōkan came to a roofless houseboat.[8] The Master received him just as if they had been old friends, and together they talked and laughed all day.

〜〜

On one occasion the Master participated in a vegetarian feast.[9]

A certain Zen teacher who was present held up his bowing mat and asked, "See it?"[10]

"I see it," the Master replied.

"What do you see?" the teacher demanded.

The Master told him, "I see you squirming in agony while you truckle to the parishioners."

〜〜

There was an old woman whose child died and who beseeched the Master to officiate at the cremation service. When the service was ended, the old woman approached the Master and said, "I have been most fortunate to receive Your Reverence's care and compassion. Please tell me, where has my child gone now?"

The Master found himself unable to reply, and the old woman, grieving piteously, left.

The Master thought, "Till now I always believed I'd attained some realization. But now, when it came to leading a funeral service, I had no idea where the deceased had come to rest. How can I call myself abbot of a Zen temple?"

And so saying, he left the temple behind and set off once more on pilgrimage.

One day on the road, crossing the ridge at Hibara, the Master encountered a monk who had realized the Way. Their incisive challenges and responses flew back and forth, the clatter of their words like thorny chestnuts, and the Master found himself unable to either advance or retreat. He asked the man his name, but the monk would not answer.

This experience inspired the Master to renewed resolve, and he set off directly for Suse in Mikawa. Here he erected a simple retreat and retired into strict seclusion, his doubt weighing on him like a mountain.[11]

Next, the Master took his well-worn meditation cushion to the mountains in Ōmi. He encountered a daimyo named Horita Shinano no Kami, who provided the Master with a secluded retreat. Here the Master would spend all day sitting in meditation on a rock and all night sitting in meditation on the platform cover over a well.

Suddenly one night the Master's meditation cushion wore through and the wood slats of the well platform supporting him snapped. At that moment he experienced realization of the koan he had puzzled over till that time and composed a *gatha*:

> Dust and dirt: the squabbling over right and wrong,
>> loss
>> and gain
> What kind of man surrenders to the other army
>> without
>> a fight?
> As night wears on, the rain lets up
> It's hard, they say, to forget the places to which one's
>> grown accustomed
> Tears without end line my cheeks.

One day the Master experienced a profound realization of the words of the monk at Hibara. "These days," he thought to himself, "there's no one who can tell a tortoise from a terrapin.[12] Rather than waste my time searching after some teacher's phony written sanction, better to obtain the invisible sanction of the buddhas and patriarchs themselves."

So saying, the Master burned incense and murmured a silent invocation: "If my experience is genuine, let all the buddhas of the three worlds and the successive generations of Zen patriarchs testify to my enlightenment![13] But if my experience is false, let me here and now suffer the punishment of all the dragons and gods and all the major and minor deities of heaven and earth!"

At that moment, day broke, the first morning of the new year. The Master recited a gatha:

> Springtime arrives in the world of men
> bestowing immeasurable blessings
> Each and every flower an offering, a thus-come
> buddha!
> Unexpectedly the lingering snow has melted away
> And everything in the vast universe beams with
> delight.[14]

During the Genna era, Nansenji was established in Edo, and Taigu was installed as founding abbot.

At this time, the daimyo Horie Yamashiro Tadaharu kept a pair of prostitutes.[15] The first was named Cricket, the second, Bell-Ring Cricket. In the daimyo's residence was a handsome young page who had just reached manhood, and the two prostitutes were always trying to catch sight of him, though with scant success. One day, however, when the daimyo had gone out, a group of pages and samurai retainers were drinking and carousing, and the young page was secretly observed by the prostitutes through a peephole. There followed an exchange of letters, and soon the three were amorously entangled, the page unable to resist the prostitutes' advances.

When word of this reached the daimyo, he was furious. The page was sent a blade and ordered to commit suicide, while the two prostitutes, terrified, fled to Nansenji, where they pleaded for assistance. Taigu hurriedly shaved their heads and gave them nun's robes, after which they hid themselves in a remote alley.

The irate daimyo dispatched samurai retainers to track down the prostitutes, and learning they had gone to Nansenji, the warriors entered the temple precincts in search of the pair.

Taigu told the daimyo's men, "I know nothing of this." To which the enraged samurai declared, "In that case, we demand to search the temple!"

Taigu allowed them to proceed, but though they searched high and low, they failed to find their quarry and returned home empty-handed.

News of these events was soon circulating in the city and thence to all the temples, including claims that the two prostitutes were being concealed at Nansenji. A greedy individual thereupon produced a woodblock print, which was hawked by a local gangster and featured two attractive Buddhist nuns, to which was later added the image of a giant Buddhist priest. By this means, false rumors were spread about, rumors that the Edo branch temples reported to the Kyoto headquarters temple, Myōshinji, in Kyoto. Taigu was consequently banned from the main temple.

Determined to clear his name, Taigu departed abruptly for the imperial capital [i.e., Kyoto], reaching the post station at Akasaka, where he hired a horse and groom.

From time to time, the groom would casually sing a ditty popular among packhorse drivers:

> Spring showers at Kitayama—
> Pay them no heed
> And they'll clear up.[16]

Deeply struck by the song, Taigu clapped his hands and told the horse driver, "I won't be going to Kyoto!" He thereupon returned to Nansenji, reflecting, "This is the best way for me to humble myself. If I appeal to the authorities at Myōshinji, the rights and wrongs of the matter will remain murky. For now I'll just stay quiet." So the Master abandoned his plan to travel to Kyoto and simply returned to Edo and Nansenji.

In the seventh month of Meishō (1636), seven years after Taigu's expulsion from the headquarters temple, Tenkai wrote to Myōshinji on the twelfth memorial of Tokugawa Ieyasu's death asking that Taigu be pardoned and praising him as an eminent monk. "While I do not know the truth or falsehood of the matter," Tenkai wrote, "if proof of guilt is lacking, Taigu should be promptly restored to full privileges at the temple lest its reputation thereby be tarnished."[17]

Myōshinji complied with Tenkai's request, and Taigu proceeded directly to the Kyoto temple, reciting a gatha before the founder Kanzan's pagoda, Misshō-an:

> Neither an ill-omened owl nor an auspicious phoenix
> Yet skilled both at concealment and freely flying
>> about
> When circumstances are right, the crooked will cease
>> to
>> conceal the straight

And the mountains of self-and-other be everywhere
Destroyed.

⌒

Praise of Taigu's realization of Zen reached the retired emperor
[Gomizuno'o], who had Master Gudō summon Taigu to an audience.

The Master, however, declared, "I can be a host; I can never be
a guest."

The retired emperor did not invite the Master again . . .

Later, the Master was heard to remark, "Had I responded to
the imperial summons, our school would likely have fallen into
the dirt!"

⌒

*Another account of the episode is included in part 7 of the Zen
master and scholar Mujaku Dōchu's (1653–1744)* Shōbōzanshi, *a
history of the Myōshinji line:*

The retired emperor was greatly taken with Zen. Master Gudō
frequently praised Taigu to His Majesty, who consequently
wished to meet the Zen master in person. Gudō communicated
the retired emperor's wishes to Taigu, who replied, "I'm just a
country priest. I'm not someone who's suited to appear before
noble persons. Nor can I be compared with teachers like yourself."

Gudō reported this to the retired emperor, who observed,
"Taigu is boastful about Buddhism."

When this comment reached Taigu, he declared, "The retired
emperor lacks a deep-seated faith [in the Dharma]. Had I presented myself at court, I'd have just spoken out spontaneously,
wildly, and gotten myself exiled for sure. That's why I don't

involve myself with people's affairs but hide from the world and keep my head down."

⌣

In the second year of Meireki (1656), the Master suffered a bout of lumbago and traveled to bathe in the hot springs of Kaga. His route led throughout the [neighboring] province of Echizen. Here there resided a certain Shimada, a samurai retainer of the domain, whose layman's Buddhist name was Hōsetsu and who came to study under the Master when the Master was in Edo. Shimada therefore prevailed upon the Master to stop at his mansion, where he tended to him devotedly. The Master remained ill and was unable to return home.

The following year, the great lord of the province, Minamoto Mitsumichi,[18] departing the imperial court, dispatched a messenger to inquire about the Master's illness. The daimyo went to call on him—the Master having now recovered—[at the home of his retainer] Shimada.

Although his illness had passed, the Master's legs remained completely numb. Unable to walk on his own, he would hoist himself on top of his bed quilt and use it to pull himself along.

The daimyo prepared to welcome the Master, who, hauling himself along on the quilt with his own hands, entered the daimyo's presence. His Lordship received the Master with the utmost reverence and devotion.

Master Gudō, too, had come to make His Lordship's acquaintance, and the daimyo exclaimed, "The chance to glimpse the *udumbara* in bloom is as nothing compared to the difficulty of meeting a single true teacher.[19] Now today I have met *two* sage-like masters!"

Gudō declared, "Your Lordship is endowed with surpassing

wisdom such as is rarely encountered and would be prized in any land."

The daimyo replied to Gudō, "I thank Your Reverence for attesting to my realization."

At this, the Master flushed and said, "Old man Gudō, you can't tell good from bad and hand out your sanction indiscriminately. What can this pasty-faced kid know about anything?"

The daimyo, visibly taken aback, thought to himself, "I am lord of the entire domain. Who is there dares reproach me to my face like this? Truly, here is one worthy to be my teacher!"

On another day, when he had invited the Master to a vegetarian feast, the daimyo told him, "It was my misfortune that my father died prematurely, so from a young age I had to assume his position and duties. Yet now it has been my good fortune to encounter Your Reverence. What I wish is to offer you a site on which to erect a temple, so that you may serve as my teacher."

The Master bowed in agreement, saying, "I receive Your Lordship's command."

The daimyo then immediately ordered his palanquin and took the Master to view the site he had in mind. His Lordship himself laid out the boundaries for the temple, which was completed in two years and named Daianji.

With his own hands, the Master himself planted auspicious shrubs and rare trees, and had countless others planted as well.

A monk asked, "What are you doing planting all these deep in the mountains?"[20]

The Master replied, "You tell me: Why do I have to do this?"

The monk said, "How about working but not getting any merit?"

The Master told him, "I'm inept; I haven't anything to teach people."

The monk stifled a laugh.

Another monk remarked, "Your Reverence does not observe

[Confucian] practices of respect and ceremony, but wherever he goes, [unobtrusively] leads the assembly of monks in performing manual labor. Is there any benefit in this?"

The Master said, "Not particularly. Just to see yourself."

The monk asked, "What do you mean by 'see'?"

The Master told him, "You don't see yourself."

～⌣～

Once the Master was at the mansion of Layman Hōsetsu. So many male and female lay adherents arrived to pay their respects that it was like a marketplace, and the Master took advantage of the opportunity to deliver a sermon.

Hōsetsu said, "Your Reverence talks about Buddhism day in and day out, but I've yet to hear you say anything about the business of our school [i.e., Zen]."

The Master told him, "If I did say anything about that, I'm afraid people wouldn't even have a clue."

～⌣～

On another occasion, the layman brought up the story of the heretic and the sparrow.[21] The layman asked the Master, "What is the meaning of the Buddha's answer?"

The Master replied, "Suppose you tell me what you would have said."

The layman answered, "If anyone were present and asked me, I'd probably shout at him, 'What a lot of meaningless noise! Sizzle, sizzle!'[22]

The Master said, "You're just talking about yourself."

The layman asked, "Your Reverence, how would you answer?"

The Master said, "The World-Honored-One had nothing particular to teach. He just wanted to settle things once and for all."

～⌣～

On another occasion the layman asked, "I've always understood the Way to lie in concentrating mind (J. *nen*). How have I failed to understand?"

The Master told him, "You have the capacity for enlightenment."

Another time, the layman asked, "I beg Your Reverence for some expedient means to guide me to realization."

Again the Master told him, "You have the capacity for enlightenment."

⌒

The daimyo of Awa invited the Master to assume abbacy of Kōgenji, declaring, "The Zen temple Kōgenji is the place of our ancestors' tombs and from generation to generation has been under our guardianship. I humbly request that Your Reverence will condescend to serve as abbot."

The Master said, "I will accept an abbacy for the sake of the Way, but never to occupy a particular office."

A monk remarked, "Kōgenji is a prestigious temple that was originally branch temple of another Zen lineage, and it is now to be granted to Your Reverence. Should Your Reverence assume its abbacy, would this not be a great coup for our line?"

The Master told him, "His Lordship is only interested in the graves of his ancestors; he has no interest in the Way."

⌒

The Master happened to run into Master Gudō [Tōshoku] in Kyoto. Gudō [subsequently] dispatched a monk to inquire about the Master's well-being. The Master then ordered his attendant to bring some sesame buns to thank the monk, but the monk would not eat them.[23] The Master then sent for more of the buns, but still the monk refused to eat.

The Master called, "Attendant, attendant, bring me my staff!

This lordly envoy declines to eat sesame buns. Perhaps I can thank our distinguished visitor by simply letting him have a taste of my stick!"

The monk fled.

︵︿︶

It once happened that the shogun Iemitsu held a grand vegetarian feast on the occasion of a memorial for his wet nurse, Her Ladyship Rinshō-in.[24] The Master was requested to deliver a sermon on Zen [at the memorial] but declared, "My particular teaching is grounded in the seat of Dharma itself. Unless a monk has been studying Zen for a long time, I do not permit him to see me for private instruction. One must not haphazardly permit beginners in Zen practice and study to interfere with others' questioning and examining with the teacher. That's why the abbots of Zen temples and teachers of advanced standing in our line just select from their assembly of monks a few dozen [capable] students. Then host and guest can confront each other, and attainment be weighed in the give-and-take of dialogue to the wonder and admiration of both monk and lay followers."[25]

The shogun told the nun Sushi, abbess of Saishōji, "For some time I have heard of Master Taigu's reputation for wisdom. Now, by good fortune he is to come. I greatly look forward to meeting him, and I am sure I can rely on you to arrange things so that this will be possible."

Privately, the Master received word of the shogun's intentions and that very night secretly left the capital.

Long afterward, the Master was questioned about this by a monk: "It is said that the Buddha's teaching must be bestowed on kings, ministers, and powerful supporters. So why, in years past, did Your Reverence run away?"

The Master replied, "Those who dedicate themselves to the Dharma do not shrink from death or destruction."

The monk said, "I am still in doubt as to Your Reverence's meaning."

The Master told him, "By nature I'm coarse in my manner and incapable of smoothing things over with consoling words."[26]

⌒⌒

Master Gudō prepared a poem to present at the three hundredth memorial service for Myōshinji's celebrated founder, Kanzan Egen, held in the second year of Manji (1659).

The poem read:

> Of the twenty-four lines of Japanese Zen,[27]
> Most, alas, have perished
> Fortunately Kanzan has Gudō
> And the torch continues to be passed on,
>   its fragrance carried across three hundred years.

Before delivering the poem, Gudō showed it to Taigu for comment.

Taigu said, "Two characters in the third verse need to be changed."

Gudō asked, "How?"

Taigu said, "What do you think about adding '. . . and fortunately Taigu too'?"

Gudō laughed and agreed to change the line to "Kanzan is fortunate to have descendants."

Taigu then declaimed his own verse to those assembled for the memorial:

> For most of the twenty-four lines of Zen
>   carried to this land by the teachers of old
> There remains neither realization nor transmission

But among the followers of the soaring dragon[28]
  on the mountain of authentic teaching[29]
Rain still leaks through the roof
  and into a woven bamboo basket.[30]

⌒⌒

The Master asked a monk, "How old are you?"

The monk replied, "Thirty-one."

The Master said, "At twenty-nine, the Buddha had already realized enlightenment, and here *you* are showing the same old face."

The monk asked, "How old is Your Reverence?"

The Master replied, "Over eighty."

"Shame on you!" the monk scolded him.[31]

The Master made a low bow.

⌒⌒

His Lordship the daimyo once asked the Master, "I have served Your Reverence with devotion, granting you land and erecting there a temple.[32] What I still can't figure out is how you're going to do something for me."

The Master told him, "As for me, empty space."

⌒⌒

Again the daimyo questioned the Master, saying, "I have heard that the *Blue Cliff Record* is the preeminent text of the Zen school. Is that correct?"[33]

The Master answered, "Yes."

The daimyo said, "I beseech Your Reverence, instruct me in one or two of the work's koan."

The Master shouted, "'Empty and boundless, nothing holy!'[34] Does Your Lordship understand?"

The daimyo replied, "I do not."

The Master told him, "My lecture is over."

The daimyo, however, persisted, and the Master told him, "Words and phrases, words and phrases—by explaining things rationally you can get some sort of toehold, but it's all idle talk, tedious blather! And I'm sure this learned priest can explain it just fine," the Master added, turning his head and indicating a nearby monk.

The daimyo's regard for the Master grew stronger by the day, and he asked the Master for a Dharma name.[35] The Master thereupon brushed the name, "His Lordship of Daian temple, the Layman Ten Thousand Virtues—Nothing! Nothing!"[36]

～～

In the fifth year of Kanbun (1665), the Master was seventy-nine and beset by the infirmities of age. He spoke to the [Echizen] daimyo, who proposed erecting for him a special detached hermitage within the temple grounds.

The Master told him, "Forget it! Even if you manage to set up such a place, I've got no more than a few days left."

The daimyo replied, "My late elder sister, the nun Jōkan, had intended to relocate from her temporary dwelling to a retreat in the mountains. If Your Reverence has no objection [to occupying the spot], I am certain my late sister would have been overjoyed."[37]

The Master acquiesced, saying, "Let's move there!"

This hermitage is today the [Daianji] subtemple Shōun-in.[38]

～～

[During his last years,] the Master would live in retreat at Hōtōji in Harima or return to convalesce at Shōunji in Echizen. One day, when the Master was eighty-five and staying at Hōtōji, he announced to the assembly of monks, "The time has arrived for me to be off on pilgrimage.[39] I'm going to Echizen."

The monks said, "In consideration of Your Reverence's great age and virtue, go to pass away in that temple."

The Master added, "Some time ago, I was in Echizen and had the opportunity to make the acquaintance of the province's daimyo." The Master then summoned his palanquin and departed.

At the time, Echizen had been ravaged by fire, reducing the daimyo's entire castle to ashes. Learning of this, the monks sent a messenger after the Master to halt his journey. But the Master told him, "Having come this far, I'm not turning back. My connection with this world is almost up. What other chance will I have?"

In the seventh month, during autumn of that year [1669], the Master had begun to show slight symptoms of illness, but his pulse was normal, and he was not experiencing any severe discomfort.[40] Some fourteen days later, he brushed his death verse:

> The Dharma heir of the western skies [i.e., India]
> The Hun-lun Mountain of the eastern seas (i.e.,
>   Japan)[41]
> One's ordinary dynamic activity
> Is the teaching of nonduality.[42]

To which the Master added the inscription, "Three days before my passing." Then, having discussed with those present the arrangements for his death, he said not another word.

The following evening, the Master summoned the attendant monk Ridatsu and asked for writing paper. Ridatsu, bearing the paper between his palms, presented it respectfully to the Master. The Master slapped him.

The next day, the sixteenth day [of the seventh month], the Master peacefully passed away.

The lord of the province told his retainer, Layman Hōsetsu, "It's bad luck that I'm down with the flu and unable to hasten to His Reverence. Please hurry there in my place."

The layman, attiring himself in the robe and headgear of the daimyo, [set off for the Master's temple]. He then stood facing the coffin containing the Master's body and prostrated himself just as he would do when the Master was alive.

Some sixteen years before the Master's passing, the daimyo had a portrait of the Master painted, which he asked the Master to inscribe.

When he had completed the inscription, the Master postdated it "sixteenth day of the seventh month." Now, in astonishment, the daimyo wondered, "How did the Master know?"

SENGAI TALES

The followers of Buddha are extolled in every quarter
The disciples of Confucius are praised throughout the land
I sit on a rock among vines and creepers
Now and then watching the drifting clouds
that pass before my eyes.

—SENGAI GIBON

Among the most beloved and eccentric figures in the history of Japanese Zen is the Rinzai master Sengai Gibon (1750–1837). Like his contemporary the Sōtō Zen master Ryōkan, Sengai was legendary for his warm and unassuming personality, his naiveté, and his close relations with the common people who were his neighbors. Sengai's friends included the Fukuoka daimyo Kuroda Narikiyo (n.d.) and his samurai retainers, local artists and literati, and assorted farmers, old ladies, drunks, and merchants—the full sweep of society in Hakata, the important port town on the northern tip of Kyushu where Sengai's temple, Shōfukuji, was located. As late as 1930, children in the area all knew stories about "Sengai-san" (Mr. Sengai), as he was affectionately referred to, and the people of northern Kyushu often spoke of him as "Sengai Bosatsu" (Bodhisattva Sengai). Exceedingly stunted and bizarre in appearance, always dressed in ragged robes, Sengai was said to have resembled a "mummified monkey," an impression borne out by several of his portraits. Besides his ready wit and abilities as a Zen master, Sengai, like Ryōkan, was celebrated for his brushwork, especially his playful drawings, which collectors went to inordinate lengths to wheedle out of him.

Little information exists regarding Sengai's early years.[1] The master himself recorded nothing on the subject, nor did his disciples leave any detailed accounts. Even Sengai's date of birth is calculated only by counting back from his age at death. We know that he was born in 1750 in the old province of Mino, now Gifu Prefecture. The master's father, a certain Itō Jinpachi (d. 1788), is said to have been a tenant farmer for a samurai family, the Kawamura. It was probably to unburden himself of an extra mouth to feed that led Jinpachi to place the ten-year-old Sengai as a novice at Seitaiji, a nearby Rinzai Zen temple patronized by the Kawamura and now part of Mino City. Here Sengai served under the temple's aging abbot Kuin Enku (n.d.), from whom, while still a child, he took religious vows as a Zen monk. Kuin was a distinguished Myōshinji-line master who had served a term as the main temple's abbot and later in life returned to Myōshinji to deliver a series of well-attended lectures on the *Blue Cliff Record*. In 1762, Kuin retired as Seitaiji's abbot, leaving the temple in the care of a disciple.

Rinzai Zen in Sengai's period was dominated by two important teaching lines, both centered on the great Kyoto headquarters Zen temple Myōshinji: the line of Hakuin Ekaku, and that of Hakuin's contemporary Kogetsu Zenzai (1667–1750/51). In 1768 Sengai traveled north to Musashi Province and sought out Kogetsu's heir Gessen Zenne (1702–1781) at Gessen's temple, Tōki-an, in what is now the city of Yokohama.[2] After several years of study under Gessen, Sengai reportedly realized enlightenment when he passed the koan "Xiangyan's 'Up a Tree'" after presenting the following verse:[3]

Three thousand years since Shakyamuni passed on
And Maitreya isn't due for another billion or more

The sentient beings of earth haven't a clue
That their nostrils are hanging right over their lips![4]

The poem is said to have been greatly praised by Gessen, who subsequently awarded Sengai his inka, or sanction of enlightenment. After Gessen's death in 1781, Sengai may have completed his Zen study under Gessen's heir Seisetsu Shūcho (n.d.), before setting off once more on pilgrimage. Later that year he returned to Mino and Seitaiji, where he had been proposed for the temple's abbacy. The appointment, however, was reportedly overruled by the temple's patrons, represented by the Kawamura, Jinpachi's employer, on the grounds that Sengai, the son of a poor farmer, was unsuited for so lofty a position.[5]

In 1788 in Kyoto, Sengai became a disciple of the Zen master Bankoku Shōteki (d. 1792), abbot of Shōfukuji, and at that time resident at the Myōshinji subtemple Unshō-in. Traditionally regarded as Japan's earliest Zen temple, Shōfukuji had been established by the monk Eisai (also read Yōsai, 1141–1215) in 1195, four years after Eisai's return from studies in Song China, where he had received his Chinese teacher Xuan Huaichang's (n.d.) sanction. In 1789, after serving for thirty-four years, Bankoku retired as abbot of Shōfukuji, conferring Dharma succession on Sengai, who at age thirty-nine became the temple's 123rd-generation abbot. At his inauguration, which coincided with the memorial of Eisai's death, Sengai recited a poem:

When Zen first arrived in our land
Twenty-four lines were handed down
Yet today where are the founders' progeny?
Our school's teaching is dead and gone
Only this blind donkey stumbles about.[6]

———

Sengai would largely remain in Hakata for the following thirty years, living in extreme simplicity and fending off repeated invitations to assume honors at Myōshinji, though he finally yielded in 1790, receiving advanced rank in the Kyoto temple and delivering a formal sermon. Further honors followed in 1798 and again in 1800, when Sengai undertook to refurbish Shōfukuji's monk's hall, now filling with students as the master's fame began to spread.[7] In succeeding years, Sengai oversaw repair and restoration of Shōfukuji's other main buildings. The master seems to have come to regard himself as custodian for the historic temple, and it is largely due to his efforts that Shōfukuji's principal structures remain intact today.

Sengai was awarded abbacy of Myōshinji in 1802, and the Kyoto temple sent a formal acknowledgment of the honor to the senior officials of the Kuroda clan, daimyo of the Fukuoka domain. In 1811 Sengai turned Shōfukuji over to his leading disciple and Dharma heir (*hassu*) Tangen Tōi (d. 1855) and retired to a subtemple, Kyohaku-in. Here he continued to live in retreat, with an occasional trip to Kyoto and beyond. In 1823 he returned to visit Seitaiji, site of his early training as a monk, and delivered to the assembly a series of lectures on the letters of Dahui.

Even at home in Kyohaku-in, Sengai by no means lived as a recluse. His acquaintances spanned the gamut of local society, including Confucians and literati, *shakuhachi* players, tea devotees, and even the occasional boisterous drunk. Sengai reputedly loved both sake and tea, and the plentiful artwork he produced during this period is in part testament to his conviviality, infused with the master's special brand of earthy humor and whimsy, and often created as gifts to friends. His paintings include a variety of subjects, from vegetables and bamboo to landscapes of mountains and rice fields, picnics under the cherry blossoms, farmers at work, local gods, birds, and animals. Even when Sengai's subject is Zen, his paintings and calligraphy reflect his playful temperament. A portrait of Bodhidharma, who on arriving in China, according to legend, practiced meditation for nine years facing the stone wall of his mountain retreat, bears the inscription, "Nine years facing a wall—what a drag!"[8] Perhaps tired of the incessant requests for samples of his brushwork, in autumn of 1823, Sengai is said to have renounced all further artistic activity and had the resolution—itself a poem—carved in stone and set up outside his hermitage:

> Here in Fukuoka in my black robes
> I'm putting down my brush for good
> Having brought only trouble and shame on myself
> As a result of all my scribbling.[9]

———

In 1837, Tangen committed some infraction for which he was removed from the abbacy of Shōfukuji and sent into exile on Ōshima, so that Sengai, at age eighty-seven, was forced to become the temple's abbot once more.[10] Later that year he was able to hand over the abbacy to another disciple and return to Kyohaku-in, where he passed away several days later. His death verse, for which he seems to have broken his ban on poetry and calligraphy, contains a pun in the use of the word "cliff," the second of the characters that make up Sengai's name—"Hermit Cliff":

> When arriving, know where you came from
> When departing, know where you've gone
> Without letting go the edge of the cliff
> The clouds are too thick to know where you are.[11]

In 1841 Emperor Ninkō (r. 1817–1846) awarded Sengai the posthumous imperial title Fumon Entsū Zenji, "Zen Master with Perfect Knowledge of All Dharma Gates."

Sengai left behind five Dharma heirs, two of whom served as Shōfukuji's abbot, along with a plethora of brush paintings and calligraphy that continue to be greatly appreciated, both in Japan and abroad.

〜〜

Sengai is the sort of figure about whom legends and folk stories naturally arise. The following are a selection of such tales from Sengai oshō itsuwasen *[Selected tales of Master Sengai] (Kyoto: Hanazono University's Institute for Zen Studies, 1999), edited by Nōnin Keidō and based principally on a 1930 collection of Sengai stories,* Sengai oshō hozoppone *(Master Sengai's Belly Button) by Kuramitsu Daigu.*[12]

The Master had a reputation for never thanking people. One rainy day, on a street not far from the temple, the thong of his *geta* broke, and observing his distress, the lady at the local tofu shop ran and purchased a new thong and hurried to him with it.[13] The Master, however, did not thank her but just bowed and returned home without a word.

Thereafter, whenever the lady met the Master, he still failed to thank her, leaving her filled with indignation.

"What a rude priest!" she thought to herself. And to an acquaintance she complained, "Everyone praises the Master for being such a worthy man, but he isn't anything of the sort. On a rainy day his geta thong broke and he was really in a bad way. But even though I went and bought him a new thong and replaced it for him myself, he never thanked me. I can't imagine a more ungrateful priest!"

The woman's acquaintance visited the temple and reported this to the Master. Sengai said, "When people finish saying thank you, that's the end of the matter right there. But I intend never to forget a kindness as long as I live."[14]

Once a day laborer noticed under the main hall of the temple fresh bones from a sea bream. Fish was forbidden in the monastery, and the worker hurried off to the Master with the evidence.

"Master! Master! Look what I found under the monks' hall!" he exclaimed. "How embarrassing to have fish bones turn up here at the temple."

"Well, well," said the Master, "the novices nowadays have certainly gotten soft. Back when I was a novice, we never left over even the bones!"

Lord Kuroda Narikiyo, daimyo of Chikuzen, prided himself on his knowledge of plants and flowers, particularly chrysanthemums and peonies. Not only did he depict these in many brush paintings, but he also raised splendid specimens in his gardens, where he would entertain guests at elaborate viewing parties.

One day it happened that a dog invaded the flowerbeds and trampled one of His Lordship's most prized chrysanthemum plants. Enraged, the daimyo held the gardener responsible and announced that he was going to execute him himself.

Learning of this, Master Sengai remarked, "Killing a man just because of a little plant—what a foolish daimyo! Very well, I have an idea."

That evening, the Master concealed his face under a broad-brimmed straw hat and, with a sharpened sickle in hand, stole into the daimyo's flowerbeds, where he proceeded to cut down every one of the precious chrysanthemums. Seeing this, a watchman raised the alarm. The daimyo, burning with rage, arrived on the scene. "Scoundrel!" he shouted, and drew his sword, posed to deliver a blow to the intruder, when he suddenly realized that the face concealed under the straw hat belonged to none other than Master Sengai.

Utterly unperturbed, the Master told him, "As long as the plants have been cut down, you can save them to use later on for fodder."

Astounded, the daimyo sheathed his sword and asked the Master why he had cut down his chrysanthemums. In reply, Sengai picked up a chrysanthemum branch that lay on the ground and faced the daimyo. Holding up the flowers beside his own face, the Master demanded, "Which life is more important?"

The daimyo suddenly realized his error. "How mistaken I've been!" he apologized profusely and, promptly pardoning the gardener, told the Master, "I would like to offer a present to Your Reverence."

"There's really nothing I want," the Master said. "But since you've expressed a desire to give me something, what about that plum tree over there?"

The plum in question was prized by His Lordship to the same extent as the chrysanthemums.

"You put me in an awkward position," the daimyo told the Master, clearly troubled. "To take away the plum tree would be like taking my head."

Sengai replied, "If it remains here at your place, I'll probably have to come back and cut it down. So if you want to see it, please come to the temple."

And with that, the Master returned home with the tree, which he planted right in front of the temple.

⌒⌒

One summer day, two old women from the village came to visit Sengai at the temple.

"My, my!" they exclaimed when Sengai appeared. "What are those red spots all over your face?"

"Oh, those," said the Master. "They're mosquito bites."

"Yes, but why should the mosquitos be biting you up so *much*?" the old ladies asked.

"To tell you the truth," the Master said, "I've already had my mosquito net stolen three times."

"Three times?" the women exclaimed. "You've been robbed three times?"

"That's right," the Master confirmed. "They took all my mosquito nets. What a headache! Every night I pull the bedding over my head for protection, but a mosquito always manages to hide inside and chew me up while I sleep. It itches like crazy!" he told them, grimacing.

The old women both expressed great sympathy for the Master, who suggested, "Ladies, if you're willing, I have a plan." Grinning broadly, he said, "Could you make me an all-white mosquito net?"

"Yes, certainly," the old ladies agreed, and pooling all their rainy-day funds, they made up the all-white mosquito net just as the Master had requested and brought it to him.

Sengai was overjoyed, and immediately taking out his brushes and ink, he set to work on the net. He covered its sides with depictions of death's heads and ghosts and its top with a terrifying picture of the thunder god accompanied by streaks of lightning.[15] At its corners he painted overturned lanterns and gravestones, ghastly hands and funerary objects. When he was done, he hung up the net and stood back to admire it. "Well, that should do the trick!" the Master announced with a laugh.

That very night, two thieves snuck up to the temple carrying lanterns. The Master was already sound asleep inside his new mosquito net. He had closed the shoji but left open the shutters.

Sliding aside the shoji, the thieves slipped into the Master's room, and shining the lantern on the mosquito net, they suddenly beheld a ghost standing before them. Trembling with fear but greedy for the net, one of the thieves approached and prepared to cut it from its hanger, when Sengai suddenly began banging his metal wash basin and shouting, "The god of thunder is here before you!"

Terrified, the two ran screaming into the night.

Hearing all the commotion, the temple's monks and the nearby villagers came running. When Sengai told them what had occurred, everyone exploded with laughter. When they entered the Master's room and looked around, they found that the thieves, in their desperation to escape, had dropped a towel, a tobacco pouch, and pipe.

～～

The Master would close his gate and on it paste a sign that read, "Out Today," meanwhile plainly sauntering back and forth in his front yard.

Once a certain samurai official of his acquaintance passed by and, noticing the Master, went to open the gate and greeted him. "Your Reverence," he called out, "I haven't seen you in some time. How have you been?"

In reply, Sengai merely pointed to the sign and told the samurai, "Please read what it says."

"But, Your Reverence," the samurai pleaded, "you're here, aren't you? You must just be kidding."

Sengai dismissed him with a wave of his hand. "That sign," he reminded the samurai, "says I'm out. It's true as anything can be." And so saying, he refused any further conversation.

Another neighbor, a farmer from the nearby countryside who was a devoted follower of the Master, came to visit him at the temple, carrying a load of Sengai's favorite sweet potatoes.[16] The Master was indoors wearing a sleeveless jacket and cooking up some rice.

"Hello!" the farmer called out from the gate. "Is Your Reverence in?"

"I'm out! I'm out!" Sengai called back.

"You're out?" the farmer repeated. "But I've brought your favorite sweet potatoes—"

No sooner had the Master heard the words "sweet potato" than he flung open the shoji, stuck out his head, and said, "No, I'm in! I'm in! Just me."

The Master was known to be immensely fond of sweet potatoes, and people, it's said, would often use them to lure him out.

⌣

Ghosts and ghost tales were a fixture of popular culture in Sengai's Japan—an interest that may be reflected in the following story.

From the time the Master became abbot of Shōfukuji, he would use any spare time he had from the temple's affairs to sit under a tree or on a rock to practice zazen. One night, a mischievous samurai of his acquaintance was passing through a pine grove near the temple when he noticed the Master deep in meditation on a rock under one of the pines, looking just like Bodhidharma.

The next evening when the samurai passed by the spot, there was the Master again, seated in meditation.

"People say that for such a runt of a man, the Master's got plenty of guts," the samurai mused. "Well, this looks like a perfect chance to find out!"

The next day at twilight, the samurai went to the pine grove, climbed a pine tree next to the rock where Sengai did zazen, hid himself, and waited for the Master to appear.

The Master, with no idea of the trap being laid for him, arrived and plunged into deep samadhi, sitting cross-legged as usual on the rock. No sooner had he begun to meditate than the samurai, in the tree above, reached down and grabbed the Master's head. But instead of being alarmed, as the samurai had expected, Sengai just went on meditating, still as a stone buddha.

Next, the samurai tried bellowing, "I'm going to get you!" But this too had absolutely no effect. Finally, feeling ashamed, he crept down silently from the tree and went off.

The following morning, the samurai went to visit Sengai at the temple. He asked to be conducted to the Master and was promptly shown into the abbot's private quarters. The instant the samurai stepped through the door the Master shouted from the shadow of the half-opened shoji, "Aha! The ghost!"

"Wha—!" exclaimed the samurai, grabbing for his sword.

The Master nearly split his sides laughing and remarked, "It's a bad business when one ghost is scaring another!"

The samurai, red in the face, slunk off.

〰

One day when the master was in front of his temple weeding the garden, two samurai appeared.

"Is Master Sengai in?" they demanded.

"He's out," Sengai replied.

"None of your lies!" they barked at the Master together. "*You're* Sengai, aren't you?"

Each samurai then grabbed one of the Master's arms and dragged him inside, where as a crowning indignity they ordered him to produce for them a piece of calligraphy. It was just the same as highway robbery!

The Master, however, remaining perfectly calm, brushed a painting of a copper coin, beside which he inscribed the following haiku:

> Two "knights"
>   dragging away a monk
> —It's a holdup!

〰

Among the Master's followers was a man who served the domain's daimyo, Lord Kuroda, as official executioner.

One snowy day when the man came to visit the temple, Sengai asked him, "You make your living cutting off people's heads. What about giving up this kind of sinful business?"

"But, Your Reverence," the man explained, "His Lordship, the daimyo, can command even my *own* execution—I'm completely blameless in this."

The Master did not reply but, changing the subject, said, "Right now it's the end of the year and I have to get the temple grounds cleaned up. I hate to ask, but could you go into the thicket over there and cut down the bamboo?"

"Certainly, Your Reverence!" the executioner instantly agreed, and entering the thicket proceeded to cut down the bamboo.

No sooner had he begun, however, than all the snow that had piled up on the bamboos' branches hurtled down with a crash on the executioner's head.

"Oh, it's cold!" he protested, brushing off the snow and returning to the Master's quarters.

Sengai told him, "The snow on the bamboo should have fallen on me, who asked you to do this; but instead it fell on you. Tell me, then: Who is guilty when you cut off someone's head? I want you to consider this carefully."

At these words, the executioner went away.

～

The Master was extremely small, and at first glance might be mistaken for an old lady or a novice priest. He disliked being recognized by people who would exclaim, "That's Master Sengai!" and he always looked scruffy and down-at-the-heels.

One day, dressed in a dingy, frayed robe, Sengai was picking tea leaves in the tea garden near his temple when a man came to ask for a piece of the Master's calligraphy.

"Hey, you—novice!" the man called out. "Where can I find the venerable Master Sengai's temple?"

Sengai, not in the least put out to be mistaken for a novice, promptly assumed the role and directed the visitor to Kyohaku-in, saying, "Yes, sir, you can find Master Sengai over there."

It's said that several times a day Sengai resorted to such stratagems in dealing with importunate visitors.

〜

On his way home from Edo, the Master arrived at the checkpoint at Hakone.[17] As he approached, the guard shouted at him, "No nuns allowed to pass this checkpoint!" and refused to let him through.

Laughing, the Master told the guard, "Very well, shall I show you my bona fides?" And pulling up his robes, he said, "Take a look! Male or female?"

〜

Once, when Sengai and the Zen master Don'ei of Sūfukuji were invited to the home of an old, established Hakata family, they noticed that the alcove was adorned by a magnificent potted orchid. Both of the masters begged to have the plant.

Their host told them, "You both want it? Then we'll have a penis contest, and whoever wins will take the orchid home."

Sengai immediately announced, "They say, 'Small man, big pecker'—so I win!" And triumphantly tucking the orchid under his arm, he went off.

〜

Someone once came and left a drawing of a penis on the gate of Sengai's temple. Sengai erased it, but the next morning an even larger penis had been drawn on the gate. Again Sengai rubbed it out, but in the morning, a still larger penis had been drawn.

Alongside appeared the inscription: "Touch it and it gets bigger."

"Ah," the Master exclaimed, "this time I've been beaten!"

⌒⌒

Among the teachers of jujitsu in the employ of the Fukuoka domain was one Shōbayashi Matashichiro. A master of ki power, Shōbayashi with a single shout could reportedly knock a man over from behind a screen or bring down a bird in flight by staring at it fiercely.[18]

One day, Shōbayashi went to visit Master Sengai.

"Your Reverence, why don't we have a little contest," he suggested. "Your samadhi power against my ki power."

"Certainly," Sengai replied. "Feel free to demonstrate your ki power at any time."

Shōbayashi chuckled sardonically. "I'm going to really teach you a lesson!" he promised, and went into the next room, where focusing his full force he gave a powerful shout—"EeeeEEEEEH!"

"I must have knocked that Zen master right on his can!" he gloated. But when he peered into the room, he saw Sengai calmly drinking tea. Shōbayashi therefore tried again, with a second great shout, but Sengai remained completely unfazed. Even the famous Shōbayashi couldn't match the power of Zen meditation.

This reached the ears of the lord of the domain, and consequently Shōbayashi's stipend was reduced by fifty koku.[19] When Sengai learned of this, he was greatly concerned about Shōbayashi's situation and secretly summoned him to the temple.

"Let's have another match," Sengai suggested. "This time I'll teach you a surefire way to win."

The Master then instructed Shōbayashi in the meditation technique of counting breaths.[20]

Returning home, Shōbayashi practiced the technique single-mindedly night and day, striving to enter the samadhi of breath counting, till suddenly he became one with his breathing:

there was no self apart from his breath, no breath apart from his self. He shouted, and the force of his shout filled heaven and earth. It seemed as if at that moment nothing existed in the vast universe. At the same time, when he shouted, the entire universe suddenly appeared.

"That's it!" he cried out spontaneously and rushed off to see Sengai, presenting his realization.

Astonished, Sengai exclaimed, "Shōbayashi, you've done it! That shout is Rinzai's jeweled sword of the Vajra King.[21] You've knocked down not only me but heaven and earth and all there is. I've lost the match!"

Through his practice of breath-counting meditation, Shōbayashi realized the indestructible diamond samadhi. Thereafter, not only was the fifty koku restored to Shōbayashi's stipend but an *additional* fifty, it is said, was awarded him.

⌒

In Hakata there lived a teacher of swordsmanship who had formerly been a retainer of the daimyo of Fukuoka but had become a ronin, or masterless samurai, and had sent his son to become a monk under Master Sengai. Later, when the sword master had once again found employment with a lord, he petitioned Sengai to allow his son to return to lay life and become the family heir. Sengai agreed, and the young man returned home, where under his father's instruction he devoted himself to the practice of swordsmanship.

One day the son returned to visit Sengai. The Master asked him, "You've been at it for some time now. Have you gotten your swordsman's credentials?"

"Not yet," the young man replied, "I'm still not qualified."

Sengai then wrote something and handed it to him, saying, "Take this back with you and show it to your father."

Returning home, he did as Sengai instructed.

When his father received the document, he was startled to read: "Between the Way of Zen and the Way of the sword there is only a difference of words, and this is itself the essence of the teaching of swordsmanship transmitted in our school. Fortunately my son has trained in the Way of Zen under Your Reverence, so that there remains no further problems."

The sword master promptly conferred on his son successorship in the school's innermost teachings.

One day a samurai named Genyū came to the temple. Demanding that the Master paint something for him, he refused to budge till Sengai complied. Having no choice, the Master took a clean sheet of paper on which he painted two circles before handing it to the samurai.

Genyū examined the painting but, unable to make out what it meant, asked the Master to inscribe it with a title.

Sengai promptly took his brush and wrote: "Genyū's balls."

Red with embarrassment, the samurai took the painting and fled.

The monks of Shōfukuji had assembled on the outskirts of Hakata to greet their new abbot. But they waited and waited, and still no one resembling an eminent Zen master appeared. Tired of waiting, they noticed a stunted, bedraggled beggar priest pass along the main road in the twilight, and they called out to him, "Hey! On the boat here, did you happen to meet the eminent priest called Master Sengai?"

Pausing, the beggar monk remained silent and then quietly replied, "Sengai . . . Yes, that's me."

The monks, taken aback, kept staring at the beggar monk. "This is the famous monk Sengai?" they all wondered.

The Master, accompanied by the monks, proceeded to his new temple. On the way, the monks stopped at a tea stall, and Sengai joined them all for buckwheat noodles in broth. When they had finished eating and were about to leave, one of the monks complained, "Those noodles we just had were made with fish stock.[22] And Master Sengai himself partook of such food." Many of the other monks could be heard muttering their disapproval as well.

Sengai told them, "I don't know anything about fish myself, but the soup tasted delicious, so I ate it. I can assume you all must be used to eating fish, and that's why you're so familiar with the taste."

The monks all looked away shamefaced.

～

There were many monks training at Shōfukuji under Master Sengai. Not far from the temple was a red-light district that attracted many monks who at night would scale the monastery wall to secretly visit the brothels. Because the wall was quite high, the monks would leave under it a footstool to help them get over and back down again on their return. Among the miscreants was Sengai's favorite disciple, Tangen, whose participation in these outings was something that the Master could not avoid learning of.

One evening, at the hour he knew the monks would be returning from their foray into the pleasure quarter, Sengai stationed himself under the wall, removing the step stool and sitting down to practice zazen and await the monks' return. Toward dawn, the unsuspecting monks tiptoed back to the temple and climbed the wall. But as they lowered themselves down on the other side, they were disconcerted to find that the footstool they always left behind was missing. Their feet groped in confusion in the darkness for the stool. Finally they managed to find something in its place that allowed them to lower themselves from the wall, and placing their feet on it, one by one they stepped down into the temple yard. As they peered around in the shadows, they were astonished to discover that the object they had used as a footstool was the shaved head of their teacher! White with fear, they prostrated themselves on the ground. But Master Sengai, in admonishing them, blamed only himself, saying their misbehavior was due to his own negligence in teaching.

～～

One year, the Hakata area was in the grip of a cholera epidemic. The head of the merchant house of Happyaku-ya,[23] a frequent visitor to Sengai's temple, arrived looking severely distressed and told the Master, "Your Reverence, this year, expecting big demand for squash, I bought up a huge quantity. But now people are saying that eating squash will give you cholera, and as a result, no one is buying. If I don't sell the squash, my family is ruined. Please, you've got to help me!"

"That's really terrible," Sengai commiserated. "Very well, I'll become your business manager and sell them for you. Please bring me all your squash."

The merchant wondered what Sengai had in mind but dutifully loaded all the squash onto a cart and brought them to the temple. Sengai then piled all the vegetables in front of Shōfukuji's main gate with a big sign that read Magical Cholera-Prevention Squash, and spreading his meditation mat alongside, he sat down and practiced zazen.

Immediately word spread throughout the area, and before long the whole district was flocking to buy the squash. By noon the squash had all sold out, and the fortunes of the firm of Happyaku-ya were restored.

～～

On New Year's Day, Sengai was roasting holiday rice cakes over the fire when a monk came to visit. Seating himself before the brazier directly in front of the Master, the monk proceeded to put forward various petty theories, challenging Sengai to engage in a Zen dialogue.

The Master remained silent and simply listened. Suddenly he grabbed the tongs and seizing the hot rice cake he'd been roasting over the flame, he hurled it smack against the cheek of the astonished monk, shouting, "You're a great talker. Try chewing on this!"

"Hot! Hot! Hot!" the monk howled in pain.

"There's no need to make such a fuss," Sengai reproved him. "Something hot is *going* to be hot."

～～

When a Shinto priest visited the Master at Kyohaku-in, the discussion turned to heaven and hell.

"Your Reverence," the Shinto priest asked, "where is heaven to be found?"

"On the Plane of High Heaven to which you pray every day," Sengai replied.[24]

"Then how about hell?" the priest demanded.

"The Plane of High Heaven's next-door neighbor."

On another occasion a monk from Buzen asked the Master, "What about heaven?"[25]

Sengai promptly lay down as if going to sleep.

"And what about hell?" the monk persisted.

Sengai closed his eyes and began to snore loudly.

"I've come all this way to question him on the Dharma, and he has the rudeness to just fall asleep!" the monk grumbled, and glaring at the Master, he started out of the room.

At that moment Sengai sat up abruptly and, pointing at the monk, remarked, "That is hell."

～～

The Master was extremely relaxed and informal. Tachibana Kanzaemon, a senior samurai official of the domain, came to call on him at Kyohaku-in in the course of visiting a gravesite.[26] The Master had just stepped into the bath but, hearing the official had arrived, jumped right out and searched around for a robe.

The official, who was waiting in the next room, called out, "Please don't trouble yourself, Your Reverence. As you are is just fine."

"Well, then, if you'll excuse me . . . ," Sengai announced, and entered the room stark naked, to the amazement of the senior official.

～～

There was a sarcastic fellow named Chōeimon who was a favorite of the Master and could provoke a fight with only two or three words. One day he came to Sengai and complained, "Your Reverence, I don't want to put on any more years."

"What's that?" said Sengai. "While you're alive it's all the same year."

～～

On another occasion, when Sengai had been sightseeing at Keya no Ooto in Itoshima, he became hungry on his way home and approached a tea shop.[27]

"Excuse me," he called out, "but I've got a young novice with me and he says he's so hungry he just can't walk anymore. Can you serve us some food?"

The tea shop owner brought out portions for two people, and Sengai contentedly polished both portions off.

Suspicious, the tea shop owner asked, "What about your novice?"

"Oh . . . well . . . ," Sengai sputtered and rapped himself sharply exactly twice on the head.

～

Sengai was extremely fond of sweet potatoes. Knowing this, the local people, when they wished to obtain pieces of the Master's calligraphy, would buy a quantity of sweet potatoes and bring them along when they visited Sengai, deliberately placing the yams to be used where he could see them.

"Your Reverence, please paint something for me," the person in search of calligraphy would ask.

"Forget that for now—where are you taking those sweet potatoes?" Sengai would demand.

"I'm bringing them someplace else," the local would reply.

"Turn them over to me and I'll paint something for you," Sengai would say.

"Very well," the man would agree, "if you paint something for me, they're all yours."

Using this sort of strategy, it is said, people would regularly wheedle paintings out of the Master.

～

One summer day, a certain sword master from Fukuoka named Toda arrived at the temple to visit Sengai. He found the Master stark naked and napping on his back. Suddenly grabbing Sengai by the testicles, Toda shouted, "What is this?"

Sengai, totally unperturbed, without even opening his eyes, replied, "A wasted possession," and then resumed snoring loudly.

～

In the eighth year of Tenpō (1837), Sengai fell ill and took to his bed. By that autumn, his life seemed to be rapidly approaching its end, and his disciples gathered around him.

One of them beseeched the Master, "Your Reverence, please leave us some final words of wisdom."

Sengai [took up his brush and wrote:] "We die alone! We die alone!"

The disciples, finding such a sentiment shockingly morbid for a revered religious teacher, pressed the Master for something else.

Above it, Sengai then inscribed: "It's true! It's true!"

⌒⌒

During the period before Master Sengai had retired to Kyohaku-in, a crisis arose in the Kuroda domain that engulfed the Buddhist priesthood of every school and was centered in Hakata. The cause of this crisis was Gōchō (n.d.), an eminent priest of the Tendai sect, who was in temporary residence at Kaidan-in in Dazaifu.[28]

Gōchō would make the rounds of all the domain's temples, defeating each of their abbots in religious debate. The keenness of his arguments was prodigious. None could stand up to his lightning retorts. It seemed [to the other abbots] that there was simply no one among them able to defeat Gōchō; and as the wild rumors of Gōchō's rhetorical powers continued to grow, the Buddhist priests of the domain felt like sparrows in the sights of a hawk.

One day the monks of the domain held a meeting, whose result was to form an alliance among themselves to expel Gōchō from the domain. One and all agreed that the only man for the job was Sengai of Shōfukuji, and a delegation of all the local abbots descended on the temple to meet with Sengai and entreat his assistance.

The Master told them, "Very well, I'll go and get him to leave, so don't worry."

The very next day Sengai went to see Gōchō at Kaidan-in, where he found the teacher sweeping the temple grounds.

Approaching him, Sengai said, "I've come to speak with you on something of a private nature."

"What?" Gōchō snarled. "Just what is it you came to tell me?"

In almost a whisper, Sengai replied, "What if I told Your Reverence that your life was in mortal danger? Well, that's the truth of the matter, and if you value your life, I ask you to make haste and escape from here."

"What's this all about?" Gōchō barked.

"There's no time to go into all that," Sengai told him. "You've got to hurry, pack your things, and get away. A crowd of men from the Kuroda domain is on its way here now to kill you!"

And having delivered his message, Sengai returned to his temple.

Like the coward he was at heart, when Gōchō heard this he started to tremble all over with fear. "Of course," Gōchō reasoned to himself, "I've been going all over the domain debating Buddhism and, without intending to, must have provoked everyone into wanting to kill me, and now there's not a moment to be lost!"

Hastily gathering up all his traveling gear, Gōchō fled the temple for good that very night.

People in the domain were convinced that Master Sengai must have bested Gōchō in debate and driven him right out of the province, and as word got about, people marveled, "That Sengai-san is really amazing!"[29]

﹏

The following story, dealing with Sengai's wayward follower Shien and his family and descendants, is by far the longest and most involved of the Sengai selections translated here. Despite the often confusing juxtaposition of timelines and characters, however, the story offers a rare glimpse of life in Japan during the early to mid-nineteenth century as well as a delightful picture of the master as seen by his Hakata neighbors.

Not far from Hakata, in the town of Katakasu, there lived a haiku poet named Kawagoe Shien.[30] A follower of Master Sengai, Shien was a frequent visitor at Kyohaku-in, where he would receive instruction in Zen from the Master and have him look over his haiku. Shien passed away in fall of the tenth year of Tenpō (1839) and was buried at Genjū-an in Hakata, receiving the posthumous Buddhist name Layman Setsuzan.

Shien's family were hereditary equerries of the Kuroda daimyo, with a stipend of five hundred koku, but for certain reasons, the stipend is said to have been reduced to some two hundred fifty or three hundred koku during Shien's generation.

One day a dejected-looking Shien came to visit the Master.

"Why so down at the mouth?" the Master asked.

Scratching his head, Shien replied, "To tell you the truth, I've done something pretty awful. I've knocked up one of our family maidservants. If this is made public, I could end up getting stripped of my stipend and having to commit hara-kiri."

The Master said, "When lascivious thoughts run wild, that's always what happens. Well, you had better just leave the matter to me." And so saying, the Master promptly left the temple.

The Master then went to talk with a Mr. Hirano, likewise a follower from Katakasu.

Sengai told him, "There's a woman I know whom I'd like you to take on as a maidservant for a little while."

"Of course," agreed Hirano, readily grasping the situation. "Anything to oblige Your Reverence."

"Ah, what a relief!" the Master exclaimed, and returned to the temple where he explained things to Shien. The maidservant was then dispatched to Hirano's, where she safely delivered a healthy male baby.

The maid had, however, contracted an infection of the nipples that rendered it impossible for her to suckle the newborn child.

Shien had not enough money to hire a wet nurse, leaving the couple[31] utterly at a loss, as they took turns cradling the infant in their arms.

One day while the Master was making his usual begging rounds, he stopped to visit Shien, whom he found once again sunk in despair.[32]

"Now then," the Master told Shien, "there's no need to get yourself so upset over this. How about letting me have the baby for a while?"

Taking up the child, the Master nestled him in the capacious sleeves of his monk's robe, balancing him tenderly in his arms.

Continuing on his begging rounds, the Master inquired if any nursing mothers had spare milk to suckle the baby, and repeated this plea every day. The citizens of the village of Katakasu, witnessing the Master's deep devotion, could not restrain their tears, and one new mother after another pressed forward to suckle the child, exclaiming, "Me too!" "Me too!" In this way there naturally developed between the Master and Shien a feeling akin to that of father and son.

Years later, I[33] heard that Shien's great-granddaughter, Ms. Kawagoe Takako, was living in the Nakano district of Tokyo, and I went to visit her.[34] Happy to receive me, she gave me the following account:

"Shien was my great-grandfather. He was born in Katakasu near Hakata, and until around age nineteen, he cared for his ailing mother, to all intents and purposes fulfilling the role of a servant.

"One day, Shien turned to his mother and pleaded, 'To this day I've been given no opportunity to study, which has left me truly at a disadvantage. So I am asking you, please allow me to begin my education.'

"Shien, whose mother had always been a lady of considerable

refinement, promptly acceded to her son's request, and from that day on Shien began to study Chinese and Japanese literature.

"Our family had served for generations as hereditary equerries to the Kuroda daimyo, with a stipend of five hundred koku. At one time, however, something happened to cause the stipend to be reduced, and by Shien's generation the family was receiving a scant two or three hundred koku. The equerry would have to travel to work from Katakasu to the daimyo's castle, a considerable distance; and I understand that when Shien turned nineteen, the household moved to the Fukuromachi section of Fukuoka.[35] Not only had his mother remained ill but the whole family was impoverished, leaving them with no choice but to obtain advance payments on the stipend from the Kuroda, till one day no payments remained, leaving them at their wit's end. One year, I'm told, they even begged the castle for a straw sack of soybeans, augmented in the same year by a gift of rice and money from the mother's family. Meager though this was, it enabled them to eke out a bare existence.

"Living on in this manner, Shien continued his studies, reading the Chinese and Japanese classics and even gaining a reputation in his own right as a haiku poet. He also began to drink heavily and to borrow money, which only compounded his poverty. Yet ever casual and self-indulgent, Shien, it is said, remained utterly unperturbed by his family's circumstances, and till well past dawn would sit up drinking sake and composing haiku with his friends.

"When Shien reached marriageable age, he was wed to a daughter of the wealthy Tomita family of Hakata. However, it was not long before he began to sell off his wife's entire trousseau—her kimono, hair ornaments, and coverlets—at the secondhand store, till the household could no longer meet its living expenses. In the end, they were supported entirely by Shien's in-laws, down to the barest necessities. All the while, Shien's friends continued to congregate at the house, lost in the composition of poetry, and at mealtimes it was they who received whatever rice there was, though I heard that nothing remained as a side dish but greens flavored with ordinary salt.

"Shien was a follower of Sengai and a diligent Zen practitioner. His devotion to the Master resembled that of a child to a parent, while, in return, the Master loved Shien like a son and is said to have given him various pieces of calligraphy, tableware, clay figurines that he'd made by hand, and the like. Until recently, Shien's home was crammed with six-panel folding screens decorated with the Master's brushwork, depicting giant goblins from whose long noses dangled bottle gourds, beneath which were drawn large sake cups.[36] Unfortunately, tears developed in the screen, leading my family to burn it. All that remains is an image of Bashō, given to me by the abbot of the Hakata Genjū-an."

And so saying, Ms. Kawagoe fetched from another room the portrait of Bashō and showed it to me. It was a figurine of light-gray unglazed pottery, the piece being altogether around one *shaku* three *sun* (fifteen inches) high and one shaku two sun (fourteen inches) wide. The back of the figurine consisted of two parts, an upper and lower. On the upper was incised, "Fourth year of Bunka (1817), image of Bashō, at the request of Shien"; and on the lower, "Evening on the banks of a pond among spring grasses / A tree frog plunges in—the sound of water.[37] Made by Sengai."

I felt mysteriously moved at seeing this image, preserving as it did the very fingerprints of Master Sengai, which remained clearly visible around the neck behind the figurine's head.

Ms. Kawagoe then continued her story: "I heard that when Shien was about sixty, he erected a house in Katakasu for a concubine. When summer guests came, Shien would pick eggplants from the fields behind the house, mashing them in a mortar as a side dish while everyone drank sake.

"Such was the state of poverty to which Shien had been reduced. But his son, Mataemon, by cultivating business relationships with the Kuroda domain, was able to restore the family fortunes, and the stipend from the Kuroda clan burgeoned with each passing year.

"Mataemon had two children, a son, Mochitarō, and a daughter, Koma. Mochitarō became a student of Kirino Toshiaki and also enlisted in the academy of Saigo-san.[38] At age twenty-three, Mochitarō perished at Shiroyama in the fighting against the imperial army.[39] The upshot was that Koma's elder daughter—myself, Takako—was designated Mochitarō's adopted child, allowing the Kawagoe family to continue.[40]

"The family retained many examples of Master Sengai's calligraphy and other articles belonging to the Master, but in the fighting of the tenth year of Meiji (1877) and the terrible panic that followed news of the advancing imperial forces, all these treasures were hidden in the well of a house where we had moved in the Su'noko district of Fukuoka and were subsequently lost."

〰

Among the Master's lay followers was one Yorozu-ya Sōhei, also known as Sakai Sōhei (1803–1881), the third son of the Sakai family.[41] He was the grandfather of Sakai Toranosuke of Hakata and great-grandfather of Sakai Munenosuke. In the first year of Tenpō (1830), Sōhei went to the house of the Kano family in Hakata and opened a sake shop. Day after day, lines of drinkers could be found pushing their way up to his shop counter.

Among these was a confirmed drunkard named Iwane, who liked to trade drinks with Master Sengai at the temple in exchange for samples of the Master's calligraphy. He was constantly badgering the Master, demanding, "I gave you a drink. Now brush me something!" And the Master, finding himself with no recourse, had to brush something for Iwane.

The shop's proprietor, who was privy to these transactions, also collected the Master's brushwork, and when Iwane would show up at the shop carrying samples of it, Sōhei would ply him with liquor and then when Iwane was unable to pay for his drinks, he would make Iwane sell him the Master's paintings. That is why, to this day, the Kano family possesses many examples of the Master's brushwork.

In his time off from the shop, Sōhei would visit the Master at Kyohaku-in, listening reverently to his sermons. And because Sōhei loved *Chronicle of the Three Generations of the Sanada Clan*, reading it every day, he also asked the Master to teach him to read classical Chinese martial arts texts, such as *The Six Secrets and Three Essentials*.[42]

It was not long before Sōhei, by applying himself to business, had become a wealthy man. The Master was heard to exclaim, "That Sōhei is a good man, even when it comes to making money!"

Moreover, Sōhei, realizing that the Master was fond of yams, would lay in a supply to give the Master in exchange for his brushwork. Sōhei then taught this trick to others, and they, too, would employ it to get the Master to produce samples of his brushwork.[43]

Once, the Master remarked to one of these people, "You've probably been told by Sōhei to come here and scrounge some brushwork from me. People like that wouldn't shrink from plucking out a horse's eyeballs or ripping out a living man's intestines and gobbling them up!"

In the Master's eighty-seventh year,[44] the year of his death, he inscribed the following cautionary verse to Sōhei, brushing it onto the bottom of a tray, which the Master then gave to him:

In My Eighty-Seventh Year

Don't get a swelled head:
Even the glory of the moon at its full
Lasts only for a single night.

—*Bodhisattva [Sen]gai*

Sōhei placed this tray on top of the shop counter where he sat every day.

In his late years, Sōhei could regularly be found in winter, seated cross-legged draped in a hand towel in front of the six-sided hibachi on his counter, puffing away at his pipe as he regaled his customers with many interesting stories.

With the overissue of new paper money by [the Fukui reformers] Hisa no Geki, Shirōzu Yōtei, and others, Sōhei was able to speculate on the Hakata rice market, using the dealings of the [competing rice merchants] Tomo'ichi of the Maru-ya and Heizō of the Takahashi-ya to his own advantage to eliminate them both from the marketplace.[45] It is even reported that Sōhei would appear at the market to manipulate the rice prices, bearing a thousand-gold-coin strongbox that actually contained nothing but an empty tea canister and some rocks and which he deployed as show money.

Meanwhile, Sōhei found himself employed by the Kuroda clan to manage the domain's finances and even lent money to the clan's chief retainers. During periods of famine, Sōhei would distribute rice to the needy, an act for which he was often commended by the daimyo himself. And yet, amid all his successes, Sōhei carried with him like a shining beacon in the depths of his heart, the words of the verse the Master had given him.

〜〜

During the Bunsei and Tenpō eras (1818–1843), there lived in Hakata a noodle-shop proprietor called Sokyū-san, whose actual name was Fukuda Hisaemon. He was known by everyone, even Edo Kabuki actors and sumo wrestlers. He was indeed a man among men, kindhearted and chivalrous, and at his establishment he could always be found tending to the needs of sumo wrestlers, Confucian scholars, Buddhist priests, and even the occasional stray cat.

This Sokyū numbered among Master Sengai's devoted adherents and is said to have frequently visited Kyohaku-in, bearing in each hand the Master's favorite bean-jam dumplings along with the first fruits and vegetables of the season.[46]

Plain and simple in his nature, Sokyū was utterly lacking in affectation about his appearance. Even when paying a visit to the Master at his retreat, he would present himself, it's said, just as he was, wearing his ordinary noodle maker's work clothes.

On one such day, Sokyū arrived to see the Master, bearing in his arms a pile of steaming bean-jam dumplings and still dressed in his usual work outfit smeared all over with noodle flour. Arriving at the entry to the temple's reception area, he called out, "Is the Reverend Master in?"

Master Sengai emerged from his quarters and exclaimed, "Well, what do you know, it's Sokyū! What can I do for you?"

Sokyū replied, "I made some bean-jam dumplings and wanted to bring them to Your Reverence while they were still warm."

The Master said, "Ah, would you mind waiting just a minute?" He then scurried back indoors, reemerging at the entryway dressed in his formal priest's robes and respectfully accepting the bean-jam dumplings.

Somewhat bewildered, Sokyū could only stammer, "Your Reverence, I'm very much honored by such formality . . ."

The Master said, "Not at all, Sokyū. You came wearing the

uniform of your vocation, and I could only greet you by putting on my Buddhist robes, the uniform of mine!"

⌒⌒

Among Sokyū's offspring were two noted eccentrics, his elder son, Kikushō, and his second son, Hisafuchi. Kikushō entered the world of Osaka sumo wrestling under the professional name Tobi-ume (Flying Plum Tree). Hisafuchi, meanwhile, received headship of the family from Sokyū, composing *waka* and haiku and continually astonishing the people of Hakata by his offbeat and original behavior.[47]

Once when his wrestler son, Tobi-ume, was returning to Hakata after a long absence, Sokyū stuck a radish into the base of his topknot and went rushing distraught through the town. Mystified by his behavior, people asked him what he was doing, and lightly brushing the top of his head, Sokyū explained, "What am I to do? My boy is coming down from the big city and all the blood is rushing up to my head!"

By which Sokyū meant to say that he had stuck the radish into the base of his topknot to stem the rush of blood to his head![48]

⌒⌒

Once Sokyū had gone to drink sake at Kohei's grog shop, the Watermill, in Hakata, when he noticed posted on the main pillar a sign that read, "Payment in advance for all drinks." Looking at the sign, Sokyū tossed back a drink and loudly declaimed an extemporaneous verse to the many other patrons crowding the bar:

> He may call himself Kohei (literally, "small peace")
> But he's really Ōhei (big arrogant bastard).[49]

Sokyū's grave lies at Zendōji in Hachisu. Carved into the tombstone is the death poem he composed:

What a laugh! It's through—
My existence in this floating world
    empty as a dried-out gourd[50]
Sobered up, passed away
The drunkenness of ignorance.

~~

It happened one year that the seventh Ichikawa Danjirō stopped for the night at the home of the noodle maker Hisaemon, popularly known as Sokyū.[51] Danjirō discussed with Sokyū his desire to make the acquaintance, however briefly, of the celebrated Zen master Sengai as a kind of memento of his visit to Hakata. Having heard the Master loudly revile actors as decadent "theater riffraff,"[52] Sokyū knew that on his own he could never be successful in going to the Master and gaining his consent to meet Danjirō. "Why not ask Sengai's bosom friend Chōeimon to speak to the Master," Sokyū thought. "Perhaps Chōeimon could succeed in arranging the meeting."

Deciding it was worth at least a try, Sokyū set off to see Chōeimon, and the latter immediately grasped the situation. "Certainly," he told Sokyū, "let's get them together, by all means!"

Chōeimon then went off to see the Master at Kyohaku-in and asked him, "How about letting me arrange for you to meet Danjirō?"

But the Master firmly declined, saying, "I don't want to meet with theater riffraff!"

Chōeimon, however, would not take no for an answer, and finally the Master relented. "All right," he said, "I'll meet him."

Yet another version of the story has it that even though the Master remained unrelenting in his refusal, the very next day Chōeimon brought the actor in tow. In any case, Danjirō arrived at Kyohaku-in in high spirits escorted by Sokyū and Chōeimon, and they all sat waiting in the anteroom of the Master's private quarters.

Yet wait though they did, there was no sign of the Master. When they finally peered inside his quarters to see what the Master was up to, he was kindling a fire under the hearth, and eventually they heard the sounds of powdered tea being prepared.[53]

Relieved, Sokyū and Chōeimon whispered to each other, "The Master may talk about 'theater riffraff,' but he's even taking out the powdered tea. Thank heaven!"

The next sound they heard, however, was that of the Master slurping the tea himself, followed by the noise of the tea things being cleared away. As Sengai had still made no sign of emerging, Chōeimon, unable to restrain himself any longer, called into the Master's room, "Your Reverence, it's taking awfully long, don't you think? Why don't you come out and just say hello, even for a moment?"

"All right, I'm coming, I'm coming," the Master grumbled. After this there was another long pause and then suddenly the sliding doors to the Master's room opened. Sengai abruptly stuck his head out, glared at Danjirō, and exclaimed, "What big eyeballs!"

No sooner had the Master said this than the doors again slammed shut and were bolted.

Sokyū and Chōeimon couldn't help feeling sorry for Danjirō. "Well, we tried, and look at the result!" they said, apologizing to the famous actor.

But Danjirō declared, "On the contrary, I've obtained a wonderful keepsake of my visit! The Master is indeed a living buddha! The eyes are the whole heart and soul of the art of the house of Ichikawa. And now I've been honored to receive the essence of the great Master Sengai's essential teaching. I am sincerely grateful for his words and wouldn't exchange them even for a chest of gold coins! I have found an awesome keepsake to carry back with me to Edo."

And so saying, Danjirō stood facing the Master's door and humbly prostrated himself.

~~

One story has it that this close friend of the Master's, Chōeimon, was very poor. Saddled with many children, he was unable to imbibe the sake he loved. At nightfall he would walk about the town to beg drinking money, guessing that this would be a busy time in every family and picking out those households with a new bride. Should the young lady refuse to help him, he would let forth with a stream of disparaging remarks, reproaching her with being a shrew, and so forth, all of which seemed to cow her into complying with his demands for drinking money. Even Sokyū, albeit without being subjected to this sort of treatment, was known to give money to Chōeimon on occasion. This technique, of course, did not work every time, and when it failed, Chōeimon would make his way to Kyohaku-in, armed with a load of calligraphy paper, and try to wheedle some pictures out of Master Sengai.

The Master was well acquainted with Chōeimon's perpetual shortage of funds and so would cheerfully brush pictures for him.

One day, hoping to get some drinking money, Chōeimon went to Kyohaku-in armed with the usual bundle of rice paper. On the stepping-stone before the entrance to the Master's quarters, he saw that the Master had left his footware as usual and, assuming him to be in, called out, as he always did, "Your Reverence, please! Master, please!" But no answer was heard from within.

Chōeimon proceeded to circle the Master's quarters, calling him as he went, but all of his cries were met with silence.

Downhearted, Chōeimon prepared to leave, grumbling as he went. "I came, thinking, 'Sengai, Sengai,'" he reflected, "but he isn't here, and now I won't have any drinking money. What am I to do?"

Just then the Master peered from the outhouse, where, in

order to see what was going on, he'd concealed himself the moment Chōeimon had arrived. Chōiemon, tired of looking for the Master, was about to depart, sighing audibly, and the Master, spying him through the outhouse window, was moved to pity.

"Hold on, Chōeimon, I'm here!" the Master shouted.

Startled, Chōeimon swung around and happily rushed to the Master's side. "Aha!" he exclaimed, exulting in his success. "So that's where Your Reverence was, eh? Now, please, let me have a piece of brushwork."

The Master selected a sheet of the rice paper, took up his brush, and promptly wrote out a poem:

> I hope you won't hold it against me
>   that I was hiding in the outhouse
> But all the folks who come here
>   are always bearing sheets of paper!

⌒⌒

During the Master's later years, when he lived in retirement at Kyohaku-in, there dwelt in the nearby village of Teranagaya a man known as Iwane, or Iwa-san. He lived with only his aged mother, to whom he was reportedly much devoted. However, his real delight was sake, and it was this that brought ruin to his family and led him to squander his fortune. Precious to him as his mother was, he also wanted to imbibe! When no money remained for drinking, Iwa saw a way out of his difficulty by visiting the Master and asking him for brushwork. So when he needed a drink, he could be found at Kyohaku-in importuning Sengai. And knowing that Iwa was a devoted son, the Master would always oblige and do Iwa a painting when he came begging like this. Afterward Iwa would promptly scamper off to the Yorozu-ya sake shop and proceed to trade the painting for sake—or when he was broke, to sell it at a good price.

The proprietor of the Yorozu-ya recalled the following:

"One summer when Sengai-san was laid up by illness, I understand Iwane came to care for him. Iwane's mode of nursing was, however, eccentric. Distinguished well-wishers from every corner of the land arrived to visit the ailing Sengai, among them eminent monks, scholars, and others, all of whom knelt at a respectful distance from the Master's sickbed, palms reverentially joined as they listened to the Master, asking after his well-being and expressing their heartfelt sympathies. Only Iwane sat right at the Master's bedside, squatting with bared thighs on the low wooden abbot's chair, which he had pulled over so that he might fan the Master's head with a round bamboo fan. So great was the casual intimacy the two displayed toward each other that it was often hard for visitors to tell which was Sengai and which was Iwa!"

⌒⌒

Among the Master's contemporaries in Hakata was an eccentric known as Gyokuran.[54] According to an aged resident of Hakata, from a young age Gyokuran would hawk soy sauce from a carrying pole balanced across his shoulders. "Soy sauce! Soy sauce!" he would call out, as he plied his business in and around the village of Torigai.

The village contained a renowned academy of the Kamei school,[55] and while Gyokuran would pause for an hour to eat his lunch and rest his weary shoulders, he would avail himself of the opportunity to enter the school and undertake study of the Chinese classics. He threw himself wholeheartedly into these studies. Yet when he would return home, he gave not the slightest indication of the erudition he had acquired. Instead, he concealed his accomplishments from one and all, patiently persevering as he mastered the reading of the Chinese classics and the practice of calligraphy.

In this fashion, unbeknownst to anyone, he passed six or seven years, till he was able to compose accomplished poems in classical Chinese and copy out formal documents. When they finally realized what a fine scholar he was, Gyokuran's parents and acquaintances were utterly astounded. A quick learner, Gyokuran went on to deepen his knowledge of classical Chinese and even to familiarize himself with the painting style of the Tosa school.[56] In addition, he loved to model in clay, making all sorts of objects.

Gyokuran became friendly with the Master, who brushed a painting of him to which he added the following inscription:

The Eccentric Gyokuran: A Short Appreciation

Oku[mura] Gyokuran delighted in modeling figures in clay. From tormenting devils in hell, hungry ghosts, beasts, and fighting demons, to men, *devas*, *sravaka* and *pratyeka* buddhas, and bodhisattvas, there was nothing Gyokuran could not make.[57] Having finished his figurines, he would arrange them on a tray and then hurl them all to the ground, reducing them to smithereens by crushing them with blows of his fist, laughing hilariously and asking, "Where did they come from? Where did they go?" Then, after several loud laughs, he would go on as normal. No one understood what he meant, so people dismissed him as an eccentric.

—*Twelfth month of the Bunsei era, Year of the Dragon [1830]*
Title and painting by Monk Sengai

〜〜

One day, a man from Hakata named Yoshiemon came to visit the Master.

"Please excuse me," Yoshiemon addressed Sengai.

"Ah, Yoshiemon, is it not?" the Master greeted him. "Good to see you. What can I do for you?"

"Well," Yoshiemon answered with hesitation, "the truth is I came to ask you something odd."

"That's all right," the Master told him. "What is it?"

"Well," Yoshiemon explained, "when I go to the True Pure Land temple and they worship the Buddha, they say, '*Naman, Naman, Naman.*'[58] But in Zen they say, '*Namu Amida Butsu!*' Which is actually correct?"

"Hmm," the Master considered, "so that's the problem. Let me have a while to give it some thought, and then you can come back."

"Very well," Yoshiemon agreed, rising to his feet, "I'll call again later." [59]

Just as he had turned and started to walk away, the Master yelled, "Hey, Yoshi!"

Yoshiemon looked back over his shoulder and answered, "Yes!"

"There," the Master told him, "that's *Naman, Naman!*"

"Aha!" Yoshiemon replied.

Then the Master shouted at him, "Mister Yoshiemon!"

Yoshiemon answered, "Yes!"

The Master explained, "That's *Namu Amida Butsu!*"

Yoshiemon, amazed at the Master's quick-wittedness, could only stammer his admiration, and after nine low bows to the Master, he departed.

⌒

Among the Master's followers in Hakata was an eccentric old rice merchant named Ōta Tadaemon. One day, Ōta dispatched a messenger to the Master, stating, "I would like to offer to Your Reverence a vegetarian meal of some humble boiled barley and rice."[60] The mention of barley and rice delighted the Master exceedingly. "I'll bet that's with grated yam!" the Master thought to himself, and set off in high spirits.[61]

But what the Master found when he arrived was a heaping tub of plain boiled barley and rice, unaccompanied by so much as a single shred of pickled radish.[62] Even the Master could not help wincing at the sight.

"Trying to pull a fast one, are you, sly old man?" Sengai thought. But without a word, the Master helped himself to a big mouthful and began to chew. Grandpa Ōta watched this all impassively, smirking and feigning complete innocence.

Finally, patting his full belly, the Master rose without a word and stomped off briskly toward the temple. Ōta, seeing this, glared angrily, visibly insulted. "Master!" he shouted after Sengai. "Is that what you call behaving like a Buddhist priest—stuffing your belly as someone's guest and just heading home without a word of thanks?"

Without missing a beat, the Master replied, "I came because I was invited for boiled rice and barley. No one ever mentioned anything about asking me to come and say thank you." And with a sweep of his hand, the Master stroked the old man's head and walked straight off without a backward glance.

"Confound it!" Ōta swore to himself. "And after all the trouble I took to outwit him! 'I was invited by you for boiled rice and barley, but you never said anything about asking me to come and say thank you' indeed! To stroke someone's head is to make a monkey out of them!" he sputtered angrily. But Ōta's chance to even the score with the Master had already passed him by.

"Woe is me!" Ōta lamented. "Isn't there any way for me to get even?"

And just then, as he was lost in brooding, who should come running into the house but the Master himself. It seems a sudden shower had caught him on the road without an umbrella, and he arrived scampering along barefoot and hitching up his robes.

"Lend me an umbrella and geta!" he pleaded.[63]

"Now is my chance to pay him back!" Ōta thought, and courteously produced the requested geta and umbrella. "Surely he'll have to say thank you this time," Ōta rejoiced. "Then I'll have had my grudge match and can stop feeling mortified." Such was Ōta's curious obsession.

Once again, however, without a word, the Master strode off briskly toward the temple.

It wasn't long before a small novice arrived to return Ōta's things. This novice happened to bear a striking resemblance to the Master, and he, too, didn't utter a word of thanks.[64]

Several days later, the Master returned to visit Ōta, who spying his chance, lit the fuse by remarking, "I dare say, the other day you must have found yourself trapped by that downpour."

"I certainly was," the Master agreed. "I had my novice bring you back the geta and umbrella."

"Yes, I received them. Very good of you, I'm sure," Ōta muttered, noting that the Master had somehow turned things around and had *him* saying thank you! The Master just smiled, but Ōta's exasperation had reached the breaking point.

"Your Reverence is certainly stubborn," he fumed. "How about just a single word of thanks?"

Quietly the Master told him, "When people say thank you, they feel the account is closed, the debt removed from the ledger. That is why instead of saying thank you with my lips, I always keep the thought in my heart. If one is kind in expectation of being thanked, or whatever, that's not real kindness."

Thus did the Master earnestly admonish Ōta in the meaning of secret virtue.[65]

⌒

One day, several samurai retainers of the Kuroda domain were discussing how they might give Master Sengai a scare. The upshot was that they invited him to a tea party. The Master, who knew nothing of the samurai's actual intentions, arrived at the party, took his place, and with both hands received the teabowl he was offered. No sooner had the Master started to take his first sip than—BANG!—a blank gun discharged loudly under the very floor where he was seated.[66] The Master, however, showed no signs of being startled, but calmly finished drinking his tea as if nothing had happened.

Afterward, when the host had finished drinking his tea, those present were assailed by an obnoxious odor.

"Something stinks!" the samurai all complained, holding their noses or covering them with the sleeves of their robes and creating quite a stir.

Then the Master, retaining his perfect composure, announced, "Oh, that smell. A bit crude, but it's *my* little gift to *you*."[67]

〰

It is said that the Master filled a mixing bowl with water and kept it beside the toilet. After relieving himself, he would wash his hands in the water. Then at lunchtime he would use the same bowl to prepare the vegetables to accompany the boiled rice, which he also added to the bowl, which thus served as his rice tub as well. Should a lay follower come by to offer some food, the Master would produce the same bowl, into which he proceeded to place the donated food. The same bowl, time and time again! Serving as a hand-washing bowl as well as a rice bowl, its uses were inexhaustible.[68]

One day a guest cautioned, "Your Reverence, are you sure it's all right to use the same bowl to wash your hands and then serve food?"

The Master replied, "When I put food into it, it's rice tub

world. And when I wash my hands in it, it's washbowl world. At the moment, I'm serving rice in it and ladling the rice from the tub 'that in all the world is alone to be revered.'[69] To you, a washbowl seems filthy. To me, there's neither pure nor polluted."

⌒⌒

Another account tells of a lay patron who went to the Master's place bearing all kinds of food and drink.

"There's a pottery bowl over there," the Master told him, "just toss your things inside for me."[70]

"But, Your Reverence," the layman protested, "please separate all the different items."

"What for?" the Master asked. "Once it goes into my stomach, it's all one meal."

⌒⌒

In Master Sengai's day, many farmers and townspeople economized on rice consumption by eating *mugimeshi*, a boiled mixture of rice and barley. Samurai and wealthy merchants, however, turned up their noses at this, objecting, "Boiled rice and barley—ugh!" and for the most part insisted on eating only rice. Indeed, most of them were picky eaters, and so one day the Master told a group of acqaintances consisting of upper-ranking samurai and wealthy merchants, "Come to my temple and I'll treat you to a meal of boiled rice and barley."

The Master's invitation had piqued the curiosity of the samurai and rich merchants, who duly assembled at the temple. Having been told that boiled barley and rice was on the menu, they all took it for granted that this would be served accompanied by a delicious cold broth[71] and waited expectantly for the meal to arrive.

But even though it was lunchtime, there was no sign of food. They waited a while longer and peered into the kitchen to see if anything were about to appear. There was not the slightest indication, however, that the meal trays were being prepared.

By this time they were all starving and waited with increasing impatience. Yet no lunch seemed to be forthcoming. As for the Master, he sat by the fireside with an air of being completely unaware that his guests were growing weak from hunger and made idle conversation about gemstones with Layman Sekishin, who was something of a connoisseur of such things.

In this way, some three hours passed, with the guests rubbing their empty bellies, when finally the individual lunch trays were brought in and set down before each of the diners. When they saw that the trays' contents consisted of nothing more than boiled barley and rice with four wrinkled shreds of pickled radish, someone asked, "Your Reverence, aren't we going to have cold broth with this?"

The Master replied, "The invitation was for boiled barely and rice. There was no invitation for cold broth."

However, in the extremity of their hunger, given that this was all there was to eat, it was agreed that the delectability of this ordinary boiled barley and rice far exceeded that of the pure white rice [to which they were accustomed].

After everyone had eaten, the Master turned to his guests and quietly admonished them, "Depending on how you go about cutting it, even an egg can be made square![72] When your stomach is empty, even boiled barley and rice tastes delicious."[73]

〰

The Master was expert at shadow sumo wrestling.[74] When at times samurai, professional sumo wrestlers, judo masters, and such would come to visit, Master Sengai would leap down into the garden and perform his shadow sumo, falling down with a great thud and exclaiming, "Well, looks like I won this match! Get it?"[75]

But no one had any idea what he meant.

The following was told to me by the Zen master Takazu Hakuju, a former abbot of the Ōbaku school:[76]

"During the Master's lifetime, my father lived in Nagasaki, working as an instuctor in swordsmanship and undertaking Zen study with Master Hakugan Enyo, the twenty-ninth-generation abbot of the Ōbaku headquarters temple.[77] It was through the good offices of Master Hakugan that my father came to visit Master Sengai at his temple in Hakata.

"Of course, when Father first went to visit, the Master was aware that he was a sword instructor and greeted him, exclaiming, 'Hey, I'm just going to do some shadow sumo in the garden. Try giving me a blow of your sword!'

"And so saying the Master leaped down into the garden and stomped his feet sumo-style, grunting, 'Yo ho! Yo ho!'[78]

"'Come on, attack me,' the Master insisted.

"Such, I understand, was the indescribably marvelous flavor of Master Sengai's unconstrained world."

⌒⌒

Among the Master's works of brush painting, one often comes across pictures of children wrestling. When asked the reason for this by an old resident of Hakata, the Master said it was because he'd always liked children. Indeed, day after day the local children would come to fish in the stream that flowed through the back of Kyohaku-in's grounds, and on their way home they would stop to play at the temple, one of their favorite places.

"Your Reverence, draw me a picture!" they would all clamor at once.

And the Master, half in jest, would tell them, "All right, but first you'll have to have a sumo wrestling competition, and whoever is the winner I'll do the picture for."

It is said that this is how the Master came, on occasion, to paint and give away the pictures of wrestling children.

～～

At Kyohaku-in, where the Master lived in retirement, every day hordes of children would come to play, climbing the pines in the garden, wrestling, and the like. The Master loved children and delighted in their play.

One day the Master called to the children, "Hey, kids, listen up! I'm offering to do a painting as a prize to whoever of you can see that crooked pine tree over there as straight."

The children were thrilled, and, screaming boisterously, they ran to the crooked pine. Some tried staring up from underneath the tree; others scaled the tree and tried looking down to the ground; yet others tried to get a view by stooping over and sticking their heads out between their legs. But no matter what they did, the crooked tree couldn't be made to look straight.

Some of the children shouted to the Master, "Your Reverence, I did it! I did it! When I looked down at the tree from above, it was straight!" Or, "When I bent over forward and looked through my legs it was straight!" and so forth. But to all of them the Master could only shake his head and say, "No good, no good."

Then a small child trailing snot from his nose came running up. "Your Reverence," he exulted, "I saw it straight!"

"How did you manage it?" the Master questioned him.

The child [whispered something into the Master's ear],[79] whereupon the Master's eyes widened in amazement.

"You are an extraordinary child indeed," the Master praised him. "You're the only one who gets a painting." And so saying he proceeded to brush a picture, which he handed to the child.

So, how did this child see the crooked pine straight? Master Hakuin used to torment his monks by telling them, "It's said, 'In under a minute one can pass straight through a narrow mountain path with forty-nine twists and turns.' Right now, at this moment, how do you pass straight through it?"[80]

～～

There was a man with blood ties to the Kuroda clan named Hakuhō-in. His present-day descendent is a man named Kuroda Naomi. At the time of Hakuhō-in's death, the Master was asked to compose the memorial inscription for the tombstone, and taking up his brush, he wrote out, "Grave of Hakuhō-in." [81]

The family of the deceased, wishing to show its gratitude, sought to reward the Master with much money and other valuables but first asked the Master what his favorite dish was.

The Master said, "I haven't any desire for gold or things, but what I really love is Kawabata candy, so just send me some of that."

This was a kind of penny candy, which even at that time was disparaged as "tartar" candy because of the way it stuck to one's teeth.

～～

In Hakata there lived a certain day laborer. On New Year's morning, his wife, thinking she would deftly prepare some rice cakes, ended up doing such a poor job that the cakes turned out mushy.[82]

"These rice cakes are simply hopeless!" her husband shouted, and seizing in one hand the iron pan in which they'd been prepared, hurled it onto the dirt floor. Unable to contain his anger, he then stormed out of the house.

He wandered aimlessly, till suddenly the thought of Master Sengai flashed across his mind, and he set off to see the Master at Kyohaku-in.

After exchanging New Year's greetings, he described to the

Master what had just occurred and how he had come in search of a way to deal with his overpowering rage.

The Master, smiling, told him, "All right, just let me handle your marital squabble. I'll draw up a one-page agreement in writing and give it to you."[83]

The Master then spread out a sheet of paper he had beside him and wrote:

> As Mount Fuji's snows
>   melt in the morning sun
> So shall your anger be melted by
>   this special New Year's morning meal.

It is said that the hired laborer received the document the Master had brushed for him and, restored to good humor, hurried home.

⌣

When Igami Kyūeimon, the samurai official governing Hakata, paid a formal visit to the graveyard at Shōfukuji, the founder's hall was in the midst of construction.[84] He thereupon proposed that he donate the cost of roof tiles for the building.[85]

The Master, however, refused.

As he subsequently explained, "People who announce they wish to donate things to the temple all just want to promote their own clan by putting their family crest on things."

⌣

Nomura Hayato, a senior councilor to the Kuroda clan, stopped to see Master Sengai on the occasion of a formal visit to the temple's graveyard.[86] The Master, however, refused to see him. Hayato, in a fury, declared, "What rudeness, refusing to see me after I went to all the trouble to visit here!"

The Master replied, "If he'd come here just to see me, I'd meet him, but I imagine his real purpose in coming was to meet the buddha."[87]

And so still refusing to meet Hayato, the Master finally had him turned away.

〰

One day, accompanied by his attendant, the Master was returning down Chūōdō Street in Hakata when he chanced upon a married couple who belonged to the temple having a quarrel in their home. The Master came to a halt in front of the house. Inquiring of a neighbor what had caused the fight, the Master declared, "Ah, surely a cause for congratulations!" and simply proceeded on his way back to Shōfukuji without attempting to intervene.

Later someone asked, "Your Reverence, a while ago on Chūōdō Street you saw a husband and wife quarreling and said, 'Ah, surely a cause for congratulations!' I don't understand what you meant."

"After all," the Master explained, "there's simply nothing so fortunate as that sort of business. Listen, when the wife is ill, she's weak and can't fight with her husband; and the same goes for him. In other words, if I'd found them on the brink of death, the two would have been in no shape to squabble with each other. But when a husband and wife are fighting together like that, it means they're both in robust health. That's why I say surely a cause for congratulations!"

〰

Among the carpenters of Hakata was a man named Jinbei. A follower of the True Pure Land school, he was continually repeating "*Namu Amida Butsu!*" even while sawing or urinating.[88]

One day the carpenter was at Kyohaku-in, and the Master, observing him repeating *Namu Amida Butsu!* even as he worked, went and stood next to him and said, "Jinbei!"

"*Nanmaida, Nanmaida,*" Jinbei continued muttering. "Yeah, what do you want? *Nanmaida, Nanmaida . . .*" [89]

"Jinbei!" the Master repeated.

"Yeah, *Nanmaida, Nanmaida . . .*"

"Jinbei!"

"Yeah, *Nanmaida, Nanmaida . . .* If you want something, hurry and spit it out! *Nanmaida, Nanmaida . . .*"

"Jinbei!" the Master called again.

"*Nanmaida, Nanmaida . . .* You're annoying me. *Nanmaida, Nanmaida . . .* Get a move on and tell me . . . *Nanmaida, Nanmaida . . .* what you want! *Nanmaida, Nanmaida . . .*"

"My, my!" the Master exclaimed. "That Mr. Amida is certainly a busy fellow!"

When Jinbei heard these words, it was as if he had suddenly been startled awake. Right then and there he stopped repeating *Namu Amida Butsu!* and from that day on, it is said, would come to the Master's room for individual Zen study. [90]

～～

There was an unusual bottle gourd, and the Master, who loved to drink, longed to own it. Try as he might, however, he failed to obtain it till finally, after three years, it came into his possession.

One day there was a certain man who begged the Master incesssantly for the gourd, and to the astonishment of everyone present, the Master casually handed it over to him.

Unperturbed, the Master merely remarked, "Whoever wants a thing, it's all the same."

～～

There was a certain Mr. Aoki who could expertly imitate Master Sengai's brush paintings. Aoki brought some of these productions to show the Master and asked him, "How about it, Your Reverence, aren't they pretty much exact copies?"

"Even *better* than the originals," confirmed the Master, wholly unfazed. "In fact, here's my personal seal—why don't you just stamp it right on?"[91]

Among the Master's contemporaries, there were some dozen individuals able to perfectly replicate the Master's calligraphy, of whom one was this Aoki. He acquired the name "Aoki Sengai" and posed a real headache for collectors of the Master's calligraphy.

Another calligrapher able to produce perfect imitations of Master Sengai's brushwork was Miyamoto Tōsai, who could also make copies of the Master's clay sculptures.[92]

After the Master's death, Tōsai received his seal, but after Tōsai's death it is said to have disappeared.

⌒

One day a rapacious collector came to see the Master at Kyohaku-in, bringing with him an outsized piece of silk that had been prepared for brushwork. He then proceeded to pester the Master to do a large painting on it for him.

"Very well," the Master told the man, "but I expect *you* to really put your back into the work of grinding up all the ink for me."[93]

Whereupon the Master produced a huge inkstone and filled it with water right to the brim. There was so much water, in fact, that [grinding the inkstone] to get the liquid dark enough was hardly possible, and finally the collector, drenched with perspiration, pleaded with the Master, "Your Reverence, it must be ready by now!"

The Master, relenting, told him, "All right, that's fine."

The Master then disappeared down the temple corridor and, after a time, returned carrying in both hands the pair of straw sandals he used for the lavatory.

"Now!" the Master exclaimed, and with a piercing shout plunged the sandals right into the middle of the ink that the man had just spent the whole day preparing. Then, getting down on all fours, the Master crawled about all over the silk till, as the collector watched, it was covered completely with ink.

"There," the Master pronounced. "It's finished! Take it home!"

The collector was outraged. "What the hell kind of painting is that?" he demanded.

"You can't tell?" asked the Master. "It's a crow flying [in the darkness]. Isn't it splendidly done?"

TALES OF HAKUIN

and His Followers

*A student asked, "What can I do
to become awakened to my own mind?"*

*The Master said, "What is that which asks such
a question? Is it your mind? Is it your original nature?
Is it some kind of spirit or demon? Is it inside you?
Outside you? Is it somewhere intermediate?
Is it blue, yellow, red, or white?*

*"It is something you must investigate and clarify
for yourself. You must investigate it whether you are
standing or sitting, speaking or silent, when you are
eating your rice or drinking your tea. You must keep at it
with total single-minded devotion. And never, whatever
you do, look in sutras or in commentaries for an answer,
or seek it in the words you hear a teacher speak."*

—KAIEN FUSETSU,
translated by Norman Waddell, *The Zen Master Hakuin*, 61–62

Hakuin was born in 1685 in Hara, a modest farming village within view of Mount Fuji that now forms part of Numazu City in the old province of Suruga (Shizuoka Prefecture).[1] Hara lay about midway on the Tōkaidō, or "Eastern Sea Road," the three-hundred-mile highway that linked the imperial capital of Kyoto with Edo, Japan's administrative capital under the Tokugawa shogunate. Originally a fishing village, then a garrison town, Edo, by Hakuin's day, had grown into a bustling commercial center. It was experiencing a celebrated flowering, associated with the popular "townspeople," or chōnin, culture of the Genroku period (1688–1704), an era roughly coinciding with the years of Hakuin's childhood and adolescence. Hakuin's family members were themselves commoners, hereditary proprietors of the Hara post station, Odakaya. Odakaya was the thirteenth of such inn-type facilities, some fifty-three in all, where travelers from Edo could change horses, hire porters, or obtain refreshments at the nearby tea stalls, which also served as roadside brothels.[2]

Although a tiny country town, Hara, situated on a particularly busy and scenic portion of the Tōkaidō, was host to a steady stream of visitors of every sort who lent the place a certain cosmopolitan character. From his vantage point at Odakaya, Hakuin was witness to a colorful cross section of Edo-period society: daimyo and their often elaborately costumed retinues, traveling from their domains to Edo for their required periods of alternate attendance on the shogun; street people, including beggars and prostitutes; performers of every description, from jugglers and acrobats to musicians, animal trainers, and storytellers—all of whom would come to figure prominently in the master's celebrated artwork.

At age thirteen, Hakuin was ordained a Rinzai Zen monk at Shōinji, the small family temple in Hara where his father was a parishioner. (Hakuin's mother was a follower of the Nichiren, or Lotus, sect.[3]) Hakuin's head was shaved and he was given the religious name Ekaku, "Wisdom Crane." Hakuin's ordination teacher, Tanrei Soden (d. 1701), was a member of the Myōshinji line, centered in the great headquarters temple in Kyoto. Tanrei was troubled by poor health, and Hakuin soon moved to another Rinzai temple, Daishōji, in nearby Numazu. Here, Hakuin spent several years in study and training, reputedly memorizing the entire *Zenrin kushū*, the phrase collection that remains indispensable in Rinzai Zen koan study.

In 1703 the young Hakuin set out on what would become fourteen years of angya, Zen pilgrimage, traveling widely to visit a variety of teachers and temples, pausing occasionally for periods of solitary retreat. His wanderings took him through both Honshū and Shikoku, two of Japan's main islands, and during this time he is said to have studied under masters of all three major Zen sects, namely the Sōtō school, founded by Dōgen Kigen (1200–1253); the Ōbaku school, introduced by immigrant Chinese masters in the previous century; and Hakuin's own Rinzai school. The last included leading students of Bankei Yōtaku, whose teachings Hakuin would later harshly denounce and whose followers were then active in the province of Mino (now Gifu Prefecture).

It was at a temple in Mino in 1704 that Hakuin chanced on a book that would change his life. Titled *A Whip to Drive [Students] Through the Barrier of Chan [Zen]* (*Chan guan cejun*; J. *Zenkan sakushin*),[4] the work had been compiled barely a century before in 1600 by the Ming Zen master Zhuhong (1535–1615). Zhuhong's short anthology assembled materials exemplifying Song-style koan practice in the tradition of Dahui and later proponents of the koan method such as Gaofeng Yuanmiao (1238–1295) and Gaofeng's noted disciple Zhongfeng Mingben (1263–1323). As described earlier, this approach involved an all-consuming focus on the huatou (J. *hattō*), or crux of the koan, especially the koan "*Mu!*" (Ch. *Wu!*), engendering a great doubt leading to sudden awakening. The fervor of the Chinese teachers described in Zhuhong's collection, their unswerving devotion to koan study, left an indelible impression on Hakuin, who thereafter, he tells us, always kept a copy of the book at his side[5]

Hakuin returned to Shōinji in 1707, intent on solving the "*Mu!*" koan. He meditated relentlessly, refusing to interrupt his practice even during an eruption of nearby Mount Fuji that sent his fellow monks scurrying for safety. The following year found Hakuin again on pilgrimage and wrestling with "*Mu!*" This despite what he describes as multiple breakthrough experiences, for which he uses the term *kenshō*, literally "seeing one's nature," an expression borrowed from Chinese Chan.[6] It was at this point, in 1707, that Hakuin's unceasing efforts resulted in his enlightenment on hearing a distant temple gong. Thereupon, in hope of finding some acknowledgment of his experience, he traveled to seek out the Zen master Shōju Rojin, the man he would revere as his true teacher. Although Shōju discounted Hakuin's breakthrough, the old master reportedly acknowledged a second enlightenment that Hakuin experienced under his instruction. He also warned the young student against contenting himself with a modest attainment and impressed upon him the importance of ongoing training to further one's enlightenment.

Taking leave of Shōju after a mere eight months, Hakuin resumed his pilgrimage, still assailed by doubts about the "*Mu!*" koan. At this juncture, physically and emotionally debilitated by his efforts, Hakuin reports meeting the recluse Hakuyūshi, who, as described in the introduction, taught Hakuin the rudiments of a Taoist-inspired hygiene in order to restore his inner energy. Rejuvenated, Hakuin resumed his rigorous koan practice, which included a period of solitary retreat in Mino around 1715. During these years, Hakuin reports many more satori experiences, once after falling into a stream he was fording, and all accompanied by an exuberant laughter that had him literally leaping for joy, "so happy I thought I was crazy."[7] Strenuous meditation was essential in the quest for enlightenment, Hakuin insisted, but true zazen, or seated meditation, also involved bouts of wild hilarity. Multiple satori, both great and small, also became a keynote of Hakuin's Zen, Hakuin stating that he had experienced so many satori that he could no longer even recall the precise number.[8]

In 1717, Hakuin's period of wandering ended with his return to

Hara and Shōinji, where, Tanrei having died, Hakuin was asked to assume the temple's abbacy. Henceforth, Shōinji and Hakuin's hometown of Hara would become the center for the master's teaching activities. The temple itself, in Hakuin's description, was in a dismal state of disrepair and sadly impoverished, its roof like a sieve in the pouring rain and its few monks clad only in paper kimono even in the depths of winter. Any ritual objects had long since been dispatched to the pawnbrokers, while meals consisted of a thin gruel swimming with maggots. None of this interfered with Hakuin's hard-driving curriculum of meditation and koan study, a curriculum observed alike by Shōinji's monks and their teacher, who still struggled with the problem of how to integrate his experience of realization with the realities of daily life.[9] At night, Hakuin would have himself securely tied to a discarded palanquin and hoisted under a tree, where he would meditate on his koan till dawn, when the temple's monks returned to lower him. Gradually, laypeople from the surrounding area—as well as monks—were drawn to the temple, and laypeople initially may have made up the largest cohort of Hakuin's early followers.

Hakuin soon received formal appointment as Zen master in the Myōshinji line, and the temple in 1718 acknowledged him as heir to Tanrei's own Dharma successor, Tōrin Soshō (d. 1754), with the additional religious name Hakuin, literally "white concealed."[10] Now a Rinzai Zen master in his own right, qualified to give koan instruction and to sanction the enlightenment of his students, Hakuin soon saw his followers increase, spreading beyond the confines of the small temple to nearby houses and abandoned shrines. But while now a recognized Zen master with his own following, Hakuin, true to Shōju's admonitions, continued his own intense koan practice.

On an autumn evening in 1726, Hakuin was reading the *Lotus Sutra* when the chirping of a cricket in the temple garden brought on his first "great enlightenment." It was this pivotal experience, he later claimed, that revealed to him the truth of Shōju's Zen, in particular the need for cultivation after enlightenment. Interestingly, there is no mention of any teacher in connection with Hakuin's initial "great enlightenment." Shōju himself was, of course, long dead by this time, so that Hakuin had not studied with or even visited the master for some eighteen years. All of which suggests that like many Myōshinji-line Zen masters who preceded him, Hakuin's first significant satori was actually "realization on his own and without a teacher" (*mushi dokugo*), making Hakuin "self-enlightened and self-certified" (*jigo jishō*)—all terms used to describe the independent awakening experiences of Bankei, Taigu, and others of the early Edo period.[11]

The 1726 experience also highlighted for Hakuin the importance of the four vows, or bodhisattva vows,[12] which enjoin helping others to reach enlightenment:

> Sentient beings are numberless; I vow to enlighten
>   them all
> Afflictions are endless; I vow to sever them all
> The gates of Dharma are inexhaustible; I vow to
>   master them all
> The Way of Buddha is ever beyond; I vow to attain it.

Hakuin's dedication to the four vows informs much of his subsequent activity, in particular his efforts to bring koan practice and enlightenment to the countless monks and lay followers that continued to flock to Shōinji. It is also the motivating force behind Hakuin's vast production of printed works and brush paintings, both frequently incorporating the popular culture of the day.

The year 1740 saw the appearance of *Kaien fusetsu*, the first of Hakuin's published works. Ostensibly a series of comments on the record of Xutang, *Kaien fusetsu* was above all a tribute to

Song koan Chan and an expression of Hakuin's determination to revive its essentials as transmitted by Xutang to his Japanese disciple Daiō, and across the generations of Ōtōkan masters to Shōju and Hakuin himself. Once again, the work emphasizes an unrelenting concentration on the koan's nub, or hattō, leading to a "great doubt" that resolves itself in sudden awakening, kenshō. Hakuin compares this process to the felling of a tree, each blow of the ax drawing closer to the core till suddenly the tree crashes to the ground.[13] Dramatic as it may be, however, kenshō is only the beginning, Hakuin cautions, and must be followed by lifelong post-enlightenment cultivation. While short on details, Hakuin does mention in this regard the need for continued koan study, focusing on what he terms the "hard to penetrate" (nantō) koan.[14]

The success of Kaien fusetsu drew increasing numbers of students to Shōinji, whose assembly steadily swelled, overwhelming the surrounding area. Among the new arrivals were two monks who would become Hakuin's principal disciples and heirs—Tōrei Enji (in 1743), for whom Hakuin would establish a nearby training temple, Ryūtakuji, and Suiō Genro (in 1744).[15] The following years saw Hakuin lecturing regularly to crowds of as many as 500—monks, nuns, laymen, and laywomen—while at other times some 150 students could be found seated in formal posture waiting in line for sanzen, their private koan interview with the master.

Now in his sixties, Hakuin undertook an intensive regimen of teaching and writing that would continue virtually till the end of his life. His teaching included travels to other Zen temples, some as far distant as Okayama in Bizen (Okayama Prefecture), a three-hundred-mile journey from the master's home base of Shōinji. It was also at this juncture, beginning in or around 1747, that Hakuin tells of a new refinement in his koan instruction, replacing "Mu!" with a koan of his own devising, the celebrated

"Sound of One Hand" (*sekishū no onjō*).[16] Hakuin explains that he found this koan infinitely more effective in raising the student's "ball of doubt," leading to the experience of kenshō, and he identified it with the authentic teaching of Zen, which had long since expired in Japan.[17] "So, what is this sound of one hand?" Hakuin writes in his eponymous book *Sound of One Hand* (*Sekishū onjō*). "When you bring two hands together you produce a sound. But when you raise one hand there is no sound. . . . You can't hear that sound with your ears!"[18] Ultimately, Hakuin presented this to his students as a two-part koan, "Hearing the Sound of One Hand and Stopping All Sounds."[19]

Those followers who realized kenshō by penetrating this "formidable barrier of the double koan 'Sound of One Hand'" were awarded dragon certificates, sanctions in Hakuin's own brushwork.[20] These depict a priest's staff metamorphosing into a dragon, possibly a reference to a famous case in the *Blue Cliff Record*, "Yunmen's Staff": "Yunmen held up his staff and addressed the assembly of monks: 'This staff turns into a dragon and swallows up the universe! Where are the mountains, the rivers, and the great earth?'"[21] Many examples of these cards remain, and Hakuin describes how on two visits to Edo between 1759 and 1761 he distributed seventy such certificates.[22] Most recipients of Hakuin's dragon certificates were laypersons, including a number of housewives, among them the wife of his longtime physician, and such individuals formed associations dedicated to promoting Hakuin's teachings. Similar cards were also bestowed on various monks, among them a number of Hakuin's leading disciples, acknowledging their having passed other koan.[23] Hakuin, however, emphasized that the cards, attesting as they did to one's initial kenshō, were only the beginning of Zen study, an encouragement to the holder to pursue a lifetime of what the master termed "after-satori" (*gogo*) cultivation.[24]

The last decade of Hakuin's life seems to have been marked by a tremendous burst of activity, and these years are responsible for the bulk of the master's surviving writings and art. As noted, many of these works show Hakuin's familiarity and even sympathy with the popular culture of the day, an extension of Hakuin's commitment to bring the teachings of koan Zen to a broad spectrum of Japanese society. In his art and published writings, Hakuin regularly invoked comic characters that were fixtures of mid-Edo street culture. One such figure, alluded to previously, is Obaba—"Grandma," the wrinkled crone with a welcoming, almost maternal expression—who is dubbed by Hakuin "Mastering-Mind Grandma" (*Shūshin Obaba*). Another familiar character Hakuin borrows from contemporary popular culture is the prostitute Ofuku, or Otafuku, literally "great good fortune." A homely, rotund, perpetually cheerful courtesan well into middle age, Ofuku projects an irrepressible good humor and in Hakuin's day served as a kind of good-luck deity. She is among the favorite subjects of Hakuin's brush paintings, where she seems to embody a wholesome, bodhisattva-like grace and warmth. Even Hakuin's female neighbors and relations might be depicted by the master as Ofuku, among these a second cousin, Otsu, who had studied Zen under Hakuin since age sixteen, and a celebrated local beauty who toiled at her father's broiled eel stand.[25]

The two, Ofuku and Obaba, make a joint appearance in Hakuin's *Grandma's Grinding Songs* (*Obaba dono kohiki uta*, 1760), an extended verse composition accompanied by Hakuin's own hand-drawn portraits of the two raucous characters.[26] The work opens with an introduction by Ofuku, and features Mastering-Mind Grandma as a vehicle for expounding Hakuin's teachings on koan study framed as a vernacular work song in alternating lines of seven-seven-seven-five syllables.[27] Despite its ostensibly vulgar format, Hakuin's intended audience for *Grinding Songs* is not neophytes or casual readers but the most advanced monks of his assemblies, with Grandma declaiming on such topics as the "hard to penetrate koan," the "'Sound of One Hand' dual barrier," and the need for continued practice after enlightenment. In Grandma's verses, Hakuin articulates through the most demotic, "down home" of formats his ultimate teaching of Zen enlightenment.[28]

As with the Song Chan classics that incorporated medieval Chinese popular language and culture, Hakuin in his large body of art and writings mined the folk traditions of his own day to communicate his teaching. The occasional supernatural, grotesque, humorous, even ribald elements conspicuous in Hakuin's surviving works reflect the ubiquity of such elements in the popular culture of mid-Edo Japan. Hence the ghost stories, tales of possession, and the stream of curious characters that crop up in the master's published writings. At times, such features seem designed merely to entertain, but often as not, they are Hakuin's means of projecting his vision of a revived Song-style Zen.

When Hakuin passed away quietly in his sleep in 1769, he left an indelible mark on Japanese Rinzai Zen, one like that of few teachers before or since. A New Year's Day poem he inscribed shortly before his death concludes:

> An elderly monk of eighty-four, I welcome in yet one
> more year
> And I owe it all—everything—to the Sound of One
> Hand barrier.[29]

Right to the end, Hakuin insisted that only koan practice made it possible to attain or transmit Zen enlightenment.[30] In this, he contrasted with luminaries of the previous century, such as Takuan and Bankei.[31] Nonetheless, it is Hakuin's forceful advocacy of koan practice and that of his disciples that has continued to shape Rinzai Zen study in Japan to the present day, not least the notion of the Rinzai training temple, for monks and laypersons alike, as a kind of satori factory. At the same time, despite differences over the unique efficacy of the koan method, Hakuin seems to have shared with his more freewheeling predecessors, such as Takuan and Bankei, a belief that the final goal of all Zen practice is nothing more than a matter of awakening to things just as they are, or as he put it, "realizing one's originally existing self nature."[32]

~~

The following anecdotes are taken from Hakuin monka itsuwasen *(Tales of Hakuin [and his] followers). This is a translation into modern Japanese of* Keikyokusōdan *(Tales from the Forest of Thorns), composed in 1829 by Hakuin's fourth-generation disciple Myōki Seiteki (1774–1848) and published in 1843. Along with the modern Japanese-language version of the text,* Hakuin monka itsuwasen *includes notes, the original Sino-Japanese (kanbun) text, and its reading into classical Japanese (yomikudashi). The book was prepared by Nōnin Kōdō and issued in 2008 in Kyoto by Hanazono University's Zen bunka kenkyūjo (Institute for Zen Studies).*

There was a certain Masa, who was the wife of a Mr. Sugiyama of Hina. After her husband's death, she lived alone with her son and strove to master Zen under the instruction of the Zen teacher Gedatsu at his temple, Muryōji. Fervently taking up her koan, she generated a great ball of doubt. There were even times when, lost all day in meditation, she forgot to prepare the family's meals. When her son returned from outside, he had nothing to eat and was fed by the neighbors, who felt sorry for him.

One day when her son returned home, Masa looked at him and inquired, "Whose child are you?"

"Mama, what are you saying?" her son asked.

To which Masa replied, "All right!" and returned to meditating.

This sort of thing continued for several days on end, when suddenly Masa experienced enlightenment. She then went to see

Hakuin. The Master proceeded to examine her on several koan, and Masa answered each one without the slightest hesitation. Hakuin then acknowledged her understanding.

⌒

The Layman Furugori Kentsu, headman of Hina, was a samurai retainer of the Inaba clan and originally a follower of the Nichiren school. One day Master Gedatsu brought him to meet Hakuin.

"This person wishes to study Zen," Gedatsu told the Master. "Won't Your Reverence please give him a koan?"

Hakuin replied, "Why bother giving and taking? Right here, in this very moment, the truth is completely manifesting!"

Gedatsu pleaded, "He is only a layman. Please offer some expedient means to guide him toward enlightenment."

Seizing a brush, Hakuin then wrote, "What is the true nature of thinking and hearing, perceiving and knowing?"

Receiving this gratefully, the layman returned home.

A year afterward, the layman experienced awakening and presented Hakuin with a poem:

> When one loses one's hold over a ten-thousand-foot
>   precipice
> One's hoe sends forth flames consuming heaven and
>   earth
> When one's body is reduced completely to ashes,
>   things spring back to life.
> The paths between the paddies are as they were
> The rice plants are putting forth ears.

Hakuin then submitted the layman to rigorous Zen training.

⌒

Yamanashi Heijirō, Layman Ryōtetsu (Penetrating Realization), belonged to the powerful Ihara family, heirs to a large fortune. By nature he was self-indulgent, sunk in debauchery. His wives and concubines were of great beauty, and even his female servants were alluring and flirtatious, so that his days were passed in laughter and amusement.

On a late spring day, Heijirō was disporting himself by the falls of Isabu.[33] Sake and fish had been set out, and there was flute and *biwa* music, making for an altogether delightful excursion.[34] Clearing mist cloaked the trees, and wildflowers bloomed everywhere in profusion. Heijirō's wives and courtesans ambled about, picking and gathering new-grown grasses. Suddenly realizing that everyone was gone, Heijirō began to stroll alone. The waters of the mountain stream and the falls poured down in a rushing torrent, sweeping along countless rocks, some of ordinary size, others as large as a foot or as small as an inch, but all vanishing in the end. Ryōtetsu suddenly perceived the impermanence of things and lamented to himself, "Human existence, too, is like this. Whether our span of life is long or short, is it really any different from a bubble?" Overcome with grief and losing all sense of enjoyment, the layman summoned his palanquin and returned home.

On another occasion, the layman happened to overhear one of his child servants reciting [a passage from] Takusui: "He who would realize the Buddha Way must first see into his own nature. Those sentient beings of dauntless courage will realize buddhahood instantaneously, while those who are feckless will never attain nirvana, even with the passing of innumerable kalpas."[35]

On hearing these words, Ryōtetsu considered, "According to Takusui's words, even a useless old nag like me must make one supreme effort to crack the whip and spur himself on!"

That very evening, Ryōtetsu went into seclusion and sat firmly in meditation. He contended with the demons of thought, and perspiration bathed his whole body. By the fifth watch [3:00

a.m.–5:00 a.m.] he had fainted from his exertions. Suddenly he revived and saw the first pale light at the corner of his window and heard sparrows twittering busily in the garden. He opened the door and stepped outside. His whole world seemed totally different. He thereupon wished to see Hakuin and, mounting his palanquin, ascended the slopes of Mount Satta.[36]

When his bearers, panting with exhaustion, paused for breath at the mountain's summit, Ryōtetsu slid open the palanquin's door and gazed at the surrounding scenery. The landscape of fields and inlets resembled a painting. All at once, without realizing it, Ryōtetsu found he had lost all traces of self. He went and saw Hakuin, who examined him with several koan, all of which Ryōtetsu answered without the slightest difficulty.

Hakuin told him, "You have experienced great penetration."

On a subsequent occasion Hakuin remarked to someone, "Not since Shigong has there been such a man as Ryōtetsu!"[37]

～

Master Chōsa Ehō was abbot of Zuiōji in Tōtōmi. He subsequently became an ardent devotee of Hakuin, longing to realize the Master's teaching. He would attend *rohatsu* every year at Hakuin's temple, with no thought to the long journey involved, always coming and joining in the intensive meditation practice.[38] Yet he had never managed to find an entrance to enlightenment.

Once, at the conclusion of the rohatsu observances, Chōsa, as was customary, came to bid farewell to the Master.

Hakuin told him, "Your being at the rohatsu every single year is just like 'ducks huddling in the water when it's cold,' traveling all this way for nothing, not even the tiniest result.[39] Don't you realize all the straw sandals you're wearing out year after year? I won't have that sort of worthless person here, so don't come back again!"

Chōsa thereupon redoubled his courage, vowing to himself, "Unless I win through to realization now, I won't return home alive! Better to die like a man trying to solve my koan once and for all!"

For seven days Chōsa secluded himself in a fisherman's hut by the seashore, practicing meditation. He neither ate nor slept, yet when the seven days had expired, he had still failed utterly to realize his goal. Preparing to throw himself into the sea and die, he removed his sandals and stood on a jetty, when suddenly he caught sight of the morning sun reflected off the ocean, which seemed washed in crimson. At that moment, Chōsa experienced great enlightenment.

Chōsa ran to the temple and entered Hakuin's room. The Master took one look at him and declared, "You have penetrated!"

～～

A novice monk of seventeen or eighteen belonging to a branch temple of Tōjiji became secretly involved with a prostitute from [Kyoto's] Kitano district. Their attachment for each other grew more intense with each passing day. One evening, believing the steward monk to be absent, the novice stole one hundred gold coins, placed them in a pouch, and accompanied by the prostitute, fled into the night.

They traveled by boat to Fushimi,[40] then proceeded to Osaka. But when the novice searched his belongings, he could not find the gold coins.

He thought, "Last night I left the pouch hanging from a hook on one of the temple pillars and must have forgotten it when I fled!" The two were overwhelmed with consternation, not knowing where to go, and in their extreme despair, the monk and his lover hung themselves from a tree.

That night, sounds of wailing and anguished moaning were heard from a room adjoining the branch temple.

"I hung the pouch here," a voice cried out, "but where is it? Oh, how terrible!"

The wailing was accompanied by the sounds of fingers running over the hooks of the temple pillars, groping along the room's walls and beams. There was also heard from time to time the voice of a woman.

Thereafter, this was repeated every evening. Hearing sounds of such misery and bitter affliction, the temple's monks were scared out of their wits and before long deserted the temple, which was left without a single monk. At this time, Master Tōrei was about to visit Tōjiji and was told in confidence of the foregoing situation. The Master [Tōrei] said, "There is no reason for distress. I will stay in the room."

The very evening of the Master's arrival at the temple, all traces of the mysterious spirits disappeared.

One night, when the Master had been invited away to another temple, the duties of caretaker were assumed by the priest Shō of Mikawa, the Master's attendant as well as an accomplished Zen student. A young maiden appeared, exceedingly lovely in appearance. Standing before the priest, her head bowed, she said, "I have come to ask a favor."

"Just tell me," Shō replied.

"I am one of the dead," she began. "I hung myself in Osaka because of forgetting some money and now am unable to free myself from the bitter round of transmigration. It is my fervent wish to beseech the great teacher of this temple to save me."

"Why don't you ask him yourself?" Shō asked.

The apparition replied, "It would be unseemly for a master of such lofty virtue to be approached by a lowly woman. How much less could I, someone from the world of shadows, dare to put to him a request?"

Shō nodded in acquiescence, whereupon the woman thanked him and departed.

When Shō subsequently conveyed this to Tōrei, the Master

said, "Such things do happen, then!" And during the sutra chanting, he had a bowl of clear water placed before him and performed the ceremony for the repose of hungry ghosts.[41]

From that time on, the ghosts never appeared again. Later, the priest Shō died an untimely death, and Tōrei is said to have greatly mourned his passing.

～～

Master Suiō Genro was born in Shimotsuke. Though by nature fond of wine, he was a man of superior talent. At age twenty-nine, Genro first met Hakuin, who perceived his endowment to be out of the ordinary and subjected him to severe and painful Zen training. Genro's private interviews with Hakuin were always conducted in the dead of night, so his traces were invisible to others. He studied some twenty years under Hakuin, but the loftiness of his wisdom remained concealed, swallowed up among the other monks of the assembly.

Genro secluded himself in a hut at Ashihara, some thirty ri from Hakuin's temple [Shōinji].[42] Unless a lecture day was scheduled at the temple, however, Genro would never go there. Indeed, as soon as the lecture was over, he would leave.

On one such day, Hakuin summoned Genro, but the attendant he sent was unable to find him. "Genro has already left," someone told the attendant, who promptly pursued and overtook Genro and told him, "The Master has sent for you. Hurry back!"

Genro replied, "The Master is doing the summoning—not me," and, sweeping his sleeves, he continued on his way.

Such was Genro's typically high-handed attitude. He had no truck with trifling matters, gave no heed to trivial things. He neither did zazen nor recited sutras. He had no fixed abode but would stretch out and sleep wherever he found himself. When drunk he considered himself happy. He loved to play go and to paint. And so he drifted along at his ease, wholly content, and no one could tell whether he was a fool or a sage.

When [in 1764] Genro received advanced rank at Myōshinji, he selected his own formal teaching name, Suiō, "Drunken Old Man."[43] Questioned as to his choice by the priest at the sponsoring Myōshinji subtemple, Genro replied, "Because I'm fond of drinking. That's why!"

The priest responded that such a name seemed highly inappropriate. He suggested instead substituting another similar-sounding Chinese character, meaning "to attain or accomplish," in place of the character "drunken."

Genro replied, "That's all right, too."

Following the ceremony, Genro traveled to Osaka, finally returning to Shōinji and offering [Hakuin] the following poem:

> On a morning in the sixth month of the first year of
>   Meiwa[44]
> I accorded with hallowed tradition at the founder's
>   pagoda[45]
> Now in the twelfth month I've come back to serve
>   as abbot of my ramshackle temple
> Having emptied completely the karmic winds, I'm
>   letting them blow as they will.

After the ceremony, Genro did not seek to stay with Hakuin but lived in solitude at Ashihara for three years. As Hakuin's health deteriorated, however, Genro returned to [Shōinji] and attended the Master by his bedside till he passed away. Genro then assumed [Shōinji's] abbacy but, willful and wayward as ever, refused to concern himself with temple affairs. To anyone who came and asked for instruction in Zen, he replied, "What do I know? Go study with Tōrei!"

In the summer [of 1789], Master Gasan was to lecture on the *Blue Cliff Record* at Rinjōin in Edo.[46] The Master wished to go, but [because of his precarious health] the monks of the temple sought to dissuade him.

Genro told them, "It's my duty to the teaching," and set off for Edo.

On the way there, however, Genro suffered from heat exposure, and returning to his temple in the sixth month, he was confined with illness to his bed and never rose from it again. He had taught the Dharma for some sixteen years.[47]

On the twentieth day of the twelfth month of the first year of Kansei [1789], the Master's attendant monk begged him for a final verse.

Genro scolded him, but the attendant returned again with the same request.

Genro wrote:

> After seventy-three years deceiving buddhas and
>   patriarchs
> What do I do for a final verse?
> *Katsu!*[48]

Genro then shut his eyes, turned on his side, and passed away.

⌒⌒

Master Tōrei was lecturing on the *Blue Cliff Record* at Tōhokuji, in Edo, when he took up the record's third case, "Sun-Faced Buddha, Moon-Faced Buddha."[49]

Among those in attendance was Shibata Genyō's[50] mother, then over sixty years of age. No sooner had she heard Master Tōrei's words than her mind seemed suddenly and spontaneously to open. After the lecture, she went to see the Master and presented her understanding. Tōrei was overjoyed.

As she lay dying, this woman instructed her granddaughter, "Though you are young, you should strive to take refuge in the Buddha's teaching. Why? Because from the moment long ago when I heard Master Tōrei present 'Sun-Faced Buddha, Moon-Faced Buddha' and suddenly experienced enlightenment right up till now, there hasn't been even a speck of dust in my mind, which has remained bright as a mirror. Now I'm dying, but I feel quite peaceful, just as if I were going home. What is there to trouble me?

"Should you fail to take refuge in the Buddha's teaching," she admonished, "you are no granddaughter of mine! Remember!"

And with these words, she simply passed away.

⌒

Master Chōdō of Chikugo studied under Kogetsu and attained realization of the "*Mu!*" koan. At that time, the Dharma teaching of Hakuin was enjoying great popularity, and monks were flocking to his temple. Chōdō, too, determined to set off there, hoping to engage the Master in a Zen dialogue, and went to take his formal leave of Kogetsu.

Kogetsu advised him, "Postpone your departure for a while."

Chōdō, however, refused, and Kogetsu then told him, "Very well, if that's how it is, I'll write an introduction for you," and writing out a note, he handed it to Chōdō.

Chōdō went off to interview Hakuin. He found the Master in the bath, but Chōdō went right into the water, introduced himself, and presented his understanding of Zen.

Hakuin told him, "One may say that your coming here was not in vain. Now withdraw."

Chōdō then thought to himself, "He's approved me!"

When Hakuin emerged from the bath, Chōdō dressed himself

in his most formal monk's robes and entered the Master's room to interview him again and present Kogetsu's letter.

Hakuin opened the seal and read the letter. It said: "It is not that this youngster lacks any merit. But he is simply a person of limited capacity. I beg Your Reverence to find some suitable expedient to teach him."

When Hakuin had finished reading, he turned on Chōdō. "Even if someone with your meager endowment and inferior spiritual potential were to realize the great matter," Hakuin angrily berated him, "what would be the use?"

At that moment, feeling that his whole realization had been snatched away, Chōdō became deranged, and from then on, he was never normal again. Hakuin was often heard to lament, "I have always taught huge numbers of students. But among these I only went wrong with two—Chōdō of Chikugo and one other, whose name escapes me."

Subsequently, Chōdō returned to Chikugo and became abbot of a temple. He erected a small monk's hall, where all alone he carried out the Zen temple observances. Every rohatsu he would bring the child priests and temple cats into the meditation hall with him to do zazen. When the cats would run out, he would grab them and hit them with the *keisaku*, berating them, "Why won't you follow the rules in my temple!" [51] In this way, countless cats died at his hands. Yet strictly maintaining his monastic practice, it is said Chōdō ended his days at the temple.

～〜

Master Gasan Jitō was a native of Mutsu. He became a monk under Master Gessen Zenne of Kōke-in in Miharu. On reaching the age of sixteen, Gasan undertook an extensive Zen pilgrimage. He traveled first to Bungo, where he undertook koan study with Korei Soō of Manjūji and attained a small realization. But even after knocking at the gates of more than thirty other Zen masters, he found none a worthy match for him. Gasan returned to see Gessen, who approved his realization and told him, "Don't go anywhere else; just stay here."

"I've completed the great matter of enlightenment!" Gasan thought to himself.

Gasan had frequently passed by Hakuin's temple, but he had lacked any interest in interviewing the Master. One day, however, he considered, "I went to see Zen masters all over Japan and couldn't find even one able to show me the Way. Hakuin is the only man left, the one master whose worth I still don't know." He therefore determined to set off to meet him.

When Gasan went to tell Gessen, the latter said, "There's no need for you to go. Why do you have to meet Hakuin?"

Gasan followed Gessen's advice and remained with him for one more year. Then he happened to learn that Hakuin was to lecture on the *Blue Cliff Record* at Tōrinji in Edo. Gasan thought, "If I fail to meet this old fellow, I can't truly call myself a man of determined spirit." He therefore resolved to go.

Gessen once more sought to stop him, but this time Gasan would not be dissuaded. Traveling directly to Tōrinji, he saw Hakuin and presented his understanding.

"What sort of bad teacher's place are you coming from, spewing out all this evil breath and smelling me up!" Hakuin railed at him. He then beat Gasan and drove him out.

Gasan, however, would not be put off and returned three times to interview Hakuin, but each time he was beaten and driven out.

"I really have experienced enlightenment," Gasan thought to himself, "but he's deliberately undermining me."

One evening, after Hakuin had concluded his lecture and Gasan had resumed his place in the meditation hall, he considered, "Hakuin is known to be among the greatest and wisest teachers in the land. How could he simply beat someone for no good reason? Surely he must have superior attainment." Thereupon, he entered the Master's room, and expressing profound contrition, he declared, "The other day, in error, I gave offense to Your Reverence and now humbly beseech your forgiveness. I beg you, bestow upon me your instruction."

Hakuin told him, "You're still young, but you'll spend your whole life hauling around a bellyful of lifeless Zen![52] However much you jabber and jabber, when you arrive at the moment of death, you'll find yourself completely helpless. If you want to be joyful your whole life long," Hakuin concluded, "you must hear my 'sound of one hand.'"

Gasan prostrated himself in gratitude before the Master and departed. From that day on he became Hakuin's devoted follower.

～～

Master Ryōsai Genmyō, abbot of Kagakuji in Mikawa, was a native of Owari.[53] He first experienced enlightenment under Master Kogetsu in Hyūga and subsequently went to see Hakuin at Shōinji.

Hakuin took one look at Ryōsai and declared, "Here comes Manjusri!"[54]

Ryōsai remained at Shōinji several years, profoundly penetrating the mysterious essence of Zen, and Hakuin formally sanctioned his realization. Subsequently, Ryōsai assumed abbacy of Kagakuji, on which occasion he delivered the following verse:

> Some grow long, some grow short—a thousand pines
> Some grow crooked, some grow bent—a dense clump
>   of bamboo
> Don't let those who come understand this as refer-
>   ring to the outside
> Ringing the gong, a monk stands amid the rays of the
>   evening sun

When Ryōsai began to teach, he attracted an assembly of over four hundred and was extremely active in propagating Hakuin's Zen. Nevertheless, Hakuin once declared, "I gave Ryōsai inka too soon. That's why he's still incomplete. If only I'd waited three more years and then given him my sanction, no one in the land would have been able to touch him!"

An attendant monk asked, "Why then did Your Reverence sanction him so soon?"

"At that time I thought I'd never find such a man again," Hakuin replied. "Ah! When it comes to conferring the sanction of enlightenment, a Zen master must take great care!"

〜〜

Daikyū Ehō was investigating the koan "Nanquan's Flower."[55] At this time, Hakuin was to pay a visit to Unzan,[56] and Daikyū accompanied him. Along the way, Daikyū presented Hakuin with his understanding of the koan.

"You couldn't even feed a dog that kind of bad understanding!" Hakuin chided Daikyū and struck him with his staff.

When Hakuin arrived at [Unzan's temple] Kongoji, he looked back, but Daikyū was nowhere to be seen. "He must have fallen behind," Hakuin thought, and he and Unzan spent the whole night talking together.

Daikyū, meanwhile, had gone to the house of the local village headman and sat in meditation until, without realizing it, he had cut off both past and future.[57] Suddenly opening his eyes he noticed that the moon had gone down, birds were singing, and the eastern sky was beginning to brighten.

At that moment, Daikyū grasped the meaning of "Nanquan's Flower." He hastened to Hakuin and presented his insight, and the Master praised him lavishly.

〜〜

Kaigan and Daikyū were staying at Hakuin's temple.

Hakuin told them, "Our temple kitchen hasn't much and can't feed you. Tomorrow, go to beg food from the villagers."

The two monks bowed in assent and withdrew.

The next morning there was fierce wind and rain, and the two were waiting in the quarters for newly arrived monks for the rain to stop when Hakuin appeared carrying his stick. "What do you think you're doing here?" he demanded.

Kaigan explained, "The rain and wind were so bad we weren't sure what to do."

"You layabouts!" Hakuin scolded them. "Are you going to be frightened off by some wind and rain? Aren't there plenty of people traveling back and forth along the Tōkaidō? Get going this minute or I'll beat the living daylights out of you both!"

Cowering in fear, Daikyū and Kaigan made their departure, turning to each other at the temple gate to exclaim, "What a harsh teacher!" Then, donning bamboo hats and straw raincoats, they set out into the pounding rain.

By noon they had reached Kashiwabara, and the sky was gradually beginning to clear. That evening they returned to the temple with some seven or eight measures of rice offered by the townspeople.

Hakuin was delighted when he saw them. "Now that's just what you young monks should be doing!" he exclaimed.

〜〜

Master Ishin Eryū was a native of Izumo. He studied under Hakuin and received Dharma transmission from the Master. His severity in training students was greater even than Hakuin's. It was Ishin's custom when receiving students in sanzen to keep an unsheathed sword at his side, and when a student showed the slightest hesitation, to brandish the sword and chase him out.

Monks would often back down, finding themselves face-to-face with the principle of Ishin's Zen.

When Reigen came to visit, he announced, "I, Etō of Tango, have come here specifically to seek an interview with the Master."

The attendant monk went and reported this to Ishin, who said, "This is one of Hakuin's students, the head monk Etō."

The attendant monk then invited Reigen to follow him upstairs to the Master's quarters, and Reigen accompanied him. Formally arranging his robes, he mounted to the second floor and presented himself before the Master.

The instant Ishin saw him, he said, "Monk Tō, let's just dispense with the formalities. I have a question for you: A demon of huge strength seizes you by the arm and is about to hurl you into the burning fires of hell.[58] How can you save yourself?"

Etō did not know what to say. Instantly, Ishin sprang up and kicked him down the stairs. Etō was stupefied. Rearranging his robes around him, he went to the latrine behind the abbot's quarters and sat there in meditation. After seven days he experienced realization and ran back up the stairs to present his understanding to Ishin.

"Since you've understood this much, our business is done," Ishin declared.

Such was the usual rigor of Ishin's style of teaching.

〰

Master Reigen [E]tō was with Hakuin for many years, relentlessly pursuing his Zen practice and living in seclusion at a hermitage some twenty ri from Hakuin's temple. He would come and go in silence, palms crossed over his chest, eyes fixed straight ahead. If he encountered one of his fellow monks, he would merely bow his head and continue on his way without exchanging even a simple word.

Once the monks of the assembly met together and said,

"Brother Tō appears to have had some sort of enlightenment experience, but there's no way to tell how shallow or deep it is."

One monk spoke up. "Wait a bit," he said, "and I'll test him and find out."

The following day, the monk ran into Reigen on the road and asked, "Brother Tō, what about the koan 'Shushan's Pagoda'?"[59]

But Reigen simply bowed his head and walked on. The upshot was that people had no way to gauge the extent of his realization.

It happened that for over one hundred days Reigen was suffering from an abscess in his navel, and in the midst of his groans and agonies he penetrated the meaning of "Shushan's Pagoda."

Reigen was frank and straightforward, without attachment to words and letters, given over entirely to hardship and struggle. It is said that is why his spiritual strength far surpassed that of others.

In later life, Reigen served as abbot of Zenshōji in Tango, and subsequently abbot of Tenryūji. Students flocked to study with Reigen, and he became a leading teacher in the [Kyoto] area.

Kaimon came to interview Reigen, whom he encountered on his way to Kyoto. Stepping forward and making a low bow, Kaimon introduced himself, saying, "This insignificant person is Kaimon, Dharma heir of Daijū."

Reigen instantly stuck out his hand, pointing it at Kaimon, and demanded, "How does my hand resemble the Buddha's hand?"

Kaimon was at a loss how to respond, whereupon Reigen kicked him to the ground.

～～

Master Kankei Sotei of Ishihara in Tōtomi studied under Hakuin and thoroughly realized the great matter. Later, he became abbot of Shōkōji. There, he lectured on the *Blue Cliff Record* to an audience of over one hundred monks. Addressing the assembly, he said: "When it comes to the koan 'Huangbo's "Drinkers of Wine

Dregs,'" in Zen temples today, they toss it aside like it was a clod of dirt.[60] My teacher Hakuin would say, 'Huangbo's "Drinkers of Wine Dregs"' must be as if it comes from your own lips; only then can you get a look at Huangbo's innards—his liver, bladder, heart, and stomach.'" Kankei added, "And not only will you see Huangbo's liver, bladder, heart, and stomach, but you'll also meet face-to-face with Master Hakuin. So, all of you, train hard!"

One day when Kankei was at Hakuin's temple, he was serving as the Master's attendant and lightheartedly asked, "Master, when you were traveling on pilgrimage, do you recall any strange happenings?"

Hakuin replied, "Long ago I was living in retreat [at Mount Iwata] in Mino. One day I climbed the mountain and strolled about. Coming upon a large, flat rock, which could easily have accommodated over ten men, I climbed up and sat a while in meditation. A few of the village farmers who were engaged in tilling some newly cleared fields shouted to me, 'Don't go up on that rock! The local *kami* have placed a curse on it!'[61]

"Hearing this, I got down and wandered about, slowly making my way through the nearly impenetrable thicket.

"Returning to my hut that evening, I sat in meditation. It was around the time of the second watch [approximately 10:00 p.m.] that I heard the sound of deliberate footsteps. Suddenly [the footsteps] had leaped down from the mountain and were right in front of my hut, which they seemed to be trying with all their might to cave in.

"'Master Hakuin!' the creatures shouted loudly, their voices shaking the trees of the forest. [They were so huge that] when I peered out at them, I could see only up to their waists. Their feet were as large as stone mortars, and they stood there towering over the house, the area above their waists wholly obscured by the edge of the eaves."

Kankei asked, "And what happened next?"

Hakuin said, "I was really tired that day, and before I knew it I'd fallen fast asleep. When I awoke and opened my eyes, the smoke from the incense stick I'd lit for my meditation had vanished and along with it all traces of those ghostly apparitions."

~~

The Zen master Daijū Zen'nyo was a native of Hōki. He was endowed with great keenness of intellect and had made a deep study of both Buddhist and Confucian texts. The only area of study he had failed to penetrate was the *Yi jing* (*Book of Changes*).[62] He therefore traveled to Edo, hoping to satisfy his curiosity under some Confucian scholar.

On his way, he passed by Hakuin's temple. Thinking, "Here is to be found the greatest teacher of the realm," Daijū asked for lodging and went to interview Hakuin.

Hakuin asked him, "Where are you off to?"

Daijū replied, "I am going to Edo."

Hakuin asked, "And what do you intend to do there?"

Daijū explained, "I have not yet fathomed the meaning of the *Yi jing* and am hoping to hear some Confucian lectures."

Hakuin told him, "As for the *Yi jing*, without any experience of seeing your true nature, you can't hope to understand it. You had better stay here awhile and strive to realize enlightenment. If you see your true nature, then I'll teach you about the *Yi jing*."

"I shall do as you command," Daijū agreed. He thereupon joined the assembly of monks at the temple and, devoting himself to exhaustive practice, finally realized the great matter of seeing into one's nature. He then served the Master over ten years, compiling *Poison Flowers from a Thicket of Thorns* (*Keisō dokuzui*).[63]

Daijū subsequently became chief abbot of Jishōji in Buzen.[64] Here, students underwent rigorous training under Daijū, who earned a reputation for extreme severity.

In instructing the assembly of monks, Daijū would only employ the koan "Doushuai's 'Three Barriers.'"

Not long after assuming abbacy of Jishōji, Daijū passed away. Subsequently, those who were his disciples also relied only on the "Three Barriers," to the complete exclusion of all other koan. Over and over, each one would repeat to his students, "When the elements of the physical body disperse . . . When the elements of the physical body disperse . . . [65] Penetrate this and your Zen studies are finished for life. I don't care if all the Zen teachers of the land criticize me!" Thus they stubbornly defended their exclusive focus on the koan.

Personally, I have some serious questions about this whole matter. [66] On consideration, does not such a dubious approach seem quite unworthy of Daijū? Here, after all, was someone who had served under Hakuin for years and even compiled the *Poison Flowers* collection of the Master's teachings, someone who had assuredly received the Master's exhaustive koan instruction in private interviews.

In all likelihood, Daijū's adherence to the "Three Barriers" koan for teaching students was no more than an expedient for those in the early stages of their Zen studies. It's what the old masters referred to as "sick bay" Zen. [67] Also, Daijū having passed away at so young an age, his students were unable to fully penetrate the innermost secrets of his teaching. Was not Daijū's untimely departure from the world the likely explanation for these things?

～～

Master Sōgai studied Zen under Hakuin and attained enlightenment. Shortly thereafter he departed for [his native province of] Hyūga and assumed abbacy of [his original teacher Sekitei's] temple. Over one hundred monks attended the intensive ninety-day meditation retreat (*kessei*), where Sōgai delivered lectures on the *Record of Linji*.

At the retreat's end, Sōgai traveled to Suruga to see Master Hakuin again.

"Previously Your Reverence favored me with his compassionate teaching," Sōgai said, "and that is what has brought me directly to where I am today."

Hakuin asked, "Since assuming abbacy of the temple, have you found someone to stay and do the cleaning for you?"

Sōgai said, "Unworthy though I am, last winter at the insistence of the more than one hundred monks attending my retreat, I delivered lectures on the *Record of Linji*—"

The words were hardly out of Sōgai's mouth before Hakuin leaped up, grabbed his stick, and, glaring fiercely at Sōgai, loudly berated him: "What's a pip-squeak like you doing sounding off with such a big mouth! And what makes you think the *Record of Linji* is easy to lecture on? You go mouthing off again and I'll beat you to a pulp!"

The force of the Master's words was like the crash of raging thunder. Prostrating himself, Sōgai expressed his profound contrition. He subsequently spent an additional three years studying under Hakuin.

Later, Sōgai lived in seclusion at Ryūkokuji in Harima [but soon found himself] surrounded by students.

On one occasion he remarked to [the Zen master] Gankyoku [Zenko], "Master Hakuin used the '*Mu!*' koan [about manifesting] original nature within karmic consciousness. Yet I have never managed to penetrate the koan. Why?"

Angrily, Gankyoku scolded, "Here you are an old man and still making up your mind! If you try to understand about manifesting original nature within karmic consciousness, do you think it's ever going to happen?"

Admitting defeat, Sōgai withdrew.

When Master Sōgai was studying under Hakuin at Shōinji, he was frustrated at his inability to rouse the ball of doubt and so would meditate with a skull placed in the palm of his [cupped] hands. Sōgai then began to advance in his practice till finally he smashed through the black lacquer bucket.[68]

For those beginning their study of Zen, this is among the primary expedients.

⌣

Master Sōten Hōsai studied under Hakuin for many years. When he subsequently assumed abbacy of Ryūshōji in Shinano Province, Sōten came to take his leave of Hakuin. As a farewell present, Hakuin brushed a picture of Bodhidharma, to which he added a verse [in Japanese]. He also presented Sōten with a self-portrait, inscribed with the following poem [in Chinese]:

> Beneath the cliff there flows a stream
> Rushing on, never ending
> If your practice is like this
> Can the moment of kenshō be far off?

This poem had been composed by the Master when he was traveling on his Zen pilgrimage and stopped at a mountain temple in Harima. There, as he watched a stream passing through a gorge, he was moved to write this verse.[69]

⌣

Master Suiō was invited to visit [the Confucian scholar Yamada] Zeigan at the latter's home. Zeigan received the master and seated him in the formal reception room, where the two talked together.

It happened that Zeigan's son, a youth of fifteen or sixteen, was on his way out, and he paused to bow to his father. Seeing him, Suiō bowed in return.

Zeigan's son angrily declared, "I'm bowing to my father. Why should I bow to a Buddhist monk!"[70]

Suiō patted Zeigan on the back and said, "What a precocious child!"

Later, Zeigan was heard to remark, "Hakuin is a true Buddhist teacher. He does not truckle to the times or seek favor with others. Suiō is merely a run-of-the-mill monk."

My own view of the matter: Zeigan is just a trivial Confucian; Hakuin is like a thunderclap sundering a stone wall; Suiō is like a man stroking one's head with hands gentle as the softest cotton. With someone like Zeigan who follows a different teaching [i.e., Confucianism], one will never be able to find common ground!

⌒⌒

We know not even the birthplace of the Zen master Sekie, "Stone Robe." The master lived in a hut some two ri from Hakuin's temple [Shōinji]. He owned no winter clothes, and on cold nights he would hold a [large stone] in his arms and circumambulate his hut, walking in meditation, only stopping when he had managed to warm himself. People called him "Master Stone Robe." Of his end, nothing is known. He was just like the eccentric sages of long ago. The stone still remains before his hut.

⌒⌒

Grandma Satsu was the daughter of Hakuin's paternal uncle.[71] On reaching the age of fifteen, she thought to herself, "It's true I'm no beauty, but thankfully I have a sound body. It seems to me I'm nearing the time for marriage. I just hope I can find a good man!" Secretly, she prayed to the Kannon of Akeno, and day and night recited the *Tennō Kannon Sutra*, even when doing the washing and sewing.[72] After several days, she suddenly experienced enlightenment.

Once, looking in on Osatsu, her father saw her in the sleeping quarters sitting crouched on [a copy of] the *Lotus Sutra*. "She must have gone crazy!" he thought.[73]

"What do you think you're doing, squatting on the *Lotus Sutra*?" he gently remonstrated with her. "You'll surely be punished by the Buddha!"

Osatsu replied, "What's the difference between the *Lotus Sutra* and my ass?"

Finding this strange, Osatsu's father reported it to Hakuin, who told him, "I've got a way to deal with this." He thereupon brushed [the following] waka [on a strip of paper] and gave it to Osatsu's father:[74]

> When in the dark of the night
> You hear the voice of the silent crow
> That is the yearning for the father before one was
>   born.

Hakuin then told him, "Go and paste that to the wall where she'll be sure to see it."

Osatsu's father went and did as he'd been told.

Seeing the paper, Osatsu said, "Why, that's Master Hakuin's calligraphy. Is Hakuin like this, too?"

Her father, still mystified, reported what had occurred.

Hakuin told him, "You bring Osatsu here to me. I'm going to question her."

The father then brought Osatsu to the Master. Hakuin examined her [understanding of Zen], and Osatsu responded smoothly to all his questions. Hakuin thereupon gave her one or two koan, and Osatsu considered them intently.

Hakuin told her, "All right, go and work on them."

Over the course of the next two weeks, Osatsu broke through several stages of koan and finally the Master assigned her the highest level of koan. Osatsu, however, would not budge from her understanding, and there was considerable arguing back and forth with Hakuin, who finally took his stick and struck her.

This sort of thing happened several times.

Half a year elapsed, during which Osatsu managed to penetrate the highest level koan and completely passed through all the most complex cases of the old masters.

Osatsu's father now found a [prospective] husband for his daughter, but Osatsu would have nothing to do with him.

The father went to Hakuin and reported what had occurred. Hakuin then summoned Osatsu and told her, "You have completed your realization of the law of Dharma. Why do you revile the law of human society? Marriage is the paramount duty for men and women. Please follow your father's wishes."

Osatsu bowed in assent.

Years later, Osatsu mourned the death of a grandchild, overcome with grief. An old man who was her neighbor admonished her, "Grandmother, why do you grieve so bitterly? Everyone in the neighborhood is saying, 'Formerly this old woman studied under Master Hakuin and realized enlightenment. Now she's overcome with grief, mourning her grandchild's death. What's that all about?' Grandmother, reflect on this!"

Glaring at her neighbor, Osatsu upbraided him, "Baldy, what do you know about it? A grandmother's weeping and mourning for her grandchild surpasses even offerings of flowers and candles. Baldy, what do you know!"

Such was Osatsu's typical acrimonious response. The monks at the temple came to dismiss her as "that old woman," while often suffering defeat at her hands in their Zen exchanges.

When Osatsu passed away at home, [Hakuin's disciple] Suiō presided at her cremation, delivering a eulogy that stated in short: "For seventy-five years she startled men from their idle dreams and with a single step trampled to bits the world of delusion."

Addressing the assembly of monks, Suiō said, "When Master Hakuin was alive there were a great many enlightened laywomen, but Grandma Osatsu surpassed them all. Even among Zen monks who have spent long years in religious practice, her equal is not to be found!"

⌒⌒

At Harajuku there lived an old woman.[75] It happened one day that she was in the audience listening to Hakuin's sermon, when the Master said: "Mind alone is the Pure Land; one's own body is Amida Buddha. When Amida manifests himself, the mountains, rivers, and the great earth, [including] the trees, grasses, and forests, will instantaneously send forth radiance. If anyone wishes to realize this, he has only to search for it single-mindedly in his own heart. As it is said, 'Within you lies the proof that mind alone is the Pure Land. What further adornment does that Pure Land need? Within you lies the proof that one's own body is Amida Buddha. What further marks of physical excellence does Amida require?'"[76]

The old woman, hearing this, thought to herself, "That doesn't seem so difficult." And returning home, she devoted herself day and night to examining [Hakuin's words], trying to resolve them whether asleep or awake.

Then, one day, while scrubbing a skillet, she suddenly broke through to realization. Tossing aside the skillet, she ran to see Hakuin, exclaiming, "I've penetrated the meaning of 'Your own being is Amida Buddha'! The mountains and rivers, the great earth, [including] the grasses, trees, and forests, all emit a vast radiance. How wonderful!" she rejoiced.

Hakuin told her, "Isn't that kind of talk just emitting radiance from your shit-hole?"

The old woman edged closer and gave Hakuin a slap, saying, "This old master still doesn't get it!"

Hakuin exploded in laughter.

∾

Master Daikyū of Iyama would tell his assembled monks, "Here before you it's already manifesting and fully alive, so what keeps you from realizing it and freeing yourselves?"

But in the entire assembly there was not one who grasped the Master's meaning, to Daikyū's deep regret.

∾

The nun Eshō was [originally] the wife of a certain man from the post station of Eijiri. Later, she became a nun, studying under Hakuin and realizing enlightenment.

Once, Eshō was seated in Hakuin's Zen room together with [the layman] [Yamanashi] Ryōtetsu. The nun questioned Ryōtetsu, saying, "I'm old and can't stand up on my own. I wonder if you could help me up—without using your hands."

Ryōtetsu was unable to reply.

The nun said, "If you can't even manage that, don't ever let me hear you say, 'I've studied with Hakuin'!"

The layman turned red.

Hakuin, observing from the side, burst out laughing.

Ryōtetsu would later realize enlightenment. And the nun Eshō would confirm his realization.

∾

[At the Hara post station] was a tea stall run by an old lady who, having studied Zen with Hakuin, was endowed with great spiritual power. Whenever Hakuin observed a Zen monk wavering, his mind lost in speculation, not having severed the roots of sentient existence, he would exclaim with a sigh, "Like this, when are you ever going to realize enlightenment? Go study with the old tea-stall lady!"

It was not uncommon that when a monk would come to see her, the old lady would immediately demand, "Studying Zen?"

"Yes," the monk would reply, and the old lady, retreating behind a folding screen, would shout to him, "Come in here!"

When the monk went behind the screen, the old lady promptly confronted him with a Zen question, and the moment the monk began to hesitate, she drove him out with a pair of iron fire tongs. Even longtime students of the Master were likely to be subjected to the same treatment, in numbers too great to recall.

It seemed that the old woman's powers of attainment surpassed those of others, just as if she were endowed with all the dexterity of a skilled Zen monk.

RYŌKAN
TALES

PLAYING WITH THE CHILDREN

Early spring
The landscape is tinged with the first
fresh hints of green
Now I take my wooden begging bowl
And wander carefree through town
The moment the children see me
They scamper off gleefully to bring their friends
They're waiting for me at the temple gate
Tugging from all sides so I can barely walk
I leave my bowl on a white rock
Hang my pilgrim's bag on a pine tree branch
First we duel with blades of grass
Then we play ball
While I bounce the ball, they sing the song
Then I sing the song and they bounce the ball
Caught up in the excitement of the game
We forget completely about the time
Passersby turn and question me:
"Why are you carrying on like this?"
I just shake my head without answering
Even if I were able to say something
How could I explain?
Do you really want to know the meaning of it all?
This is it! This is it!

—TAIGU RYŌKAN, RZ 1:149

Despite the quantity of tales and legends surrounding Taigu Ryōkan (1758–1831), many of the facts of his life remain unclear. We have occasional hints in Ryōkan's poems (almost all undated) and in cursory biographies by friends and contemporaries but few actual dates or details. The master himself seems rarely to have touched on his past. That many parts of Ryōkan's biography remain sketchy is hardly surprising given that he led his life as a shabby beggar monk in a remote corner of Japan, never founding or serving as abbot of a temple and having no disciples or heirs to record their teacher's "words and deeds."[1]

Ryōkan was born in Izumozaki, a once bustling coastal town in the old province of Echigo (now Niigata Prefecture), Japan's snow country. The area had long served as a penal colony, with its long winters, deep snows, and brutal natural environment. Izumozaki itself, however, was a scenic spot on the Sea of Japan facing the island of Sado, a haunt of artists and writers as well as home to a prosperous middle class of merchants, brewers, and doctors. Rich veins of gold had been discovered on Sado, and Izumozaki had served as the transshipment point for the precious metal along with regional commodities such as rice and fish, the town's pier areas jammed with rice boats and brothels. By the time of Ryōkan's birth, however, Izumozaki had begun to decline and was already being bypassed for the neighboring port of Amaze, which was better situated to handle the Sado gold trade.[2]

Ryōkan was the eldest son and heir of Yamamoto Tsunamichi (1736–1795), Izumozaki's headman (*nanushi*) and one of the town's leading citizens. A locally known haiku poet under the literary name I'nan, Tsunamichi, born to a country farming family, had been adopted by marriage into one of Izumozaki's wealthy merchant clans, the Yamamoto, which operated under the shop name Tachibana.

From ages ten to nineteen, Ryōkan attended a nearby academy, where he and his peers studied Chinese literature and culture, with an emphasis on poetry, under a noted Confucian scholar and poet, Ōmori Shiyō (d. 1791), studies interrupted by Shiyō's departure for Edo. It was during this period, too, that Ryōkan seems to have begun studying Zen at a local Sōtō temple. By age sixteen, Ryōkan was assisting Tsunamichi in the family business and helping his father in his duties as headman. This was a trying time in Echigo, which had recently been stricken by drought (1770) and then devastated by plague (1772). Eleven years later the province would be convulsed by a great famine that saw food riots in the streets of Izumozaki.[3]

After only a year as his father's understudy, Ryōkan renounced his position as the Yamamoto heir and abandoned Izumozaki to enter Kōshōji, a Sōtō Zen temple in Amaze. There he became a novice, adopting the Buddhist name Ryōkan (Virtuous and Tolerant). Whether Ryōkan's decision to enter the temple was motivated by what he had seen of life as a businessman and village official or by his newfound enthusiasm for Zen is unknown. In retrospect, Ryōkan only observed, "People all say, 'Become a monk and then study Zen.' But I studied Zen and then became a monk."[4]

In 1779 Kōshōji was visited by the Sōtō Zen master Tainin Kokusen (1722–1797), the abbot of Entsūji, a well-known training temple in western Japan in what is now Okayama Prefecture. Kokusen, who had assumed Entsūji's abbacy in 1769, was a member of a distinguished Sōtō lineage that included Gesshū Sōkō (1618–1696), the teacher of the celebrated Zen master and scholar Manzan Dōhaku (1635–1714). Both Gesshū and Manzan were key figures in the early Tokugawa reform movement that shaped the present-day Sōtō school, with its emphasis on the sect's medieval founder Dōgen Kigen (1200–1253), especially Dōgen's writings on Zen and his formulation of monastic rules. When Kokusen departed for Entsūji, Ryōkan accompanied him on the nearly four-hundred-mile journey.[5]

We know nothing of Ryōkan's studies under Kokusen, but the monastic rules at Entsūji, an establishment with a reputation for strictness, included the regular periods of zazen and two annual intensive meditation retreats (*ango*, or *kessei*) typical of Zen training temples, along with chanting of Buddhist texts, group begging, and chores such as cooking, cleaning, and gardening.[6] Ryōkan eventually advanced to the rank of *shuso*, meditation hall supervisor of the annual retreats.

In 1790, at age thirty-two, Ryōkan, along with several of Kokusen's other students, received the Zen master's inka in the form of a Chinese poem, which Ryōkan kept with him throughout his life, along with a staff of wild wisteria. At this time Ryōkan may also have received the second Buddhist name Taigu (Great Fool).[7] Ryōkan was also permitted by Kokusen to begin studying a collection of Dōgen's writings.[8]

With Kokusen's death the following year, Ryōkan seems to have drifted away from Entsūji and, despite his recognition by Kokusen, would never reenter the Sōtō temples. As he had rejected the prospect of succeeding to leadership of the Tachibana clan and its enterprises or to the office of Izumozaki headman, Ryōkan never seems to have been comfortable for long as a member of any organization or hierarchy, however advantageously placed within it he may have been, and remained instead a determined loner.

By his own account, Ryōkan next spent years wandering Japan on pilgrimage or simply drifting from place to place. Our only source for this period is the record of a brief encounter of Ryōkan and the Edo poet and scholar Kondō Banjō (1776–1848), included in Banjō's 1845 collection *A Bedside Companion* (*Nezame no tomo*). Traveling through the old Shikoku province of Tosa (present-day Kōchi Prefecture), Banjō is caught in a rainstorm and forced to seek shelter in a ramshackle hut. The hut is occupied by a solitary monk, who willingly shares his simple food and accommodations. The monk rarely speaks, and when questioned only smiles, leading Banjō to conclude that he is probably crazy. Banjō cannot help noticing, however, the impressive samples of calligraphy scattered about and the monk's Chinese edition of the Taoist classic *Zhuangzi*. When after two nights the rain finally lets up, Banjō prepares to continue on his journey, offering his reticent host—whom in retrospect he realizes to be Ryōkan— some money in appreciation. The monk, however, refuses the proffered cash, remarking, "What am I going to do with that?" He is nevertheless delighted by Banjō's gift of some calligraphy paper and poem cards.[9]

By 1795 Ryōkan had returned to his native area, where he was discovered living as a beggar in a lean-to on the beach.[10] During his absence, things had not gone well for the Yamamoto family. After Tsunamichi's retirement in 1786, Ryōkan's younger brother Yoshiyuki (also read Yūshi, 1762–1834) had taken over the family business and the position of Izumozaki headman but proved an inept administrator.[11] Tsunamichi, meanwhile, abandoned the family to drift about the country and lead a life of drink and dissipation, culminating in his suicide by drowning in Kyoto's Kamo River in 1795.

Ryōkan refused all attempts by his family to lure him home, moving on to a series of vacant huts on the grounds of local temples. By 1800 the master had retreated to Mount Kugami, a picturesque peak some twelve miles north of Izumozaki. By 1804 he had settled into Gogō-an, a hut in the precincts of a Shingon temple on the mountain's western slope. The retreat would remain Ryōkan's home for the next dozen or so years and is the subject of many of his poems.[12]

While Gogō-an's solitude was among its attractions for Ryōkan, his life there was hardly that of an anchorite, and into old age he continued to wander the area, often staying with friends. Eventually he established a second hut on the foothills of Mount Kugami in the precincts of a deserted Shinto shrine, Otogo *jinja*. Situated in a cryptomeria forest and surrounded by a grove of bamboo, the Otogo hut probably served as Ryōkan's permanent residence after 1816. The year before, the master had been joined by a fourteen-year-old Shingon monk, Henchō (1801–1876), who served as Ryōkan's attendant for the next ten years, aiding him in performing some of the more exacting chores and watching over the hut while Ryōkan was absent.[13]

Ryōkan's routine on Mount Kugami varied with the weather. On rainy days, or when trapped indoors by Echigo's legendary snows, Ryōkan would occupy his time composing poetry, performing zazen, practicing calligraphy, smoking his pipe, reading sutras, or studying the ancient Chinese and Japanese classical poets. Among his favorites were the poems of Hanshan (*Hanshan shi*, "Cold Mountain poems");[14] *Manyoshū* (Collection of the myriad ages), the earliest collection of Japanese verse, compiled in the mid-eighth century;[15] and *Kokinshū*, the first imperial anthology of poems, particularly waka, completed in 905. Ryōkan even undertook studies of Chinese and Japanese phonetics, for which his handwritten notes remain.[16]

On clear days, however, Ryōkan would take his staff and bowl and walk down the mountain at dawn, begging his way from village to village and not returning to his hut till nightfall. Times were hard—harvests in Echigo were devastated by a succession of blizzards, floods, and earthquakes, contributing to widespread famine—but Ryōkan's neighbors freely shared with him whatever they had.[17] Unlike the strictly ordered group begging that was routine for monks at Zen monasteries, Ryōkan's begging was unstructured and relaxed. He was always ready to interrupt his rounds to play with the village children, pause to drink sake with a farmer, stop by to visit acquaintances, or pick flowers and wild vegetables by the wayside, the last an activity in which the master was frequently joined by the local boys and girls and even their parents.

As the modern Ryōkan anthologist and scholar Tōgō Toyo-haru suggests, begging was essential to Ryōkan's practice. It was not merely the Buddha's time-honored tenet for a monk to sus-tain himself but Ryōkan's principal means of teaching through actual face-to-face contact with his neighbors.[18] Not surpris-ingly, Ryōkan became a regular fixture of the area around Mount Kugami, welcome at festivals and wine shops, and a particular favorite of the local children, who would swarm him on sight, insisting he join them in endless games of handball, tag, hide-and-seek, or sumo wrestling.[19] Mercilessly teasing the indulgent master, the children would often detain him till sundown, so that Ryōkan was left with no chance to beg and found himself return-ing home with an empty bowl. "The Master is always accompa-nied by children," we read in the earliest biography of Ryōkan, an 1811 account by his friend the Confucian scholar Suzuki Bundai (1796–1870). "When he is out begging, he can be found playing with them in the shade of trees and in the fields, tugging at blades of grass,[20] sumo wrestling, and bouncing balls. His mind is like a mirror, looking neither forward nor backward."[21] And in 1895, Bundai's adopted son Tekiken (1836–1896) recalled:

> Whenever the Zen Master went out, children would follow him. Sometimes they would shout at him loudly, and the Master would shout back in surprise, throwing up his hands, reeling backward and almost losing his balance. Whenever the children found the Master, they were always ready to do this. Ordinary people frowned on the Master's behavior. My late fa-ther once questioned him about it. The Master laughed and said, "When the children surprise me this way,

it makes them happy. When the children are happy, it makes me happy. The children are happy, and I'm happy too; everyone is happy together, and so I do it all the time. There's no truer happiness than this!" This happiness of the Master's was itself a manifestation of the ultimate truth.[22]

Ryōkan's particular combination of simplicity, naiveté, and warmth endeared him to the local population and gave rise to endless tales about the master, some of which remain staples of Japanese children's literature. A pervasive ingredient of these stories was Ryōkan's absentmindedness, which led him to constantly forget his belongings. Ryōkan's poems and letters attest to this, and the master tells of forgetting his walking stick, his precious begging bowl, his books, even his underwear, despite a checklist of personal items he carried with him (and promptly forgot).[23]

Ryōkan maintained a wide circle of admiring friends drawn from every strata of local society, from amateur literati to wealthy merchants, and including doctors, brewers, and unlettered peasants. His love of sake was legendary, though the poems make plain that his drinking was rarely solitary but in the company of others. "When people offer the Master sake," a contemporary notes, "he can imbibe and remain completely relaxed. If people urge him to get up and dance, he doesn't hesitate. When he's had enough, he simply leaves without a word."[24]

Despite the delight Ryōkan took in his neighbors and rustic accommodations, he remained essentially an impoverished beggar, and his life was a hard one. The master had to haul his own water, firewood, and other necessities up Kugami's treacherous slopes. He often faced starvation, and when ill or snowed in and unable to go out begging, he had to depend on friends and neighbors, sometimes themselves in dire straits. Most of Ryōkan's roughly two hundred surviving letters are appeals for help or thank-you notes, often disarmingly blunt, with no traces of pleading or unctuousness, and an occasional poem attached.[25] From the letters we know that the master's needs included food, clothes, medicine, bedding, candles, sake, tobacco, even cash, but especially calligraphy supplies. Indeed, Ryōkan's brushwork, still treasured for its childlike freedom and directness, was appreciated, collected, even forged for sale during the master's lifetime.[26]

Besides poverty, Ryōkan was burdened by poor health, which was aggravated by his increasing age and the rugged conditions on the mountain. By 1826 the master was forced to accept the hospitality of his prosperous merchant friend Kimura Motouemon (1778–1848) and move to a small, detached cottage, a former workshop, on the grounds of the Kimura family mansion in the village of Shimazaki. Although only seven miles south of Mount Kugami, the move was a painful dislocation for Ryōkan, who hated being in a town, removed from old friends, and longed for the mountain home where he had passed some thirty years.

It was at this difficult juncture in his life that Ryōkan met a beautiful young Buddhist nun, Teishin (1798–1872). Widowed early in life, Teishin had become not only a nun but an accomplished waka poet and had sought out Ryōkan for his instruction in Japanese poetry. At the time they met, Ryōkan was sixty-nine, Teishin twenty-nine, yet the two seem to have fallen deeply in love. Teishin faithfully nursed the master during his final illness, which left him bedridden with severe diarrhea and abdominal pains and often unable to sleep. The moving poems the two exchanged during the four years of their association are preserved in Teishin's 1835 collection *Dew on the Lotus* (*Hachisu no tsuyu*).[27] Teishin and Kimura were at the master's bedside when, shortly after New Year's, 1831, Ryōkan passed away seated in meditation posture "just as if he were falling asleep."[28]

Among the best sources for Ryōkan's daily life is his poetry. None was published in his lifetime, though manuscript copies circulated widely among local literati. By the end of the nine-teenth century, some of the poems had begun to appear in pub-lication, but it was only in the twentieth century that interest in Ryōkan was dramatically revived, largely through the widely read 1918 biography *Great Fool Ryōkan* (*Taigu Ryōkan*) by the writer Soma Gyōfu (1883–1950), who devoted his later life to the study of the master. Soma's book was based on tales about Ryōkan, part from the *Curious Accounts of the Zen Master Ryōkan* (first pub-lished in 1918) and part from oral traditions surviving in Echigo. This was followed in the twenties and thirties by works from lo-cal historians who collected and published Ryōkan's writings and related biographical materials.

The postwar period witnessed a "*Ryōkan būmu*" (Ryōkan boom) with numbers of tales and legends collected and the for-mation throughout Japan of Ryōkan societies and study groups. A 1975 survey of Japanese elementary school children found that 99 percent were familiar with Ryōkan; and the century between 1885 and 1985 saw 3,600 books on Ryōkan published in Japan, 362 in 1983 alone.[29] Although his life was spent largely as an obscure beggar priest in his native area, Ryōkan has somehow come to epitomize those qualities that the Japanese still like to feel are the timeless essence of their national character: simplicity, trust, goodness, and sincerity.

It is worth recalling that the title *zenji*, or Zen master, was bestowed on Ryōkan not by the emperor in a formal rescript,[30] as was customary in premodern Japan, but by the friends, fami-lies, and nameless individuals in Ryōkan's locality, including even his brother Yoshiyuki[31]—a kind of informal sanction from those with whom he shared his Zen on a daily basis. Ryōkan certainly never referred to himself in this manner. While contemporary Sōtō school lineage charts recognize Ryōkan as his teacher Koku-sen's Dharma heir, Ryōkan never "taught" Zen but lived it, his admirers would contend, sharing it freely among his neighbors.[32]

Nor did he ever deliver sermons. Kera Yoshishige (1810–1859), who studied poetry under Ryōkan and whose family regularly welcomed the master at their home during Kera's childhood and young adulthood, recalled:

> The Master stayed several nights at our home. Young and old became harmonious, and a peaceful atmosphere filled the house for several days after his departure. Just one evening of talking with the Master made us feel that our hearts had been purified. The Master never held forth on the scriptures or classics or the importance of ethics. Sometimes he would be in the kitchen tending the fire, sometimes in the parlor practicing meditation. In his conversation he never alluded to classical poetry or ethical teachings, and his manner was indescribably casual and relaxed. It was just his own innate goodness that naturally guided others.[33]

Ryōkan, it is true, went his own way. After his training, he never returned to the Sōtō monasteries or became abbot of a parish temple. But we know he regularly practiced zazen, albeit in an informal setting, whether in his hut or by the rushing streams of Mount Kugami. He also continued to revere the Sōtō school's founder, Dōgen, and his writings. Like Dōgen, he venerated the *Lotus Sutra*, which he tells us was always at his side and on which he composed a series of devotional poems.[34] Ryōkan's favorite bodhisattva, Jofukyō Bosatsu (Bodhisattva "Despising No One"), appears in the sutra's twentieth chapter, which describes him bowing down to and revering each person he meets, because each individual contains buddha nature.[35]

The relation of Ryōkan's life and poems to his Zen attainment is a source of necessarily subjective speculation—speculation on which academic, if not popular, opinion may differ. Some modern literary scholars have taken the position that Ryōkan's frequently ironic, self-deprecating tone betrays a crippling self-doubt. Analyzing Ryōkan's Chinese poetry, for example, Iriya Yoshitaka, a highly regarded expert on Chinese language and Zen texts, views the master as a great poet haunted by his father's suicide and his own history as a dropout and serial failure in both the secular and religious worlds.[36]

Such views, to me at least, take at face value in certain of Ryōkan's poems what is a standard pose of classical Chinese poets with whom Ryōkan was intimately familiar, a mood of melancholy, regret, and isolation. It likewise appears to me that, in other poems, scholars have mistaken the openness and honesty of Ryōkan's expression as the sign of an unawakened mind. Instead, as my friend Professor Abe has so often observed to me, Ryōkan's poetry, his Zen, his eccentric and haphazard way of life are all of one piece. The master's willingness to reflect in his verse the full range of human feelings, from joy to moodiness and despondency, was not an admission of defeat but an essential part of Ryōkan's genius. It represents his personal actualization of the unity of ordinary experience and enlightened mind that underlies not only Zen but Mahayana classics such as the *Heart Sutra* and *Awakening of Faith*.[37] Similarly, in the stories, Ryōkan's refusal to protest when mistreated or falsely accused does not bespeak a somber fatalism or resignation but a graceful acceptance of things as they are, however foolish or misconstrued.

For those of Ryōkan's neighbors who preferred to see a sermon rather than to hear one, this was the precious teaching the master had to offer. As Tōgō Toyoharu remarks, unlike the literati and aesthetes who admired Ryōkan's art, the reverence in which the common people held the master, conveyed in the many stories and tales about him, was based not on his poetry or calligraphy but on the actual character of Ryōkan's daily life, which charmed and amazed them, just as it continues to delight Japanese of our own day.

⌒

The materials here are drawn largely from the Ryōkan den, *by Matsushima Hokusho (1814–1844). Like the* Ryōkan zenji kiwa, *translated elsewhere,[38] the work is among the earliest accounts of Ryōkan and similarly served as the basis for many of the later stories that circulated about the master. In a brief introduction,[39] Matsushima describes how he had heard the accounts from a certain native of Echigo, one Miura Hakukō (n.d.), a doctor and Confucian scholar studying in Edo. Matsushima laments that Ryōkan is little known outside of his home province of Echigo and hopes that a record of tales about the master will remedy this situation and preserve Ryōkan's memory. Nōnin Keidō, editor of* Ryōkan zenji itsuwashū, *from which these accounts are taken, used a photographic reproduction of a woodblock edition of Matsushima's text in the collection of Kansai University. Nōnin notes in his foreword that the anecdotes are an important source for the study of Ryōkan because they began to be recorded within ten years of the master's death and so are not simply fanciful tales and fabrications but important materials for our understanding of Ryōkan's enduring legend as an eccentric, poet, and Zen master, and of his special place in the Japanese imagination.*

The Master was originally a samurai in the Nagaoka domain.[40] His secular name was Ogawa Sazaeimon.[41] As a child, he did not mingle with the other children, and as a young man, he was little afflicted by lust. He pursued no particular occupation and grew habituated to indolence so that he was unable to associate with others in a dignified manner.

⌒

At age nineteen, on the pretext of poor health, the Master resigned from all his duties.[42] One day, he accompanied his friends to a brothel, where they became boisterously drunk, sang, shouted, and dropped one hundred gold coins on the spot. Thereupon the Master shaved his head and gave himself the Buddhist name Ryōkan. He traveled to Kyoto, where he remained for three or four years before returning home, erecting a small hermitage, and settling among the hills of Nagaoka, drifting about at his leisure.

⌒

On one occasion when Master Ryōkan was out begging, he approached a home. It happened that an object had recently gone missing at this house, and the householder, suspecting the Master of the theft, bound him hand and foot. The Master only hung his head in silence.

Just then, an acquaintance of the Master's happened by and was able to have him released.

"Why didn't you tell them you were innocent?" he berated the Master.

Seemingly lost in thought, the Master replied, "Even if I'd explained, I wouldn't have been let off. Best not to make any explanations and just hope for the best."

⌒

There was a wicked child who, hearing that Master Ryōkan would tolerate any sort of children's misbehavior, secretly got aboard a boat with the Master and then came up behind him and pushed him into the water. The Master barely escaped drowning but showed no sign of resentment.

⌒

Always dressed in a ragged robe, Master Ryōkan would stroll about town. When offered a good robe as a replacement, the

Master would immediately put it on without the slightest demurral. When cold or hunger afflicted the world, however, the Master would take off his robe and give it away, along with all the food in his begging bowl.

〰

One evening a thief stole into Master Ryōkan's hut, but seeing nothing but the four bare walls, he could not find anything to steal. The Master took off his robe and gave it to the thief, sending him on his way.

〰

Master Ryōkan was skilled at both Chinese and Japanese poetry and was especially adept at grass script, the varying movements of his brush seemingly divine.[43] He was, however, unwilling to casually write out samples of his work for people.

In the village was a wealthy man who raised peonies in his garden. Each year when the blossoms appeared, the Master would arrive to admire them, and he never left without breaking off a branch to take with him. The proprietor had long sought a sample of the Master's brushwork, but although the Master had agreed, the rich man had never succeeded in obtaining one.

Now there occurred to him a scheme. The rich man dispatched a servant to report to the Master that the peonies had come into bloom. The Master hurried over and once again broke off a cluster of blossoms for himself. The rich man, pretending to be incensed, had the Master confined in a room, which had been furnished with ink, paper, and brushes. In a loud voice, he instructed the guard assigned to hold the Master, "If he does any brushwork, release him. If not, don't let him out!" The Master then proceeded to inscribe a folk ditty, which said, in effect, "A gentleman may be deceived but cannot be impugned."[44] The rich man was dumbstruck.

On his way back, the Master brushed open a green banana leaf whose color looked to him like lapis lazuli. Jumping for joy, he yanked out the leaf and set off for home.

〜〜

Master Ryōkan loved to play ball. The result was that when people wanted to get a sample of his calligraphy, they would trick him into it by first sending along a ball. The Master would then cheerfully take up his brush. Other gifts that were sent for this purpose, even those as precious as gems, he simply ignored.

〜〜

Kameda Bōsai, a man of Edo, was traveling in Echigo.[45] Seeing a sample of Master Ryōkan's calligraphy, he was amazed and went to visit him. Finding the Master seated in zazen, Bōsai knelt there and waited for half a day. Then, quickly realizing that Bōsai was no ordinary practitioner, the Master engaged him for some time in a friendly and openhearted discussion. When he was about to leave, Bōsai exclaimed, delighted, "I have truly been able to advance another step in my brushwork!"

For someone like Bōsai, celebrated for his grass script throughout the land, to speak like this makes one realize the extent of the Master's skill with the brush.

〜〜

Master Ryōkan passed away in a certain year of the Tenpō era (1830–1844) at age sixty.[46] Several days before the Master's death, he was visited by the headman of Aozu, a certain Mura'osa. Smiling, the Master asked him, "Some years back I left a bundle of things at your house. Do you still recall it?" The headman had no idea what the Master was referring to but, searching through his home, finally turned up a traveling bag, which, on close inspection, was found to contain thirty small gold coins, which the

Master had apparently carried with him to provide for funeral expenses.[47]

Regarding these coins, another story has come down to us that the granddaughter of Kimura of the Shimazaki Noto-ya related at age eighty-two:[48] "According to my elderly relations, when I was only one or two, the Master, in his spare time from religious practice, would care for me tenderly, carrying me on his back and rocking my cradle. However, the Master passed away when I was no more than three. In disposing of his bedding, there were discovered some forty small, bright gold coins secreted among the bottom layers of his futon. Everyone, from my family members to the assembled onlookers, was happily surprised, struck with admiration at the care of the Master's preparations and esteeming him all the more. For with these funds the Master's funeral was conducted, his memorial services carried out, and a gravestone erected. And despite the Master's bedding having been reduced to tatters, several of these fragments were carefully preserved."

The magnificence of the Master's funeral ceremony was an expression of people's lasting respect and reverence for him. When he had nothing, the Master would beg, and when he had anything, he would give it to others; yet these coins he carried with him as if sealed away in a purse. In all likelihood, when the Master was still living in Tamashima,[49] he had received the coins from his parents, so that in case he should die, whether in the fields or among the mountains, if someone took care of burying him this money could be used, thereby benefiting both himself and others.

〜〜

Master Ryōkan was born a son of Yamamoto, village headman of Izumozaki, and given the childhood name Eizō.[50] He was by nature exceedingly dull and careless, wholly incapable of such things as straightening his garments when meeting others. That's why, it's said, the local people nicknamed him "the headman's 'lantern in broad daylight.'"[51]

This happened when Master Ryōkan was six or seven:

One day the Master slept late and was scolded by his father. The Master looked up and stared at his father intently, and his father told him, "Anyone who glares at his father like that will surely turn into a flounder."

Hearing this, the Master fled suddenly from the house and by nightfall still had not returned. Worried, the whole household searched everywhere for him, but the Master was loitering, dejected, on a cliff by the ocean.

When the searchers finally found the Master, they shouted at him, "What are you doing here?"

The Master is said to have asked them, "Haven't I turned into a flounder yet?"

～～

As a youth, the Master's only joy was reading, and he would keep himself shut up at home. One evening during the Bon festival, a crowd of people performing a Bon dance happened to pass by the front of the family mansion.[52] The Master's mother seized the opportunity to urge her bookworm son to get outside and join in the festivities. Making a sour face, the Master silently left the house.

As the red lanterns of the festival passed through the street, the Master's mother thought she would step into the garden, but when she glanced about she noticed a mysterious figure in the shadow cast by the stone lantern. Hastily concluding it must be a robber, she returned to the house and reappeared holding a curved halberd (*naginata*) with which she approached the intruder. However, examining the figure at close hand, she was startled to recognize her own son, lost in his reading of the *Analects*.[53]

The following episode presents a wholly contradictory picture of the young Ryōkan's attitude to the Bon dancing.

On the seventeenth day [of the seventh month], during the Bon festival, the young Master, who delighted in the [Bon] dances, seemed to be dancing happily as always, while drinking sake all night long. However, the next day, it is said, he suddenly shaved his head and entered Kōshōji.

It is said that Master Ryōkan got married in the period before entering the monastery but only lived with his wife for some six months before abandoning lay life.

Master Ryōkan's family had served for generations as headmen of Izumozaki. As the oldest son and head of the family [after his father's retirement], the Master, too, was originally expected to succeed to this office. However, one day, it is said, he was called on to attend the execution of a thief and, after witnessing this scene, returned home and promptly became a Buddhist monk.

This following version of the Master's path to the priesthood was handed down within the Master's family, the Yamamoto:

At age seventeen, following the family tradition, Master Ryōkan became headman of Izumozaki. At this time, however, there arose a dispute between the shogunal magistrate and the local fishermen, a dispute that proved particularly intractable. In such cases, matters had to be submitted to the village headman for mediation. The Master began his mediation efforts but would convey to each party in the dispute exactly what was said by the other, reporting to the magistrate every bit of foul language and abuse heaped on him by the fishermen, and then reporting to the fishermen every angry and slanderous word expressed toward them by the magistrate. The result was that the gulf between the two sides only grew wider and deeper, till any resolution became impossible.

Scolded by the magistrate for his simple-minded honesty, the Master lamented, "A man has to be honest. Fortunately, I was able to avoid distorting the truth about this. Today's world is degenerate, with people morally superficial and shallow-minded, so that those who lie to others are hailed as clever. A rootless world, alas, with nothing one can count on!"

And fleeing straight to Kōshōji, he became a monk.

～～

When the Master was training to be village headman, the shogunal magistrate for Sado was preparing to set sail for the island from Izumozaki. However, such was the length of the handles on the magistrate's palanquin that it could not be accommodated on any local boat, and the Izumozaki boatmen were at their wit's end.[54] Seeing this, the Master suggested, "You'd better shorten those handles," whereupon the boatmen proceeded to cut away the handles of the palanquin.

When he saw what was happening, however, the magistrate was furious, and this caused a breach between the magistrate and the headman. It was this that led directly to the Master becoming a monk.

～～

In the seventh year of the Kansei era (1795), when the Master was thirty-seven, his father, Yamamoto I'nan, committed suicide, drowning himself in Kyoto's Katsura River. At that time, I'nan entrusted to a friend a bundle, with the instructions, "After my death, a monk named Ryōkan is sure to come from western Japan asking about me. Please give him this." And so saying, he plunged into the Katsura River.

Afterward, the Master was visiting Kyoto and was given this package as a remembrance of his father. In it, he found a haiku inscribed on half a sheet of Chinese drawing paper:

> The silk tree's flower[55]
>   sunk one step lower
> In the morning mist.

With this was another haiku composed on a small vertical poem card (*tanzaku*):

> The evening frost
>   will be gone
> Even before the ivy's crimson flowers.

Reading these two haiku, the Master grieved over his father's death, adding a waka in small characters at the margin of the first poem:

> The brush's traces
>   grow hazy through my tears
> As I think back
>   over things of long ago.

The Master then proceeded to Mount Koya in order to perform the funeral service for I'nan and from there made a pilgrimage to the Ise Shrine.[56] Throughout his life, it is said, the Master always kept these memorabilia of his father.

〜

An old man has passed down the following account, which dates from the final year of the Kansei era (1801):

A short distance from Teradomari lies the village of Gōmoto.[57] Formerly there lived in this village a beggar monk, lodged in a thatch hut. It is not known when this mysterious monk arrived there or from where he came. His possessions consisted of a bedraggled robe and straw hat, along with a monk's begging bowl and staff. On rainy days he would sleep, on clear days he would go out to beg, and he was always to be seen at play with children.

The monk's behavior was out of the ordinary, and the villagers all wondered at him. Someone said, "Why, that looks like the son of the Tachibana firm of Izumozaki, the one who became a monk!" The firm was notified and, when the monk was pointed out, agreed that it was the Master after all. A Tachibana representative was promptly dispatched to welcome him back into the family, but in the blink of an eye, the monk had vanished, leaving behind only a single dented cook pot. Seeing they were unable to dissuade the Master from his purpose, the Tachibana [retainers] gave up and returned home.

〜

The Master enjoyed perusing the *Analects* of Confucius. One day, happening upon a portion of the text that was unclear to him, the Master asked Suzuki Bundai. Bundai told the Master, "It must be explained in the commentaries. Has Your Reverence read them?"

To which the Master replied, "I've always made it a point not to read commentaries. One can be misled reading such things and instead end up increasing one's doubts."

〜

Once, someone asked the Master, "Of all the ancients, whom did you study the most? Priest Saigyō? Priest Kisen?"[58]

The Master told him, "I don't study the well-known works of anyone. I try to study those works that everyone overlooks."

The man then asked, "Nevertheless, you must have given some study at least to [the poetry of] Master Ikkyū."[59]

"Yes," the Master replied, "that's true."

"Well," the questioner persisted, "which aspects [of Ikkyū's works]?"

"This," said the Master, drawing from the pocket of his robe a copy of the Confucian *Analects*.

~~

Among the three things Master Ryōkan liked best were children, boys and girls; playing ball; and shooting marbles.

Children he liked because in their innocence they did not lie. When people would beg the Master for samples of his calligraphy, he was extremely reluctant. But when it came to children, if one would bring him a ball or a piece of shell used as a marble, the Master would beam with delight and would immediately decorate these items with his calligraphy.

~~

From time to time Master Ryōkan would visit the entertainment district and would join the circle of prostitutes shooting marbles, participating freely in the fun. Learning of this, the Master's younger brother, Yūshi, sought to remonstrate with him by way of a waka:

> While wearing a Buddhist monk's black robes
> You fritter away your days
> Playing games with whores
> —such is your mind.
>
> —*Yūshi*

To which the Master wrote in reply:

> Frittering away one's days
>   as life transpires in this floating world
> Even if I say, "Fine, who cares?"
>   others will scold about brothel girls!

> —*Ryōkan*

Wholly dissatisfied with his brother's response, Yūshi dispatched a second poem:

> "Fine," you say, "so I fritter away life in this world—
>   who
> cares?"
> But what sort of thought
>   can you be giving
> To the world that's yet to come?[60]

> —*Yūshi*

The Master replied again:

> Frolicking my way through life
> Even in this world
> What sort of thought am I to give
> To a world that's yet to come?[61]

> —*Ryōkan*

⌒⌒

Master Ryōkan had only a single wooden bowl, which he used to grind miso and then to wash his face, hands, and feet.[62]

⌒⌒

One year, bamboo shoots sprouted under the floorboards of the Master's hut. The Master then tore up the floorboards to help the shoots grow. In time, the bamboo shot up and then pushed their way through the Master's roof. Untroubled by this, the Master simply continued about his daily life, meditating under the bamboo.

〜〜

This happened at the Seba ferry crossing in Jizōdo.[63]

A notorious ferryman, an outlaw, plied his trade there. Knowing Master Ryōkan to be gentle, meek, and inoffensive, the ferryman took him aboard. But once he had left the shore behind, the ferryman deliberately rocked the boat, tumbling the Master into the water. Then, seeing the Master on the verge of drowning, the boatman became alarmed and rushed to his aid, plucking him from the water.

Thereupon, the Master, believing the boatman had saved his life, thanked him profusely for his act of selfless kindness.

〜〜

[The following story was collected from Koetsu Masaharu, a modern descendant of Koetsu Chūmin, resident in Natsudō:]

In Natsudō, in the town of Teradomari in the district of Mishima, lived a doctor by the name of Koetsu Chūmin. Chūmin was returning home to Natsudō one day, his medicine box in his hand, when he chanced to pass the beach at Gōmoto. For some reason, a crowd of villagers was setting up a great clamor, and when Chūmin approached to have a look, he found a single bedraggled monk being buried alive in a hole.

It seems that a salt-cooking hut had burned down,[64] and there was no doubt in the villagers' minds that it had been burned by the beggar monk.

"Wait, hold up!" Chūmin shouted. "Let me deal with this!" Distributing sake and food to the villagers to mollify them, the doctor managed to extricate the Master from the crowd and return him to his own home.

Though he had barely escaped being buried alive, the ragged monk seemed rather unconcerned, and Chūmin asked, "Why didn't you say anything?"

The Master told him calmly, "What would have been the point? Since everyone was convinced I was responsible, what could I do but accept the fact?"

The ragged monk was Master Ryōkan.

The Master remained at Chūmin's home for some time, during which Chūmin became utterly enchanted by the Master's boundless erudition.

Brought together by such fortuitous circumstances, the Master stayed at the Koetsu home for nearly two years, often playing with the doctor's youngest son and, it is said, even teaching him to read and write with a primer he produced himself.

～～

Once, in a nearby farming village, a complaint was lodged with the local official that a sneak thief was breaking into homes in broad daylight.[65] The villagers declared, "It must be the work of that monk who's been hanging around here lately," and the official promptly took the monk into custody for questioning. However, no matter what the monk was asked, he would not say a single word. Finally losing patience, the official accused the monk of the crime and ordered the villagers to dig a hole and bury the monk alive.

Just at that moment, a wealthy farmer of the village happened to be passing and, horrified by what was happening, took pity on the monk and told the official, "The fact that the prisoner will say nothing, even with things having gone this far, shows he is no ordinary person. I've heard lately about the presence of a training monk from Entsūji. Outwardly, it's said, he looks just like a regular person, but in actuality he is one who has experienced deep enlightenment. Perhaps this is that monk."

Thereupon the official questioned the prisoner all over again, and for the first time the monk opened his mouth and replied that he was indeed the Entsūji monk. He then went on to say, "Once people's suspicions have been aroused, however much explaining you do, in the end, is no more than useless apologies. Knowing this, I resigned myself to taking responsibility for this crime of some sort that no one had actually witnessed, resolved to endure in silence, and prepared to submit to whatever torment awaited me."

Thereupon, the villagers and the official humbly apologized for their error and promptly released the monk, who, it is said, was none other than Master Ryōkan.

⌒⌒

According to the Master's student and anthologist Henchō (1801–1876), Dr. Koetsu Chūmin's prized possession was a rosewood netsuke, a toggle that he wore and that became the subject of the following satirical verse:

> The rare rosewood
> How exquisite its color and patina.
> But rather than rosewood
> Better put your back into your work![66]

⌒⌒

At some time or other, Master Ryōkan had borrowed a copy of the *Kusha ron* from Man'inji in Izumozaki.[67] After reading the work, he returned it to the temple, along with a present of tofu as an expression of thanks, appending the following waka:

The wild geese and ducks
have flown off and left me behind
Thankfully there are no feathers
in the tofu!

〜〜

The piece of calligraphy described below, along with the explanation appended to the lower portion of the mounting by Ryōkan's
friend Suzuki Bundai, still survives. It is dated the sixth year of
the Kaei era (1853) and resides in the Fujisaki family collection.
Bundai's inscription states:

Besides his erudition, Master Ryōkan excelled in the composition of both Chinese and Japanese verse and was a matchless
calligrapher. A collector able to obtain even a single character
brushed by the Master on a sheet of rice paper cherished it as
a priceless treasure. As a result, dishonest dealers in calligraphy
would defraud collectors, mixing genuine articles with fakes.
Having myself been long associated with the Master, I can attest
that many people came begging him to inscribe for them even a
single word.

There is a piece owned by a Mr. Tōju of the Tsubame post station. One day, Tōju came and told me the following: "Once when
the Master came to Tsubame to beg, a young boy approached
him, holding out a piece of paper, and said, 'Please, write something on this paper for me!'

"The Master asked, 'What are you going to use it for?'

"The boy said, 'I want to use it to make a kite. Please write the
four characters, "High in the sky a great wind" (J. *Ten jō tai fū*).'

"The Master complied and handed it back to the child. Lately
the piece has come into my possession, and I have had it mounted
to display as a scroll. I would like to request that you set down [on
the bottom of the scroll] an account of this."

Now, unrolling the scroll and looking it over once more, I

cannot help but be struck by the simplicity and selflessness of the brushstrokes. I recall those years long ago when [the Master and I] would talk and laugh and, filled with regret, take up my brush and set down this account.

Sixth year of Kaei (1853)
Layman Bundai.[68]

⌒⌒

Master Ryōkan had a high regard for farm work. "From one seedling," he would say, "myriad plants." [That is,] when one rice seedling is sown, myriad plants will be produced. Such was the Master's view of the farmers' hardships. He would brush pictures depicting the farmers at work, breaking the ground for planting and bringing in the crop at harvest time. The Master would then paste these on the walls of his hut, burning incense before them and making offerings of flowers.

The Master composed a waka that says:

> Soon, it seems, it will be time
>   to transplant the rice seedlings
> And in my hut
>   I'll be painting pictures of the scene
> And offering flowers and incense.

⌒⌒

Master Ryōkan loved the craftsmanship of carpentry and consequently was extremely fond of carpenters.

"In the world," he would often remark, "there is nothing so honest as carpentry."

The Master's calligraphy turns up in all sorts of places, and he seems to have inscribed in black ink the six Chinese characters for the invocation "*Namu Amida Butsu!*" (Praise to the Buddha Amitabha!) on an undistinguished paulownia box. According to a certain eminent priest, this was probably inscribed by the Master to express the notion that the craftsman had the same frame of mind in fashioning the box as one has in reciting the invocation to Amida Buddha.

⌒⌒

The Sōtō master Dainin Rosen, like Master Ryōkan, hailed from [the town of] Amaze in the Mishima district.[69] [Dainin,] who was abbot of the Kyoto temple Kōshōji in Uji,[70] was Dharma heir to the Zen master Reitan Roryū, the twenty-third-generation abbot of Keifukuji in Edo.

Dainin was a poetry companion of the Master, and once when Dainin had left Edo to visit his native area, the Master happened to stop by his lodgings. However, not a single word was exchanged between the two, who just sat together in silence for several days writing out linked waka.[71]

They say that after the Master had returned home and Dainin had departed for Edo, the members of the household entered Dainin's quarters to sweep up and found the whole room crammed helter-skelter with linked verses the friends had tossed off on pieces of paper.

⌒⌒

The following account is from the period when Master Ryōkan had settled at the Otogo shrine.

One evening, a sneak thief broke into the Master's hut. However, he could not find a single item there worth stealing, and he was about to give up and return home empty-handed when the Master called him back. Shedding the old cotton-quilted bedclothes he was wearing, the Master sent the thief off with them. Just then, noticing that the moon had risen over the eastern mountains, the Master composed the following waka:

Left untouched
by the thief in his haste—
The moon in the window.[72]

～～

Master Katsugen Taiki, the twenty-seventh-generation abbot of Tokushōji in the village of Yoita, revered Master Ryōkan for his high spiritual attainment and would frequently visit the Master at his Shimazaki hermitage, receiving his instruction.

On one of these visits, Master Ryōkan said, "I'm going to gather something we can use to make soup for lunch," and taking a small bucket, the Master approached a cremation ground and began to gather wild celery.

Returning home, his basket brimming with wild greens, the Master set to work using them in a miso soup, which he then offered to Master Katsugen. Katsugen balked but, fearing to show disrespect to a senior priest such as the Master, could barely swallow a single bowl of the stuff. However, seeing Katsugen's expression, and his reluctance to down even half a bowl of the soup, Master Ryōkan carefully questioned the Zen teacher as he pressed on him a second helping.

"How is it that while you pronounce 'delicious' vegetables that have been manured," the Master demanded, "when it comes to wild celery growing near a cremation ground, you find it objectionable and claim it's unclean?"

Master Katsugen, on hearing this, is said to have attained enlightenment and proceeded to happily down several bowlfuls of the soup.

This probably explains why Master Ryōkan left final instructions asking Katsugen to officiate at his funeral service.

～～

Even when people asked him to do so, Master Ryōkan was extremely reluctant to provide samples of his calligraphy. Yet when seized with enthusiasm, he would brush calligraphy with abandon.

Once, while visiting a wealthy farmer in the village of Shichi-nichi, the Master, perhaps because the mood had struck him, immediately borrowed brush and ink and set about inscribing a waka entitled "Iron Begging Bowl" on the sooty sliding screen in the maids' quarters.[73] Looking over the ink marks he had just spattered on the screen, the Master couldn't help giving a smile of satisfaction and, without a word, promptly left and returned home.

~~

Once Master Ryōkan stayed the night at the Satō home in the village of Nakayama. The sliding doors had been newly repapered. Seeing this, the Master was roused to his usual propensity, so that by first light he was up and covering the length and breadth of the screens with his brushwork, after which he promptly fled.

~~

The following is another story of an occasion on which the Master simply could not restrain himself from brushing the calligraphy that just seemed to well forth from his fertile imagination.

Freely wielding his brush on thick Chinese-style paper and sliding-screen paper, the Master let his brush move as it wished, spontaneously and without constraint, drawing such large characters that the dripping ink marks spread beyond the paper and onto the tatami.

According to a certain person's account, this seems to have occurred at the home of Mr. Yamada of Yoita, who subsequently, it is said, had the pieces of calligraphy mounted as scrolls and kept them as treasured possessions.[74]

~~

The Niigata calligrapher Makiri Yōko returned from Edo to his native province of Echigo at a time when his fame as a master of brushwork was nearly universal.[75]

It happened that a certain wealthy man had commissioned Makiri to decorate a pair of gilded folding screens with his calligraphy. Having completed the first screen, Makiri retired to another room to rest. Into the now vacant room stepped an old monk. Brandishing a calligraphy brush, the monk freely proceeded to cover the remaining screen with characters and then departed.

When the members of the household saw what had happened, they reported it to the owner, who, scowling, went together with Makiri to have a look.

When Makiri examined the calligraphy, he saw that the brushstrokes truly possessed a forcefulness and vivacity that distinguished the work as a rare masterpiece.

Makiri exhorted the master of the house, "Let's quickly go after him!" and they started off in pursuit of the old monk. In the meantime, Master Ryōkan, seeing people from the house chasing after him and having no idea why, abruptly seated himself on the bare ground and began to plead for his life, beseeching his pursuers, "For heaven's sake, spare me!"

"You've got it all wrong," they reassured him, escorting the Master back to the house as they explained.

The proprietor treated the Master with the warmest cordiality and, joined by Makiri, expressed his heartfelt gratitude for the Master's calligraphy on the second screen. Indeed, the full pair, with one panel by the Master and the other by Makiri, has been preserved, a proud possession of the family.

~~

Master Ryōkan's brush painting could not be mistaken for that of an amateur. He is said to have received the art by studying with a monk named Ugan, who had erected a hermitage at Tsubame.[76] Ugan had studied the Kano school of painting, and his own artwork is said to have displayed tolerable skill.[77]

Like Ryōkan, Ugan was also a noted eccentric, as the following story attests.

When the monk Ugan was serving as abbot of Mannōji in Tsubame, an old cherry tree stood in the temple garden. One spring, Ugan was gazing up at the tree's blossoms, beneath which he had propped the handle of the broom he used to sweep the garden. Just then a traveling monk arrived and said to Ugan, "I have come from Saga in Hizen, and our town's temple, Kōdenji, has no abbot.[78] Since Your Reverence has some lineage connection with the temple, we all discussed the matter and I have come to invite you to assume the abbacy."

Ugan replied, "As a Buddhist monk, I have no fixed abode, so I'll be glad to go. I'll be leaving later, so you go on ahead."

It wasn't long, however, before Ugan had utterly forgotten his promise.

During cherry blossom season the following year, as Ugan gazed once again at the flowering trees, he suddenly remembered the promise he had given the year before. And so, equipping himself for travel, he hastily set off for Kōdenji in Saga, only to find when he arrived that another abbot had already been installed. He casually departed, making a pilgrimage through various provinces and then returning to Echigo, where he is said to have lived in retreat at Tanomo-an in Niida village.

～

One day before Master Ryōkan's death, he inscribed a waka on various sheets of paper, which he cut into small pieces and distributed among his friends and acquaintances. The poem said:

What keepsake have I to leave?
In spring, the cherry blossoms
In summer, the warbler's song
In autumn, the maple's crimson foliage.[79]

〜〜

Master Ryōkan's funeral service was attended by a large number of mourners. Apart from Master Katsugen, who officiated at the service, there were some 80 monks from fifteen Buddhist temples who chanted sutras, as well as 295 ordinary mourners. According to traditions preserved within the Kimura family, who hosted the event, the funeral procession was so long that even once the officiating priest had reached the cremation ground, Master Ryōkan's coffin had still not cleared the door of the Kimura home! The distance from the Kimura residence to the cremation grounds was approximately three *chō*.[80]

ABBREVIATIONS

BGD   Nakamura Hajime, ed. *Bukkyōgo daijiten.* 3 vols. Tokyo: Tokyo Shoseki, 1976.

BJ   Ui Hakuju, ed. *Bukkyō jiten.* Tokyo: Daitō Shuppansha, 1978.

BZ   Haskel, Peter. *Bankei Zen.* New York: Grove Atlantic, 1984.

BZZ   Akao Ryūji, ed. *Bankei zenji zenshū.* Tokyo: Daizōshuppan, 1970.

DNBZ   Suzuki Gakujutsu Zaidan, ed. *Dai Nihon bukkyō zensho.* 94 vols. Tokyo: Kōdansha Hatsubai, 1970–73.

GF   Abe Ryuichi and Peter Haskel. *Great Fool: Zen Master Ryōkan.* Honolulu: University of Hawaii Press, 1996.

HKD   Mangen Shipan. *Honchō kōsōden* (v. 63 of DNBZ).

HMI   Nōnin Keidō, ed. *Hakuin monka itsuwasen.* Kyoto: Zen Bunka Kenkyūjo, 2000.

HON   Katō Shōshun, ed. *Hakuin oshō nenpu.* Kyoto: Shibunkaku, 1985.

HOZ   Goto Mitsumura, ed. *Hakuin oshō zenshū.* 8 vols. Tokyo: Tokyo Ryūginsha, 1967.

HZHZ   Yoshizawa Katsūhiro, ed. *Hakuin zenji hōgo zenshū.* 15 vols. Kyoto: Zen Bunka Kenkyūjo, 1999–2003.

LG   Haskel, Peter. *Letting Go: The Story of Zen Master Tōsui.* Honolulu: University of Hawaii Press, 2001.

ROI   Nōnin Keidō, ed. *Ryōkan oshō itsuwasen.* Kyoto: Zen Bunka Kenkyūjo, 1999.

RZ   Tōgō Toyoharu, ed. *Ryōkan zenshū.* 2 vols. Tokyo: Sōgensha, 1959.

SOI   Nōnin Keidō, ed. *Sengai oshō itsuwasen.* Kyoto: Zen Bunka Kenkyūjo, 1999.

T   Takakusu Junjirō et al., eds. *Taishō shinshū daizōkyō.* 100 vols. Tokyo: Taishō Issaikyō Kankokai, 1924–34.

TOG   Nōnin Keidō, ed. *Taigu oshō goroku, shūi, gyōjitsu.* Kyoto: Zen Bunka Kenkyūjo, 1999.

TOZ   Takuan Oshō zenshū kankokai, ed. *Takuan oshō zenshū.* 6 vols. Tokyo: Zen Culture Research Institute, 1928–30.

ZD   Miura Isshū and Ruth F. Sasaki. *Zen Dust.* New York: Harcourt, Brace & World, 1966.

ZS   Hori, Victor. *Zen Sand.* Honolulu: University of Hawaii Press, 2003.

ZZ   *Dai Nihon zoku zōkyō.* 150 vols. Kyoto: Zōkyō Shoin, 1905–12.

ZB   *Zen bunka* magazine

NOTES

INTRODUCTION

1 The story can be found in the *Jingde Era Transmission of the Lamp* (*Jingde chuan-deng lu*, see below), T 51:219b. An earlier version appears in the late-eighth-century *Record of the Jewel of Dharma through the Ages* (*Lidai fabaoji*, T 51:181a), an early Chan text discovered among the many documents at Dunhuang, a network of fourth- to fourteenth-century cave temples in the western Chinese province of Gansu, on what was originally the Silk Road connecting medieval China and the West.

2 T 48:348a. That is, hulling rice with a heavy foot-operated pestle (*tatui*). The expatriate Japanese Zen master Sokei-an (Sasaki Shigetsu, 1882–1945) gives a notional description of Huineng working the device: "The mortar was a very big stone, and the pestle was made of heavy wood with a very long shaft. Two crosspieces were balanced with stones, and when you stepped down the stone crashed down. The Sixth Patriarch was treading on this shaft every day. As he was a small man, his weight was not enough to press the pestle down, so he carried a large stone around his waist." See Sokei-an's commentary to the sutra in *Original Wisdom: Zen Comments on the Sixth Patriarch's Platform Sutra* (Bloomington, IN: iUniverse, 2010), 17–18.

3 Again, the account regarding the hunters appears not in the Dunhuang version but in the 1291 "Yuan," or "Ming," text, T 48:349c.

4 The work survives in a Korean edition published in 1245 and discovered in a Korean temple in the 1930s. There is no evidence that the text was ever printed in China, where it apparently went for the most part unread. *Zutang ji* has been extensively studied by modern Japanese scholars, and a facsimile of the Korean text was published by Hanazono University in Kyoto in 1960. Some Japanese scholars have theorized that despite its given date, *Zutang ji* is actually a creation of the same period of the Song that produced the early "lamp" histories. ZD, 369.

5 ZD, 359.

6 The first edition of the *Jingde Era Transmission of the Lamp* (*Jingde chuandeng lu*), published in 1011, no longer exists. References are to the second edition, published in 1132 (T 51, no. 2076). As Thomas Y. Kirchner observes, the work constituted a major source for Zen koan. See Ruth F. Sasaki and Thomas Y. Kirchner, *The Record of Linji* (Honolulu: University of Hawaii Press, 2009), 393. The *Extensive Tiensheng Era Transmission of the Lamp* (*Tiensheng guangdeng lu*) is the Taiwan edition of the Japanese *Zoku zokyō*, 78, no. 1553. Altogether, the last three of the five "lamp" collections were issued in 1101, 1183, and 1202, respectively.

7 Iriya Yoshitaka, *Baso no goroku* (Kyoto: Zen Bunka Kenkyūjo, 1985), iii.

8 Albert Welter, *Monks, Rulers, and Literati: The Political Ascendancy of Chan Buddhism* (New York: Oxford University Press, 2006), 188–90.

9 The term *yu lu* seems fairly elastic and, in the view of some scholars, describes many varieties of Chan literature, including the "lamp" histories and the dialogues with which they are associated. Albert Welter, *The Linji lu and the Creation of Chan Orthodoxy* (New York: Oxford University Press, 2008), 46.

10 T 47:504b. Translated in Sasaki and Kirchner, *Record of Linji*, 311. The Sasaki and Kirchner version is based on the standard 1120 printing of the text, the *Zhenjou Linji huizhao chanshi yu lu* (T 47, no. 1985). The evolution of the Linji text is well covered in Welter's *Linji lu*, which traces the work's development over time toward the brusque, often shocking words and behavior with which we are familiar from the 1120 version.

11 John R. McRae, *Seeing through Zen: Encounter, Transformation, and Geneology in Chinese Chan Buddhism* (Berkeley: University of California Press, 2003), 67.

12 Iriya, *Baso no goroku*, iii.

13 Welter, *Linji lu*, 149. In his earlier *Monks, Rulers, and Literati*, Welter examines the means by which this new Chan and its texts formed part of an "imagined tradition" adapted to the tastes and preferences of the Song court and bureaucracy. Welter, *Monk, Rulers*, 77–102, 125–26, 171–80. See also Wendi Adamek, "The Lidai fabaoji [Record of the Jewel through the Ages]," in *The Zen Canon: Understanding the Classic Texts*, ed. Steven Heine and Dale S. Wright (New York: Oxford University Press, 2004), 83, 86–87, 96–98. For a dissenting view, see Mario Poceski, *The Records of Mazu and the Making of Classical Chan Literature* (New York: Oxford University Press, 2015). Poceski calls for a more balanced picture of Mazu and his descendants, one that credits the very real importance of Tang Chan, even while acknowledging

the effects of reinterpretations during the subsequent Five Dynasties and Song periods. See, for example, Poceski, *Records of Mazu*, 30–37, 138–41. That is, while rejecting the traditional or sectarian approaches that accept all Chan materials at face value, Poceski cautions equally against distortions arising from the "overly aggressive debunking, deconstructive applied analysis, unnecessary obfuscation, or overinterpretation" that are unquestioningly applied in some recent academic works on Chan history (36). Poceski thus presents his book on Mazu and Chan as a corrective of sorts, while concurring that there is absolutely no evidence in Tang records of the distinctive iconoclasm of the Chan encounter dialogues of the sort identified with Mazu and his followers. See chart in Poceski, 155, and accompanying remarks.

14 Welter, *Linji lu*, 107, 163.

15 Ishii Shūdō, a Japanese authority on Song Zen, states categorically that the koan method is a Song invention, "systematized" in the early twelfth century by Dahui Zonggao (see below). "Koan Zen is not a method that dates from the early period of Chan development," he writes. "There is no evidence at all of its existence during the Tang dynasty." "Kung-an Ch'an and the Tsung-men t'ung-yao chi," trans. Albert Welter, in *The Koan*, ed. Steven Heine and Dale S. Wright (New York: Oxford University Press, 2000), 111. For more on this subject, see Albert Welter, "Mahakashyapa's Smile: Silent Transmission and the Kung-an (Koan) tradition," in *The Koan*, ed. Steven Heine and Dale S. Wright (New York: Oxford University Press, 2000), 75–109; and T. Griffith Foulk, "Form and Function in Koan Literature," in *The Koan*, ed. Steven Heine and Dale S. Wright (New York: Oxford University Press, 2000), 15–45; as well as McRae, *Seeing through Zen*, 123–32.

16 *Hsialu* from the *Blue Cliff Record* (T 48), cases 79 (305a), 36 (174), and 21 (161a), respectively.

17 Another koan favored by Dahui in his letters to students, or *Dahui shu*, an important source for the master's teaching, is the twenty-first case of *Wumen guan*, "Yunmen's 'Piece of Dried Shit (*Yunmen ganshijue*)'": "A monk asked Yunmen, 'What is the Buddha?' Yunmen said, 'A piece of dried shit.'" T 48:296c. The expression, which also appears in the *Linji lu* (T 47:496c), has been variously interpreted to mean "a piece of shit," "a shit-wiping stick"—a bamboo device used for wiping up after using the monastery latrine—a worthless blockhead, filth, etc. See Yanagida Seizan, *Rinzai roku* (Tokyo: Daizō Shuppansha, 1973), 52; and Sasaki and Kirchner, *Record of Linji*, 131; as well as Dahui's "Reply to Minister Lu," *Dahui shu*, T 47:930b. Yunmen refers

to the Chan master Yunmen Wenyan (864–949). Well into the early twentieth century, poor farmers in the southern United States would employ "shit-wiping sticks" in their outhouses. Hence the ironic American expression, "Getting left with the brown end of the stick."

18 T 48:292c. Zhaozhou is the Chan master Zhaozhou Congshen (778–897).

19 Jeffery R. Broughton, *The Chan Whip Anthology* (New York: Oxford University Press, 2015), 129–37, has given *huatou* the intriguing translation "cue," as in "to cue up" the koan to one's attention, "to pull the cue [into full conscious awareness]." Broughton, *Chan Whip Anthology*, 136. The term is rendered as "crucial phrase" in Welter's translation of Ishii, "Kung-an Ch'an," 111, while Morten Schlutter, in *How Zen Became Zen* (Honolulu: University of Hawaii Press, 2008), defines *huatou* as the koan's "crucial punch line" (107, 115). Because of Dahui's technique of total engagement with the huatou, Schlutter maintains that Dahui "invented a whole new kind of Chan," but he cautions that Dahui himself never claimed his approach to be new. *How Zen Became Zen*, 116–17, 215n27. It should be noted that in other contexts, Chinese and Japanese, *huatou* is used simply as a synonym for "koan."

20 "Reply to Palace Chamberlin Lu," *Dahui shu*, T 47:930a.

21 For Dahui's conception of relentless, wholehearted practice as the "shortcut" (*jing jie*) to enlightenment, see Robert E. Buswell Jr., "The Short-Cut Approach of K'an-hua Meditation: The Evolution of a Practical Subitism in Chinese Ch'an Buddhism," in *Sudden and Gradual Approaches to Enlightenment in Chinese Thought*, ed. Peter N. Gregory (Honolulu: University of Hawaii Press, 1987), 348–55.

22 Iriya, *Baso no goroku*, ii.

23 Unlike the Japanese Confucian model of the Edo period, where the military caste composed a hereditary elite, classical Chinese Confucianism saw warriors as the lowest stratum of society. Government, ideally, and in premodern China often in practice, was to be headed by bureaucrat-intellectuals chosen in competitive examination for their cultivation in poetry and the Confucian classics. Jacques Gernet, *A History of Chinese Civilization* (Cambridge: Cambridge University Press, 1982), 144–48.

24 *Keisō dokuzui*, HOZ 2:9–10.

25 See, for example, the criticism by the Confucian Kumazawa Banzan (1609–1691) in his *Usa mondō*, where he repeatedly attacks Buddhism for devastating the nation's agriculture by drawing money and labor from the farmers

and consuming arable land for temple construction, all to support a corrupt and exploitative priesthood. Atsuo, *Banzan zenshū* (Tokyo: Meicho Shuppan, 1940), 5:293–94, 320–21; and *Shūgi gaisho*, *Banzan zenshū* (Tokyo: Meicho Shuppan, 1940), 2:39–40, 52, 237, 293. For an extended treatment of the anti-Buddhist debate during the Tokugawa period, see Tsuji Zennosuke, *Nihon bukkyōshi*, 7th ed. (Tokyo: Iwanami Shoten, 1992), 10: 1–403.

26 Both teachers are descended from the Linji line of Yuanwu Kechin (1063–1135), the celebrated author of the lectures that formed the basis for the *Blue Cliff Record*. Dahui was an heir of Yuanwu, and Xutang, a member of a branch of Yuanwu's Dharma line established by the Zen master Mian Xianjie (1118–1186). Because the pioneering Japanese Zen teacher Nanpo Jōmyō (Daiō kokushi, 1235–1308) was among Xutang's heirs, it is this Yuanwu Mian branch from which virtually all Japanese Rinzai masters of the Edo period, including Hakuin, trace their descent.

27 Phillip B. Yampolsky, *The Zen Master Hakuin* (New York: Columbia University Press, 1972), 27.

28 The wrinkled crone Obaba, or as Hakuin at times refers to her, Shushin Obaba, "Mastering-Mind Grandma."

29 Ikkyū as a quick-witted child novice was even the subject of a popular children's cartoon series, *Ikkyū san*, in which Ikkyū uses his Zen-inspired intuition to solve problems for people at all levels of medieval Japanese society, from shogunal retainers to farmers and merchants. The series ran on Japanese television from 1975 to 1982.

30 Hakuin's most detailed account of the story appears in his autobiographical *Wild Ivy* (*Itsumadegusa*); see Norman Waddell, trans., *Wild Ivy* (Boulder: Shambhala Publications, 1999), 89–112; HZHZ 3:17. The Hakuyūshi story is also recounted in other Hakuin works, including *Oradegama*, HZHZ 3:220–30, and Tōrei's *Nenpu*. Norman Waddell, *Hakuin's Precious Mirror Cave* (Berkeley: Counterpoint, 2009), 177–79; HON, 121–22. In Hakuin's accounts, he refers to Hakuyūshi's techniques by the term *naikan*, "inner contemplation."

31 See Waddell, *Wild Ivy*, 152–54, and *Hakuin's Precious Mirror Cave*, 86–87. The facts regarding Hakuyūshi have been established by the Japanese Zen scholar Itō Kazuo. Although an initial article on the subject by Itō ("Hakuyūshi no hito to shi," ZB, no. 6 [November 1956]: 48–68) claimed to confirm the truth of Hakuin's account, later detailed research by Itō seems to have credibly debunked Hakuin's story of meeting Hakuyūshi in Shirakawa. Itō's later

arguments are contained in *Hakuyūshi: Shijitsu no shintankyū* (Kyoto: Yama-guchi Shoten, 1960).

32 The episode is recorded in *Oradegama*, HZHZ 9:427; *Yaemugura*, HZHZ 7:153; and *Itsumadegusa*, HZHZ 3:172.

33 *Nenpu*, HON, 92–96. *Oradegama*, HZHZ 9:428–29.

34 Mu'nan did not become a monk till 1654, following years of grueling koan study as a layman under Gudō Tōshoku, whose Dharma heir he became. Mu'nan spent nearly his entire teaching career in a small hermitage in the Azabu section of Edo, and his instruction seems to have been directed largely to the local men and women who made up much of his following. The chief source for Mu'nan's life is *Shidō Mu'nan zenji gyōroku* by Hakuin's heir Tōrei Enji. Koda Rentarō, ed., *Shidō Mu'nan zenji shū* (Tokyo: Shunjūsha, 1956), 195–206. For Mu'nan's life and teaching, see also Furuta Shōkin, *Gudō, Mu'nan, Shōju* (Tokyo: Kōdansha, 1944), 67–177; Furuta's article "Mu'nan no anshū zen," ZB 77 (June 1975): 58–64; and in the same commemorative issue of ZB, Ōmori Sōgen, "Shidō Mu'nan no zen," 38–45; and Hōseki Genjō, "Shi-dō Mu'nan," 48–53. For English translations of Mu'nan's principal vernacu-lar works, see Kobori Sōhaku and Norman Waddell, "Sokushinki," *Eastern Buddhist* 3, no. 2 (October 1970): 89–118; and *Eastern Buddhist* 4, no. 1 (May 1971): 116–23; and Priscilla Pedersen, "Jishōki," *Eastern Buddhist* 8, no. 1 (May 1975): 96–132; and Eduardo Cuellar, "Tokugawa Zen Master Shidō Mu'nan" (master's thesis, University of Arizona, 2016), which includes translations from Mu'nan's 1666 work *Ryūtakuji hōgo*, 28–31. The original text of the *hōgo* is contained in Ichihara Toyoto, ed., *Nihon no zen goroku: Mu'nan* (Tokyo: Kōdansha, 1979).

35 Hakuin proclaims his descent in this line in *Kaien fusetsu*; see Waddell, *Essential Teachings of the Zen Master Hakuin: A Translation of the Kaien Fusetsu* (Boulder: Shambhala Publications, 1994), 15; HOZ 2:11 (internal numbering).

36 Waddell, *Hakuin's Precious Mirror Cave*, 194; *Nenpu*, HON, 160.

37 See, for example, Hakuin's statement in *Sokkō roku kaien fusetsu* (1743) that he is only continuing Shōju's efforts toward reviving authentic Song koan study as embodied by Xutang (Sokkō), whose record is the ostensible sub-ject of the lectures that constitute the work. HOZ 2:75. The only written evidence that Hakuin received Shōju's inka is a memorial inscription of 1782 erected by Hakuin's heir Tōrei at Shōju's temple, Shōju-an. Tōrei's inscrip-tion states that "My late teacher [i.e., Hakuin] received the master's [Shōju's] sanction of attainment [*shōin*]." Hanazono Daigaku Hakubutsukan, *Hakuin*

zenji nihyaku gojunen onkinen (Kyoto: Hanazono Daigaku Rekishi, 2017), 137. See also Audrey Seo and Stephan Addiss, *The Sound of One Hand: Paintings and Calligraphy of Zen Master Hakuin* (Boulder: Shambhala Publications, 2010), 25.

38 As indicated by a handwritten memo dated 1788 that survives at the master's Kyushu temple. *Sengai oshō* (Fukuoka: Shōfukuji Bunko Kankōkai, 1963), 13.

TAIGU TALES

1 *Honchō kosōden*, DNBZ 63:273. Following his independent enlightenment in 1631, Ungo is said to have lived a largely humble and reclusive existence till urged by Taigu in 1636 to assume abbacy of Zuiganji in northern Matsushima (Miyagi Prefecture), the domain of the powerful daimyo Date Masamune (1567–1636), who died later that year. Ungo served two terms as Myōshinji abbot, in 1620 and 1645, but by his death in 1659 he had retreated to a secluded hermitage in Sendai (Miyagi Prefecture). Ungo's Zen involved koan study and, at least in teaching laypersons, a melding of Zen and Pure Land elements. Ungo's long religious poem *Ōjōyōka* (Song of the essentials of rebirth in the Pure Land), composed in 1649 for Masamune's widow Yōtoku-in (d. 1653), is said to have sparked objections among certain Myōshinji priests for its Zen–Pure Land synthesis. Amakuki Setsu'nan, *Myōshinji roppyakunenshi* (Tokyo: Daihōekyoku, 1930), 388. The poem is included in Nōnin Keidō, ed., *Ungo oshō goroku* (Matsushima: Zuiganji, 2009), 641–47.

2 See Nōnin's remarks in "Angya," *Ungo oshō goroku*, 136. Information here is based principally on Nōnin's *Taigu oshō goroku* (Kyoto: Zen Bunka Kenkyūjo, 2012); his four-part article in ZB, "Edo zenki no san daizensho," pts. 1–4, no. 225 (2012): 25–28; no. 226 (2012): 132–37; no. 229 (2013): 136–41; 230 (2013), 70–72; the biography in HKD 63:276; and Matsukura Zentei, "Taigu Sōchiku zenji no gyōjō," *Zengaku kenkyū* 52 (1963): 40–82.

3 The 1768 Nansenji manuscript's full title is *Taigu oshō gyōjitsu narabi ni toteiki* (Master Taigu's Complete Biographical Record and Dharma Heirs).

4 That is, the Battle of Sekigahara (in present-day Gifu Prefecture), the key battle in which Tokugawa Ieyasu defeated his rivals, leading to the establishment of the Tokugawa shogunate. The chronology of Gudō Tōshoku (*Gudō nenpu*) describes how he and Taigu wandered together through the ravaged area of the battle, carrying their books on their backs as they picked their way through the corpse-strewn fields. Quoted in TOG, 189n1.

5 It was customary for Buddhist monks to carry their written religious

materials in a kind of portable library on a wooden frame that could be hoisted backpack-style.

6 Missing from the account is any overt mention of an enlightenment experience resulting from Taigu's years of pilgrimage and Zen study. But reading between the lines, one may probably assume that such a realization is implied in Taigu's sanction by Chimon and his subsequent recognition as a Zen master in his own right, able to assume the abbacy of temples and to train and sanction students of his own.

7 Now Nara Prefecture. Yoshino and its picturesque and mountainous landscape was often the site of retreats for recluse Buddhist monks and followers of the syncretic Esoteric Buddhist and Shinto cult known as Shūgendō.

8 A *ri* (Ch. *li*) is an old unit of linear measurement, equivalent to approximately 2.44 miles. Myōkan has thus traveled a considerable distance—nearly 250 miles—presumably on foot, to meet Taigu.

9 *Sai.* Vegetarian meals traditionally provided to Buddhist monks by lay patrons as an act of merit.

10 "Bowing mat," *zagu.* The mat a monk always carries neatly folded and which he spreads on the ground to perform prostrations before Buddhist images or eminent masters.

11 As noted earlier, in Zen and, in particular, koan study, a strong sensation of "doubt," or *gi,* sometimes also referred to as the "great ball of doubt" (*daigidan*)—a kind of single-minded questioning—is often considered necessary to the experience of awakening.

12 J. *kibetsu.* An old Chinese expression of disdain. A tortoise is, of course, a land turtle, and a terrapin is an aquatic turtle.

13 "All the buddhas of the three worlds," *sanzen shobutsu.* That is, all the myriad enlightened beings of the past, present, and future.

14 Like many Japanese Zen poems, Taigu's various gatha, composed in classical Chinese, are often a pastiche of poems by a variety of earlier Chinese Zen monks and poets. For Taigu's particular sources in this gatha, see TOG, 56nn2–3. Such "borrowings" were not intended or regarded as plagiarism but rather sincere tribute to one's forebears.

15 Horie Yamashiro Tadaharu (n.d.), a daimyo of the Matsue domain (present-day Shimane Prefecture). Daimyo in the Tokugawa period were required to keep often elaborate residences in the Tokugawa capital, Edo, where they

would spend part of the year "in attendance" on the shogun, leaving behind their families in the capital as a kind of assurance of their fealty when they returned to their provincial domains.

16 Kitayama (literally, "north mountain") generally refers to a northern district of Kyoto. Nōnin links the horse driver's verse to a phrase in case 19 of the thirteenth-century koan collection *Wumenguan* (T 48:295b.):

> In spring, the myriad flowers
> In autumn, the moon
> In summer, refreshing breezes
> In winter, snow
> If the mind is not tied up in useless matters
> It's always a fine time to be alive!

Nōnin Keidō, "Edo zenki no daizensho," pt. 3, ZB 229 (2013): 141.

17 Tenkai (1536–1643), a Buddhist priest who was an important advisor on religious affairs to the early Tokugawa shoguns. He had also been instrumental in engineering Takuan Sōhō's recall from exile in 1632, on the occasion of the death of the second Tokugawa shogun, Hidetada. Memorials of the passing of a shogun were often the occasion for pardons to be issued by the authorities, attesting to the magnanimity of the deceased and augmenting his merit in the afterlife. The text of Tenkai's letter is included in Kawakami Kozan's history of the temple, *Myōshinji shi* (Kyoto: Myoshinjiha kyomu honjo, 1917), 2:432–33.

18 Actually, Matsudaira Mitsumichi (1636–1674). Mitsumichi had succeeded to the Fukui domain as ruler of Echizen in 1645 at age nine. He was thus only twenty years old on meeting Taigu for the first time and had only been daimyo of the Fukui domain for eleven years, during the majority of which, due to his extreme youth, affairs must have been managed largely by the domain's senior retainers. TOG, 33n4.

19 *Udumbara* (J. *udonge*), an Indian flower said to blossom only once in three thousand years. A metaphor for the rarity of a buddha's appearance in the human world and, by extension, the difficulty of encountering an enlightened teacher.

20 Quoting a famous passage in the *Record of Linji*. When Linji was planting pines, Huangbo asked, "What are you doing planting all these deep in the mountains?" Linji said, "First, to make a suitable setting for the temple gate. Second, to make a model for those who will come later." T 47:505a. Huangbo

is Linji's teacher, Huangbo Xiun (d. 850?). Translation based in part on Sasaki and Kirchener, *Record of Linji*, 317.

21 Case 65 of the *Blue Cliff Record* (*Piyan lu*). A heretic, approaching the Buddha with a sparrow concealed in his fist, asked, "Please tell me: Is this sparrow in my fist dead or alive?"

The Buddha mounted the threshold of the temple gate and asked the heretic, "Tell me, am I going out or coming in?"

Unable to reply, the heretic prostrated himself before the Buddha.

The actual origin of the story is unknown. T48:149c–150a.

22 Referring to a phrase in case 5 of the *Blue Cliff Record*: "For such a person, one who has attained solid faith [in mind], who can grasp things and not accept the delusions of others, the words and teachings of the buddhas and patriarchs are just meaningless sounds." T 48:166c. The expression translated here as "meaningless sounds" (J. *netsuwan myoshō*) refers literally to the sizzle of boiling liquid being poured into a bowl but in colloquial Chinese signified "meaningless" or "senseless." BGD 2:1078b.

23 *Kobyō* (sesame buns), according to Nōnin, is an ornate way of referring to a simple wheat roll. Such rolls, sprinkled with sesame seeds, were said to have originated in India and were produced in China, where they are referred to most notably by Yunmen Wenyan (864–949) in the *Blue Cliff Record*, case 77. T 48:204b–205a. In the koan, a monk asks, "What is it that transcends buddhas and patriarchs?" To which Yunmen replies, "A sesame bun." Urs App, in *Master Yunmen* (New York: Kodansha International, 1994), translates this as "sesame flatcake" and notes that the bun in case 77 refers to "a baked flatcake four to six inches in diameter, made from wheat flour dough, baked plastered against the inner side of an earthen oven, and sprinkled with sesame seeds." App observes that "this is one of the most celebrated instances in Chan literature of presenting everyday reality as the highest doctrine" (114n2). In the Japanese context, along with the allusions to the *Blue Cliff Record*, it may simply constitute a literary way of referring to an ordinary bun with sesame seeds.

24 Tokugawa Iemitsu (1604–1651), the third Tokugawa shogun. Iemiitsu was a great patron of Buddhism and of various Zen teachers, of whom perhaps the most notable was Takuan Sōhō. And Rinshō-in is the posthumous Buddhist name of Kasuga no Tsubone (1579–1643). At a future shogun's birth, a wet nurse would frequently be chosen from among the daughters of the Tokugawa's leading vassals. Kasuga no Tsubone was credited with promoting Iemitsu's fortunes over those of his siblings, and she was always treated with

great reverence by Iemitsu following his succession to the shogunate. The name Kasuga no Tsubone is a court title bestowed upon Risshō-in in 1629 by Emperor Gomizuno'o (1596–1680), no doubt at Iemitsu's urging. The year 1629 was also the time of the still-influential Gomuzuno'o's abdication—at the insistence of Iemitsu's father, Shogun Hidetada—and it is unclear whether the title was bestowed on Risshō-in prior to or after this event.

25 *Hinju shoken.* "Host" and "guest" are common terms in Zen, used by teachers such as Linji Yixuan to distinguish subject and object.

26 Again, Taigu implies that wherever he is, he remains true to himself, so that Iemitsu—known for his touchiness and quick temper—would probably find Taigu's behavior insupportable and might even order him executed for lacking suitable respect for the nation's ruler.

27 According to tradition, twenty-four lines of Zen were introduced to Japan from China during the Middle Ages.

28 The Zuiōsan Ryūshōji, a temple founded by Nanpo Jōmyō (1235–1308), the master of Kanzan's teacher Shūhō Myōchō (1282–1337) and thus the progenitor of Kanzan's line. The two Chinese characters of Ryūshō mean literally "dragon soaring aloft." The temple was erected at the western edge of Kyoto as Nanpo's mortuary temple but was moved within the Daitokuji precincts in the sixteenth century. See ZD, 206.

29 Shōbōzan. The "mountain," or formal, name of Myōshinji.

30 A reference to Myōshinji's founder, Kanzan, with whose reputedly crusty behavior Taigu seems to have empathized. According to *Shōbōzan rokuso den*, "Kanzan's abbot's quarters were in extreme disrepair. The roof leaked, and when it rained there was nowhere to sit. One day, it suddenly began to pour, and the teacher [i.e., Kanzan] ordered, 'Someone bring something to fix the leak.' A young acolyte quickly came with a [loosely] woven bamboo basket, and the teacher praised him extravagantly. Another acolyte then arrived with a wooden tub. Enraged, the teacher exclaimed, 'You shilly-shallying dolt!' and struck him and chased him from the room." A related story in the text records that "a certain Takanashi of Shinano Province [now Nagano Prefecture], a patron of the teacher's [Kanzan's] lineage, visited the temple to pay his respects to the abbot. But seeing the rain leaking into the abbot's quarters, he withdrew and told the teacher's attendant monk, 'The roof of the abbot's quarters is leaking. Why hasn't it been repaired? I hope you will permit me to donate whatever trifling costs may be incurred for the purpose.' The attendant monk reported this to the teacher,

who furiously exclaimed, 'That layman! He says he wants to see *me* and then asks what's going to be done about repairing my roof. Don't let him in here again!'" Quoted in TOG, 90n4. Composed by the Myōshinji master Tōyō Eichō (1438–1504), *Shōbōzan rokuso den* (Biographies of the Six Patriarchs of Myōshinji) consists of biographies of six leading Myōshinji Zen masters of the medieval period. For a modern edition, see Ogisu Jundō, *Shōbōzan rokusoden kunchū* (Kyoto: Shibunkaku, 1979).

31 The historical Buddha, Shakyamuni, is said to have died at age eighty. Nōnin suggests the monk here is castigating Taigu for overstaying his time. TOG, 218n13.

32 Apparently the Echizen daimyo Minamoto Mitsumichi, referred to earlier.

33 Because of its importance in Zen, the *Blue Cliff Record* is often accorded the accolade employed here by Mitsumichi, "preeminent text of the [Zen] school" (*Shūmon dai ichi no sho*).

34 J. *kakunen mushō*. The title of the first case of the *Blue Cliff Record*, "Bodhidharma's 'Empty and Boundless, Nothing Holy.'" Emperor Wu of Liang asked Bodhidharma, "What is the ultimate meaning of sacred truth?" Bodhidharma said, "Empty and boundless, nothing holy." T 48:140a. The Liang dynasty in South China extended from 502 to 557, and Emperor Wu, the dynasty's founder, is said to have reigned from 502 to 549.

35 *Hōmyō*. A Buddhist name bestowed by a teacher on a priest or dedicated lay student.

36 Bankyū MuMu Koji. The curious religious name that Taigu assigns the daimyo is perhaps an ironic reference to the same case (case 1) of the *Blue Cliff Record* that the master cites in the previous section, "Bodhidharma's 'Empty and Boundless, Nothing Holy.'" In the course of his interview with Bodhidharma, Emperor Wu is said to have asked what merit he, as emperor, has accrued through his many virtuous activities in support of Buddhism, to which Bodhidharma replies, "No merit at all!" (*pingwu gongde*). *Jingde chuan deng lu*, T 51:219a. The same phrase appears in an earlier version of the story in the eighth-century *Lidai fabaoji*, T 51:180c.

37 That is, the spirit of the daimyo's late sister would be delighted at having a revered Buddhist master installed in her retreat.

38 Shōunji is a now-defunct temple in Echizen Province, present-day Fukui Prefecture.

39 In Zen texts, "setting off on pilgrimage" (J. *angya*) is often employed as a euphemism for dying.

40 Japanese of the premodern period observed the lunar calendar. The seventh month of autumn was approximately equivalent to late August by modern Western reckoning.

41 Hunlun shan (J. *konron*). A mountain range in western China, used in Zen literature to symbolize a state of complete nondistinction, or primordial chaos. See Inagaki Hisao, *Glossary of Zen Terms* (Kyoto: Nagata Bunshōdō, 1991), 207.

42 *Funi no hōmon*. The Buddhist principle of the oneness of the phenomenal and absolute realms enunciated in such classic Mahayana scriptures as the *Vimalakirti Sutra* (J. *Yuimakyō*) and the *Awakening of Faith* (J. *Kishinron*).

SENGAI TALES

1 The following capsule biography of Sengai is based on material in Nōnin Keido, *Sengai oshō itsuwasen* (Kyoto: Zen bunka kenkyūjo, 1999); Miyake Shukudō, *Hakata to Sengai* (Tokyo: Bunken Shuppan, 1978); Uratsuji Kendō, *Hakata Sengai* (Fukuoka: Nishi Nihon Shinbunsha, 1990); Obata Buntei, ed., *Shōfukuji shi* (Fukuoka: Shōfukuji Shi Bunko Kankokai, 1964), 73–74; Fujita Takushi, "Shi ni tomonai: Sengai Gibon," *ZB* 224 (2012): 46–56; Furuta Shōkin, *Sengai* (Sydney: Trustees Art Gallery of New South Wales, 1985); and Furuta Shōkin, *Sengai: Master Zen Painter* (Tokyo: Kodansha International, 2000), with notes and commentary by Reiko Tsukimura; Shōfukuji Bunko Kankokai, *Sengai oshō* (Fukuoka: Shōfukuji Bunko Kankokai, 1963), which includes a chronology (*nenpu*) of Sengai's life by the native Fukuoka historian Miyake Shukudō (11–37); Miyake Shukudō, *Sengai goroku* (Tokyo: Bunken Shuppan, 1979), which contains a similar *nenpu*; and Nakayama Kiichiro, *Sengai: Sono shōgai to geijutsu* (Fukuoka: Fukuoka shi Bijutsukan Kyōkai, 1992). Sengai's longest-known written work, *Tenganyaku* (Eye medicine), a composition in *kanbun* (Sino-Japanese) on the subject of Zen, is included in Kuramitsu Daigu's *Sengai oshō ikō* (Tokyo: Kōgeisha, 1931), 27–49 (a volume I have unfortunately been unable to locate).

2 Another disciple of Kogetsu was Hakuin's Dharma heir and biographer Tōrei Enji, who, following Kogetsu's retirement, left to join Hakuin's assembly. Kogetsu and his students were particularly active in western Japan and are said to have been influenced by the recently imported Ōbaku school, particularly

that school's views on the precepts. Michel Mohr, "Hakuin," in *Buddhist Spirituality*, ed. Takeuchi Yoshinori (New York: The Crossroad Publishing Company, 1999), 2:314–15.

3 Case 5 of the thirteenth-century koan collection *Gateless Gate*. Zen Master Xingyan Zhixin (d. 898) describes the predicament of a man in a tree, hanging from a high branch by his teeth, his hands and feet dangling helplessly. At this moment, another man asks him the purpose of Bodhidharma's coming from the West. If the man hanging from the branch doesn't answer, he fails in his duty. If he does answer, he falls to his death. T 48:239c. For a chart showing Sengai's place in his Rinzai lineage, see Miyake, *Hakata to Sengai*, 250–54.

4 Fukuoka shi, *Shōfukuji shi*, 73–74. Shakyamuni (J. Shakya) is the historical Buddha, Gautama. Maitreya (J. Miroku) is the buddha who will appear in the future.

5 Miyake nenpu in Shōfukuji Bunko Kankokai, *Sengai oshō*, 12.

6 "Blind donkey" refers to the dying Linji's parting words to his disciple Sansheng Huiran (n.d.): "Who would have thought that my True Dharma Eye would be extinguished upon reaching this blind ass!" *Linji lu*, T 47:506c. Translated in Sasaki and Kirchner, *Record of Linji*, 340.

   Furuta interprets Linji's words here as a backhanded compliment (of which Zen boasts a great many) and argues that the poem extends Linji's supposed accolade to Shōfukuji's founder, Eisai. Furuta, *Sengai*, 11. But a straightforwardly pejorative tone can also be given to Linji's last words, and by extension Sengai may be humbly transferring the celebrated metaphor to himself.

7 There seems to be some difference among the accounts of Sengai's biography as to whether he accepted or stalwartly rejected honors and advanced rank at Myōshinji. I have followed the information in Furuta, *Sengai*, 1–16, and the nenpu compiled by Miyake Shukudō, in Shōfukuji bunko kankokai, *Sengai oshō*, 14–16. Nōnin's brief biography in SOI, 5, states that Sengai refused all honors at Myōshinji, as does Michel Mohr in his essay "Sengai's Multifaceted Legacy," in *Zen Master Sengai*, ed. Katharina Eppreck (Zurich: Scheidegger and Spiess, 2014), 17. (The book is an accompanying volume to an exhibition of Sengai's painting at the Zurich Rietberg Museum.)

8 *"Kyūnen menpeki iya na koto!"* Furuta, *Sengai*, 25.

9 SOI, 216. Sengai's painting of the monument is included in Suzuki Daisetsu, *Sengai, the Zen Master* (Greenwich, CT: New York Graphic Society, 1971), 33.

10 The largest of a chain of volcanic islands that make up the Izu archipelago, Ōshima lies a short distance east of the coast of Honshu in the Philippine Sea. Until the mid-Edo period it served as a penal colony and then as a place of exile. Tangen's infraction is said in some accounts to have been a dispute with Nomura Hayato, a senior advisor to the Kuroda clan, over the Nomura family's meager temple donations. See below, p. 207, n. 86.

11 SOI, 216. A photograph of Sengai's death verse, brushed in the master's clearly faltering hand, appears in Shōfukuji Bunko Kankokai, *Sengai oshō*, 3, no. 5.

12 Published in Tokyo. A second, 1937 edition bears the title *Sengai oshō itsuwa*.

13 Geta are Japanese platform clogs, often worn in wet or snowy weather.

14 A further example of the master's refusal to acknowledge gratitude in the conventional manner appears later in connection with the eccentric merchant Ōta (pp. 88–90).

15 The thunder and lightning god, known in Japan as Raiden *sama* or Raijin. He is commonly depicted as a terrifying demon, clad in a tiger-skin loincloth and draped by a ring of drums, which he beats with drumsticks grasped in his hands to produce claps of thunder. Among the most well-known depictions of Raiden is that by the seventeenth-century artist Tawara-ya Sōtatsu (n.d.) on a panel of folding screens at the Kyoto Zen temple Kenninji.

16 *Yama no imo. Dioscorea japonica*, or Japanese yam. Unlike the American variety, it tends to be yellowish white inside and have a subtler, sweeter flavor.

17 Today, a scenic town in the mountains of western Kanagawa Prefecture. In Sengai's day, Hakone was a station on the Tōkaidō, the highway connecting Edo and Kyoto and the site of a key checkpoint (*Hakone sekisho*), where travelers to and from Edo had to have themselves and their baggage cleared by shogunal officials. The date and purpose of Sengai's trip to the capital is unknown, as is the reason for turning back nuns at the checkpoint, though in some cases, women of daimyo families were expected to remain in Edo as de facto hostages to insure the daimyos' loyalty to the Tokugawa regime—a situation reflected in the saying, "[No] women out, [no] guns in" (*De onna— iri teppō*). Any attempt to bring guns into the capital or sneak hostages out could be construed as a possible plot against the Tokugawa government. By the eighteenth century, however, such measures were no longer being seriously enforced. See Marius B. Jansen, *The Making of Modern Japan* (Cambridge MA: Harvard University Press, 2000), 139–40.

18 *Ki* (Ch. *qi*) in East Asian tradition is a kind of vital force, or breath, the dynamic physical manifestation of mind. The concept remains important in many Chinese and Japanese martial arts. In China, the term was associated with Daoism, Han Confucianism, and Neo-Confucianism and has been variously translated "vital force," "material force," "spirit," "energy," as well as "breath" and "vital breath," the latter the meaning implied here.

19 A koku (also read *seki*, approx. 5.2 bushels) is an old unit of measure for rice used as an index of wealth and, as here, to calculate the stipends of samurai, including daimyo.

20 *Susoku*, literally the "counting of breaths"—beginning, for example, with "one" and proceeding up to "ten" without distraction—a common technique recommended for neophyte Zen practitioners.

21 An expression found in the *Linji lu* section known as "The Four Shouts" (*shihe*), in which the master questions a monk about four different kinds of shouts he, Linji, employs. The first of these is likened to the "Jeweled Sword of the Vajra King," a symbol of admantine power and sharpness that severs all delusion. T 47:504a.

22 Buddhist monks were supposed to be vegetarian.

23 *Ya* is a common Japanese suffix indicating a business or shop name.

24 *Takama ga hara*, "Plane of High Heaven," is the homeland of the gods in Japanese creation myths.

25 Buzen is an old province in what is now Fukuoka Prefecture.

26 In premodern Japan, it was customary to pay regular visits to the graves of one's relations or clan leaders. Such graves were almost always located on the grounds of Buddhist temples, such as Shōfukuji, of which Sengai's retreat was a subtemple.

27 A basaltic cave along the shoreline of Itoshima City (Fukuoka Prefecture), Keya no Ooto is a huge pointed rock long noted as a scenic spot for sightseers. Today it is contained within Kyushu's Genkai National Park, some twenty miles north of Sengai's temple in Hakata.

28 Tendai (Ch. Tiantai) is one of the principal schools of East Asian Buddhism. It was founded in China by the priest Zhiyi (538–597) and introduced to Japan by Saichō (Dengyō Daishi, 767–822). Its major text is the *Lotus Sutra* (*Saddharma-pundarika*).

29 *San*, as noted earlier, is used in Japan as a kind of suffix, with the common

meaning of Ms. or Mr., but when used with a first name or a priest's informal name, as here, carries with it a kind of affectionate familiarity. Ryōkan, for example, was often referred to by the neighboring villagers as "Ryōkan-san" and is still referred to as such in children's stories about his openhearted naiveté.

30 Haiku, the traditional compact Japanese seventeen-syllable poem, was popularized in the Edo period by Matsuo Bashō (1644–1694) and his followers and remains popular in Japan to this day. Shien was probably the poet's literary name, Kawagoe his family name.

31 Presumably referring to Shien and the maidservant, the latter seeming to have returned to Shien's home following the child's birth.

32 *Takuhatsu.* Literally, "to receive in the bowl," the traditional begging practice in which a line of black-robed monks wearing wide-brimmed straw hats wends its way chanting through towns, cities, and villages in search of alms from passersby and parishioners. It is unclear here whether Sengai's *takuhatsu* is the usual group practice or an individual begging expedition.

33 The identity of the narrator here is unclear. It may be Kuramitsu Daigu, whose *Sengai oshō heso no hone* served as the principal source for Nōnin's *Sengai oshō itsuwasen.* (See Nōnin, *Sengai oshō itsuwasen,* i.)

34 Nakano is one of the city's wards, or *ku.* Apparently this event occurred after the Meiji Restoration (1868), when the capital's name was changed from Edo to Tokyo (literally, "Eastern Capital").

35 Site of the castle town from which the Kuroda daimyo ruled their domain from 1600 to the time of the Meiji Restoration. This move would presumably have shortened Shien's commute from the Hakata area.

36 "Goblins" (*tengu*) said to bedevil lonely travelers in the wilds. Fond of pranks, they are generally depicted with long human noses or beaks and were reputed to have been endowed with mysterious skill at traditional martial arts. The twelfth-century Japanese warrior hero Yoshitsune, for example, is said to have been taught by the tengu, who were also frequently associated with the *yamabushi,* mountain monks who practiced a form of syncretism involving Esoteric Buddhism and Shinto. Tengu disguised as yamabushi are a common theme of premodern Japanese folk art.

37 Although composed in Sino-Japanese (*kanbun*), Sengai's poem for Shien is an obvious reference to the most celebrated of Bashō's haiku: "An ancient pond / A tree frog plunges in / the sound of water" (*furuike ya / kawazu*

tobikomu / mizu no oto). This haiku was probably written by Bashō between 1686 and 1691. See Ueda Makoto, *Matsuo Bashō* (New York: Twayne, 1970), 52. The first line of Bashō's poem is also shorthand for a familiar Chinese verse by the southern Song Confucian Zhu Xsi (1130–1200) recalling the evanescent joys of youth.

38 Kirino Toshiaki (1838–1877), a late-Edo samurai and master swordsman, served as a senior commander in the Satsuma forces of the imperial army that unseated the Tokugawa shogunate and installed a new government under Emperor Meiji. Later, however, Kirino turned against the Meiji government and joined the revolt known as the Satsuma Rebellion, led by his fellow Satsuma samurai Saigo Takamori. Kirino's wife, Hisa, also a martial arts expert, followed him into battle but, unlike her husband, who was killed in the rebellion, lived on until 1920. Saigo Takamori (1827–1887), though continuing to proclaim loyalty to the Meiji emperor himself, opposed the clique of military leaders around the emperor who were assuming political power in Japan. It took the government forces some six months to subdue the Satsuma Rebellion, in which both Saigo and Kirino perished. See Jansen, *Making of Modern Japan*, 346–70. Academies (*juku*) such as that mentioned here were often established during the late Edo period by anti-shogunate samurai like Saigo and continued into the early Meiji period. Young men at these academies would be imbued with their teachers' pro-imperial values as well as being frequently instructed in Confucianism and the traditional martial arts.

39 In early September 1877, the remnants of Saigo's army withdrew to Shiroyama (Castle Mountain) near present-day Kagoshima City, the capital of the eponymous prefecture. Saigo refused to surrender and perished in the fighting but in 1889 was issued a posthumous pardon by the Meiji emperor. Even in his lifetime, Saigo was admired for maintaining the traditional samurai virtues of courage and determination, and he remains an object of reverence and romance to many Japanese.

40 Presumably because Takako's husband would change his birth name and assume the Kawagoe name along with management of the family business.

41 Yorozuya would have been Sōhei's commercial or shop name, Sakai his actual family name.

42 The Sanada were a celebrated warrior family of the sixteenth and seventeenth centuries. *Sanada sandaiki* is an illustrated account of famous warriors of the clan written under the inspiration of Chinese models by Ryusuitei

Takekiyo (1821–1907) and published in Tokyo in 1882 in woodblock edition. A copy is in the holdings of the Waseda University Library. The original illustrated text is available at www.wul.waseda.ac.jp. The dates, well after Sengai's death, suggest that the account here is referring to an earlier version of the work or has perhaps mistaken its title. *The Six Secrets and Three Essentials* (Ch. *Liu tao san lue*; J. *Rikutō sanryaku*) is an early Chinese military work, probably dating to the Sui dynasty (581–618). See Chengfeng Sima *Zhongguo ren de mou lue* (Guangzhou: Guangdeng lu yu chu ben sho, 1991).

43 The implication may be that Sōhei, being a canny and successful businessman, hired people to trade yams to Sengai in exchange for the master's brushwork, thereby augmenting his own collection.

44 Literally, eighty-eighth year (*kome no toshi*). In East Asia, one is considered a year old at birth.

45 In the late Tokugawa period, Fukui, like other domains, found its financial position precarious, and a series of new policies were attempted from the Tenpō era (1830–1843) by Confucian-inspired reformers, many of originally humble commercial backgrounds. Hisa no Geki (1703–1790) was a chief retainer of the ruling Kuroda clan who instituted reforms during the early years of Tenpō. Shirōzu Yōtei (n.d.) was appointed by the Kuroda daimyo Nagahiro on his succession in 1834. Originally a provincial eye doctor, he was chosen for his keen understanding of the Osaka markets. Among the reforms introduced from the mid to late Tokugawa period was the use of paper money. David Douglas Brown, "From Tempo to Meiji: Fukuoka Han in Late Tokugawa Japan" (PhD diss., University of Hawaii at Manoa, 1981), 97–99. Brown's dissertation presents a detailed discussion of the Fukuoka reforms.

46 *Batamochi*, literally, "peony rice cake." A rice-cake dumpling coated with bean jam, its name is said to derive from its resemblance to a peony blossom. It is prepared by boiling together glutinous and nonglutinous rice that, while hot, is shaped into balls and covered in red-bean jam or soybean flour.

47 Waka, literally "Japanese poem," is the traditional Japanese thirty-one-syllable verse form, generally consisting of units of five, seven, five, seven, and seven syllables.

48 That is, to calm his nerves. Much like the major league sports figures and prizefighters of our own time, sumo wrestlers were the pampered celebrities of their day in Japan, especially in the large commercial cities of Osaka and Edo. As Kikushō did with Tobi-ume, it was and remains common for sumo wrestlers to assume separate professional names.

49 A pun on the saloon keeper's name. *Hei*, though literally the Chinese character for "peace," was a common component of male names in premodern Japan, with no particular significance. *Ko*, here, is the Japanese reading of the character for "small," while *Ō* is the reading for the character "big." The Japanese word *ōhei*, though written with different characters, means "arrogant," "pushy," and so forth. The translation is somewhat free to convey the humor of the pun.

50 *Hisago*. Generic term for any kind of dried gourd. Such gourds, emptied of their pulp and dried, were sometimes equipped with a plug and used as a flask for sake, constituting an apt metaphor for the wine-loving Sokyū.

51 Ichikawa Danjirō is the professional name borne by a celebrated line of Kabuki actors famed for its portrayal of ruffian (*aragoto*) and heroic characters (*tachiyaku*). Such roles call for a special attention to the movement and expression of the actor's eyes. Faubian Bowers, for example, describes the *mie*, a pose in which the villain and hero confront each other, the latter opening his eyes wide and crossing one eye while the other eye glares dramatically straight ahead—the crossed eye determined according to whether the villain is positioned to the hero's right or left (if to the left, the right eye is crossed, and vice versa). See Faubian Bowers, *Japanese Theater* (New York: Hermitage House, 1952), 138, 191–92. The seventh Ichikawa's dates are 1791–1859.

52 *Kawara kojiki*. As in early modern Western Europe, actors in Edo-period Japan, albeit famed Kabuki performers, were simultaneously celebrated as stars and scorned as members of a kind of immoral demimonde. They were often called *kawaramono*, literally "riverbed beggars," after the homeless beggars who traditionally congregated in dry riverbeds under urban bridges—said to be the original locales of Kabuki performances. The term is now synonymous with stage actors, and it is invoked here by Sengai, who apparently concurred in this prejudice against theater folk.

53 Matcha. Powdered green tea, often used in premodern Japan for formal occasions, to conduct the tea ceremony, and to serve distinguished guests.

54 Literally, "Jade Orchid."

55 Reference is to the teaching of the late Edo period Confucian scholar Kamei Shōyō (1773–1836).

56 A traditional school of landscape painting said to have been established in Kyoto in the fifteenth century and continuing through the Edo period. Tosa school artists were often the official painters of the imperial court, and their

paintings frequently illustrated classical Japanese literary works, such as the eleventh-century *Tale of Genji*. The Tosa style was characterized by extensive use of gold and bright colors and, in the Edo period, came to include subjects based on Chinese models, such as bird and flower paintings.

57 Although only nine are listed, reference is to the ten types of beings, or ten realms (*jikkai*), a common feature of Buddhist teachings: hell dwellers (*jigoku*), hungry ghosts (*gaki*), beasts (*chikushō*), fighting demons (*shuras*), men (*ningen*) and devas (heavenly beings), sravaka (*shōmon*) and pratyeka (*engaku*) buddhas, bodhisattvas (*bosatsu*), and buddhas (*butsu*). These are viewed literally as realms of rebirth or metaphorically as constituents of being that may be elicited according to the workings of inner and outer circumstances.

58 That is, the popular Japanese school of Pure Land Buddhism founded by Shinran (1173–1262). It is particularly identified with worship of the Buddha Amitabha, one of the "eternal buddhas," and Amitabha's vow that all who call his name will be reborn in the Pure Land, a kind of Buddhist paradise in the western heavens. Associated with Pure Land belief is the *nenbutsu*, the incantation "*Namu Amida Butsu!*" (Praise to the Buddha Amitabha!). Nenbutsu recitation was practiced widely in both China and Japan, as forms of prayer and meditation. "*Naman, Naman, Naman*" is apparently a somewhat crude and abbreviated form of the nenbutsu, contracted to enable constant repetition.

59 It would have been customary in premodern Japan to kneel when addressing an important person, such as a daimyo or Zen master.

60 *Mugimeshi*, or *bakuhan*. Originally a humble rural staple now widely popular in Japan, the barley (*mugi*) is often presteamed or presoaked so that it can be cooked together with the rice. As Japanese peasants in Sengai's day paid taxes in rice, the rice for their own consumption often had to be supplemented with barley, making the concoction slightly chewy. Today, *oshi mugi* (pressed barely) is commonly used, and despite its humble origins, mugimeshi is sometimes touted as something of a health food and offered at upscale restaurants. In keeping with the formal tone of his message, Ōta uses the word *sai* (or *toki*), referring to a vegetarian meal for Buddhist priests, often offered by lay donors as an act of merit.

61 *Inokake*. Probably referring here to a dish made with peeled and grated Japanese yam (*imo*). On grating, the yam becomes a thick, white mucous-like substance that is then poured over cooked rice and mixed in with chopsticks before consuming. Yams, it will be recalled, were a favorite of Sengai's.

62 *Takuan.* Various kinds of pickled radish (daikon) are a common accompaniment to Japanese rice. The dish is sometimes said to have been invented by the eponymous Zen master Takuan Sōhō (1573–1645), and it is a fixture of Japanese Zen temple cuisine.

63 The umbrella (*kasa*) here would be a traditional parasol of oiled paper stretched over split bamboo ribs.

64 As mentioned earlier, Sengai, because of his small size, was often mistaken for a novice.

65 *Intoku.* Literally, "hidden or private virtue." The expression is used in both ordinary Japanese and in Buddhism, particularly Zen, where anonymous acts of kindness (*injigyō*) are considered part of the training of the Zen monk. Nishimura Eishin and Satō Giei, *Unsui* (Honolulu: University of Hawaii Press, 1973), 67.

66 Firearms, including mortars and matchlocks, were introduced to Japan from Europe in the mid-sixteenth century and quickly came to play an important role in warfare, replacing arrows as the leading cause of battlefield casualties until the unification of Japan under Tokugawa rule. By Sengai's day, however, after some two centuries of peace and isolation, firearms had become far less common, with handguns used more for sport than defense. For the early history of firearms in Japanese warfare, see Karl F. Friday, "Off the Warpath: Military Science and Budō in the Evolution of Ryūha Bugei," in *Budō Perspectives*, ed. Alexander Bennet (Auckland: Kendo World Publications, 2005), 253–54; and Suzuki Masaya, *Katana to kubitori: Sengoku kassen issetsu* (Tokyo: Heibonsha, 2000), 151.

67 Tea gatherings in premodern Japan were rather formal occasions, with the guests admiring the tea ware and appreciatively sipping the powdered green tea whisked to a froth by the host in his tearoom or tea hut. Needless to say, gunshots would not normally be in keeping with the overall refinement of such an occasion, nor a Zen master breaking wind.

68 *Jūyū fujin.* Reference is to case 3 of *Gateless Gate*, "Juzhi's Finger." Juzhi (n.d.) is said to have raised one finger in response to any question about Zen. Before dying, he reputedly told his followers, "All my life I used this one-finger Zen, but I never could use it up (*jūyū fujin*)." T 48:193b. The implication here is that Sengai's all-purpose mixing bowl is the culinary equivalent of Juzhi's finger.

69 *Tenjō tenge yuiga dokuson.* Referring to what were reputedly the Buddha's

words at birth. The newborn Buddha is said to have taken seven steps, looked in the four directions, pointed with one hand to heaven and the other to earth, and declared, "In all the world, I alone am to be revered!" See, for example, *Sarvastivada Vinaya*, T 24:298a. The phrase also appears frequently in Chinese Chan texts, including the *Blue Cliff Record*, case 6, "Yunmen's 'Every Day Is a Good Day,'" T 48:193b.

70 *Donburibachi*. A deep, thick ceramic bowl, often used to serve rice topped with special items such as grilled eel (*unagi donburi*). In Japanese restaurants, the term *donburi* still lends such dishes, and the use of this sort of bowl, a "homestyle" resonance.

71 *Hiyashiru* (reading uncertain). A local specialty in which cold broth was added to the boiled barley and rice.

72 [*Marui*] *tamago mo kiriyō de shikaku*. A Japanese proverb implying that the result of any situation depends on the way you approach it.

73 A similar story involving the Zen master Takuan Sōhō appears in *Manshōsoroku*, TOZ 6:192. It is translated in Peter Haskel, *Sword of Zen* (Honolulu: University of Hawaii Press, 2013), 119.

74 *Hitorizumo*. Literally, "by oneself sumo." Like Western shadowboxing, but here referring to sumo, the popular Japanese wrestling form has its roots in Shinto practice. Essentially, the wrestler summons all his strength, physical and spiritual, to display his skill without a visible opponent present. Hitorizumo is still practiced at certain Shinto shrines, such as the Oyamazumi *jinja* (shrine) in Imabari, Ehime Prefecture, where the solitary wrestler's invisible opponent is the rice deity. An official, dressed in sumptuous shrine priest regalia, referees, with the winner declared in the best of three successive bouts. Generally, in such entertainments, the deity is allowed to win two out of the three bouts in order to gain his or her cooperation in ensuring sufficient rainfall and an abundant rice harvest.

75 Typically a Zen temple garden would be placed below a wooden veranda on which monks would circulate and at times meditate by night.

76 The smallest of Japan's Zen sects, the Ōbaku school was founded in the seventeenth century by immigrant Ming Linji (Rinzai) monks from mainland China.

77 That is, Manpukuji, headquarters temple of the Ōbaku sect, founded by the Ming Zen master Ingen Ryūki (Yinyuan Longqi, 1592–1673). The temple is located at Uji, in Kyoto. Chinese abbots remained the rule at Manpukuji

till the mid-eighteenth century. After 1740, Japanese Ōbaku priests were permitted to serve as abbots, and since 1786 the temple's abbots have all been Japanese. Hakugan's dates are 1767–1836. He became Manpukuji abbot in 1831.

78 *Shiko o fumu.* Before a sumo match, each wrestler squats with legs apart and places his hands on his knees. He then raises each leg in turn, keeping it as straight as possible, and forcefully stomps on the ground. Originally, when the matches were performed as offerings to the gods, this was said to have been a means to dispel malevolent forces.

79 My emendation here is suggested by the nine ellipses in the text, where the child's answer should be (167, line 3).

80 I have been unable to locate this question by Hakuin or the source of the phrase upon which it is based.

81 Apparently a descendant of the Kuroda daimyo family of the Fukushima domain, referred to earlier. His dates, like those of Hakuhō-in, are apparently unknown. The *in* (literally, "temple" or "retreat") portion of the name could indicate that the individual is living in retirement or serving as priest or abbot of a temple, or it could be a posthumous religious name.

82 Toasted rice cakes (mochi) remain a traditional treat on New Year's Day in Japan. Premodern Japan followed a lunar calendar, and New Year's Day was equivalent to approximately February 4 or 5 in the modern Western calendar. It was a day on which, among other things, outstanding debts were paid, old grudges forgiven, and disputes resolved.

83 *Ichimai azukari shōmon.* A written receipt, an agreement in writing. A similar Japanese poem, titled "Receipt Proof of [Resolution] to a Husband and Wife Quarrel" (*Fufu kenka no azukari shōmon*) is included in Miyake, *Sengai goroku*, 314.

84 This samurai official (*machibugyō*) was a kind of combination mayor, chief constable, and magistrate, appointed in all likelihood by the daimyo of the province from among his samurai retainers. It was traditional for Japanese to visit the graves (*hakamairi*, literally, "grave visit") of relatives or deceased superiors such as clan leaders or daimyo on regular occasions. Invariably such graves were located in Buddhist temples with close and important ties to the samurai families interred there, ties both political and economic. *Kaizandō*—a hall dedicated to the temple's founders. Shōfukuji's founder, Eisai, as noted previously, was particularly celebrated, having been the progenitor of what is now the Rinzai sect of Japanese Zen.

85 Roof tiles on Japanese temple buildings—heavy and elaborate ceramic tubes sometimes bearing the crest (*mon*) of the donor at both ends—may be costly items.

86 Nomura Hayato (n.d.) was a cause of difficulties for both Sengai and his heir Tangen (d. 1855), who succeeded Sengai as abbot of Shōfukuji on Sengai's retirement in 1811. Tangen tended to be of a principled, uncompromising, and outspoken nature, and an 1837 dispute with Hayato over what he viewed as the latter's meager donations for temple repairs led Hayato to order all the Nomura family gravestones removed from the temple. The end result was Tangen's forfeiture of his abbacy, house arrest, and exile to the island of Ōshima for violating his arrest in order to travel on pilgrimage. Tangen was not pardoned till 1852, when he withdrew into retirement. Sengai, meanwhile, had to resume abbacy of Shōfukuji at age eighty-seven. Ōshima is a small island in what is now Fukuoka Prefecture. SOI, 12–13.

87 The character read *butsu* or *hotoke* in Japanese can be understood as Buddha or buddhas or, more broadly, the deceased—here, the clan or family members buried in the temple graveyard.

88 Shinran Shōnin's True Pure Land school, referred to earlier, a prominent feature of which was devout repetition of the nenbutsu, the invocation "Hail to the Buddha Amitabha!"

89 Apparently yet another contraction of the nenbutsu, to allow for faster repetition.

90 *Sanzen*, literally, "studying Zen." In the Rinzai school today, the term refers specifically to the regular private interviews in which Zen students study koan under a Zen master.

91 *Hanko*. Traditionally, calligraphers, painters, and collectors in East Asia authenticate works by placing on them their unique personal carved hand seal. The seal often bears an abstract arrangement of the creator's or owner's name within a cartouche, which is sometimes stamped in red ink on a carefully chosen spot on the work. Sengai's seal, as seen on his many surviving paintings, bears the Master's name in blockish "seal characters," often just beneath his brushed abstract signature, consisting of the second character of his Buddhist name, [Sen]Gai. Often referred to in the West by the Hindi-derived term *chop*, such seals were also employed by individuals for use in contracts and other such transactions. Possession of a parent's or employer's seal could be equivalent to granting a person power of attorney.

92 Miyamoto Tōsai (d. 1874) was a Hakata doctor, follower, friend, and go partner of Sengai's, living not far from Kyohaku-in.

93 *Sumi*, the black "india ink" made from charcoal that is used for calligraphy and painting in East Asia. It is traditionally prepared by rubbing down an ink stick on an ink stone containing water—an arduous task if, as here, a vast amount of ink is required.

TALES OF HAKUIN AND HIS FOLLOWERS

1 Besides his key role in formulating Japanese Rinzai Zen as we know it today, Hakuin (1686–1769) stands out among premodern Zen masters not only for the sheer volume of his writings—over three dozen published works—but also for the large amounts of autobiographical material he provides. The master's two key autobiographical works deal with the first part of his long life, including his quest for enlightenment before establishing himself as a teacher. Both works are in Japanese: *Wild Ivy* (*Itsumadegusa*, 1766), an extended, colorful account that freely alternates between preaching, sarcasm, and humor; and the similar *Tales of My Childhood to Spur on Students* (*Sakushin osana monogatari*, 1762). The other key contemporary source for Hakuin's life, *Chronology of the Zen Master Jinki Dokumyō* [i.e., Hakuin] (*Jinki Dokumyō zenji nenpu*, 1820), was composed in Sino-Japanese (*kanbun*) by Hakuin's heir Tōrei Enji (1721–1792) during Hakuin's lifetime, probably carried out under the master's supervision as a kind of collaborative effort. (See Katō Shōsun's comments in his introduction to HON, "Hakuin to sono shōgai: Hito to shisō," 3–36.) All three have been translated by Norman Waddell, the latter two in Waddell's collection *Hakuin's Precious Mirror Cave* and the first as a single volume, *Wild Ivy*. The original texts are to be found, respectively, in volumes 3 and 7 of *Hakuin zenji hōgo zenshū* (Kyoto: Zen Bunka Kenkyūjo, 1999–2003), Yoshizawa Katsuhiro's multivolume annotated edition covering most of Hakuin's Japanese works; and in *Hakuin oshō nenpu* (Kyoto: Shibunkaku Shuppan, 1985, edited by Katō Shōshun).

While consulting the original texts as needed for this brief biography, I have benefited greatly from Waddell's many Hakuin translations and their supporting materials, together with Philip B. Yampolsky's pioneering *The Zen Master Hakuin*; Seo and Addiss's *The Sound of One Hand*; and Yoshizawa Katsuhiro's *The Religious Art of the Zen Master Hakuin* (Berkeley: Counterpoint, 2009), a compilation of material from Yoshizawa's articles focusing on Hakuin's art and Edo folk culture, selected, translated, and edited by Norman Waddell. (The articles appeared originally in the periodical *Zen bunka*, a publication of Hanazono University's Zen bunka kenkyūjo, where Yoshizawa serves as director of the Hakuin Studies Center.)

Hakuin, as noted in the introduction, regarded all his written works as primarily a means of spreading his Zen teaching and in many instances did not hesitate to embroider, exaggerate, or even invent the facts of his early life to provide his readers a livelier and more dramatic account. This would not have seemed at all suspect in Hakuin's day, and a certain amount of such literary license was probably assumed by Hakuin's audience. Tōrei, in turn, relied exclusively on Hakuin's own versions of the master's early life. The story of Hakuin's training and enlightenment experiences till about age forty-one, which make up the first part of Tōrei's biography, are designated "formative experiences" (ingyō kaku); while the second half of Hakuin's career, from about age forty-three till the master's death—a portion of the master's life to which Tōrei was himself witness—was largely composed under Hakuin's oversight.

Because Hakuin was born on December 25 of the old, or lunar, calendar, employed in premodern Japan, some confusion has attended his dates, which are occasionally given as 1686–1769. See Heinrich Dumoulin, *Zen Buddhism: A History* (New York: World Wisdom, 1990), 2:394n1.

2 Interestingly, Hakuin's "grandfather" in Zen, Shidō Mu'nan, the celebrated teacher of Shōju Rojin and an important earlier popularizer of Zen, was also born into a family that managed a post station (*juku*, or *shuku*) on the Tōkaidō. See Pedersen, "Jishōki," 96.

3 *Hokkeshū.* A sect of Japanese Buddhism basing itself on the *Lotus Sutra* and founded by the priest Nichiren (1222–1282). Known for its militancy and its intolerance of other Buddhist teachings, the school stresses the unique efficacy of the recitation of the title (*daimoku*) of the *Lotus Sutra* and forbids its adherents to recite any other sutra. In the Tokugawa period, all families were required to maintain connections with a parish temple as proof that they were not secret Christians. Although generally families had to affiliate with the father's sect of Buddhism, objections were voiced by Confucians and others that this gave inordinate power to the Buddhist sects, and cases of families, such as Hakuin's, including different sect affiliations were not unknown. See Nakamura Hajime et al., *Ajia bukkyōshi: Nihon ben* (Tokyo: Tōkyō Shoseki, 1972), 7:37, 47.

4 T 48:1098a–1109c.

5 *Itsumadegusa*, HZHZ 3:162. In addition to his enthusiasm for Dahui-style koan study, Zhuhong was also an advocate of the Zen–Pure Land syncretism

that came to dominate Ming Zen, a tendency for which Hakuin excoriated Zhuhong and his ilk in several vicious and long-winded diatribes. See, for example, *Orategama zokushū*, HOZ 1:5 (translated in Yampolsky, *Zen Master Hakuin*, 147–49).

6 An early use of the term *kenshō* (Ch. *jianxing*), for example, appears in the Tang priest Zongmi's (780–841) *Prolegomenon*, in the context of a description of the existing schools of Zen. T 48:402b.

7 *Itsumadegusa*, HZHZ 3:172.

8 *Itsumadegusa*, HZHZ 3:233–34. Elsewhere, Hakuin speaks of experiencing eighteen great and countless small satori, a statement sometimes attributed to Dahui. See, for example, *Yukichi monogatari*, HZHZ 7:222.

9 In *Oradegama*, for example, Hakuin paraphrases Dahui on the signal importance of practice in the midst of daily activity: "Practice in the midst of activity is worth ten thousand million times more than practice in quiet." HZHZ 9:198. The statement also appears in Hakuin's calligraphy (Hanazono Daigaku, *Hakuin*, no. 51, pp. 38 and 159). In *Oradegama*, Hakuin also notes that continual, uninterrupted practice was a feature of Shōju's instruction. HZHZ 9:243–44.

10 Combining with Hakuin's ordination name Ekaku, "Wisdom Crane," the two names together are possibly an allusion to a verse in *Zenrin kushū*: "When a heron stands in the snow, it's colors are not the same" (*Roji yuki ni tatsu dōshoku ni arazu*). Translation by Victor Hori in ZS, 311:7, 495. At Myōshinji and other Edo-period Zen temples, priests generally received second names when they became Zen masters. As a rule, such a second name would precede the ordination name.

11 Ungo Kiyō and Isshi Bunshu (1607–1645) are additional examples. Kimura Seiyū, "Tokugawa shoki ni okeru Rinzai zen no teimei to sono dakai," in *Zengaku ronkō*, Yanagida Seizan ed., (Kyoto: Shibunkaku Shuppan, 1977), 437–47. Kimura suggests that belief in the need for self-reliance in the quest for enlightenment in the absence of enlightened teachers may be one reason for the emergence of so many individual teaching styles in the early Tokugawa period. For an overview of the mushi dokugo and jigo jishō phenomena in early Tokugawa Zen, see LG 19–21, 131–32nn67–70.

12 *Shi guzeigan* (also read *seigan*); in the Sōtō school read *shi kuseigan*. The four vows are recited in all the principal East Asian Mahayana schools, some of which have their own formulations. The vows' earliest appearance in a Zen text is in the Dunhuang text of the *Platform Sutra* (T 48:338b), a version of

the vows that itself may derive from earlier Chinese sources and is closest to that recited in Japanese Zen temples. ZD 227–28.

13 *Kaien fusetsu*, HOZ 2:74.

14 Waddell, *Zen Master Hakuin*, 30; *Kaien fusetsu*, HOZ 2:389. For more on the nantō koan, see also ZS, 22–24.

15 Although he appears prominently in most Rinzai lineage charts as among Hakuin's foremost Dharma heirs, Suiō—to whom, Tōrei tells us, Hakuin entrusted his affairs at death (*Nenpu*, HOZ 122)—is unaccountably dropped from the lineage chart in the original edition of ZD (508–9). Whether this is due to embarrassment at Suiō's reportedly unconstrained behavior, some revisionary reading of Hakuin's life, or merely an error of omission seems unclear.

16 At times, Hakuin also refers to the koan as *katate no koe*. See, for example, *Obaba dono kohiki no uta*, HZHZ 13:22, 34. Hakuin's koan may allude to Xuedou's comment on case 18 of the *Blue Cliff Record*, "The National Teacher's Monument": "A single hand by itself produces no sound" (*Du zhang bu lang ming*). T 48:157c. Xuedou Chongxian's dates are 980–1052.

17 "Ball of doubt," *gidan* (Ch. *yituan*). Sometimes given as "great ball of doubt" (*daigidan*; Ch. *dayituan*), it has also been translated "great doubt block" in Jeff Shore's unpublished 2010 article "Great Doubt." Shore's article offers an overview of the term in Chinese and Japanese Zen, and a translation of and comments on the Ming Zen master Bohan's (1575–1630) *Exhortations for Those Unable to Arouse the Doubt* (*Shiyiqingfapuqi jing lu*). "The one-hand koan . . . is none other than the true Dharma, which has been dead in Japan for five hundred years." *Osana monogatari*, HZHZ 7:218.

18 HZHZ 2:45–46. *Sekishū no onjō*, composed in 1753, is also known under the title *Yabukōji*.

19 "*Sekishū no koe o kiki, onjō o todomaru*." *Yukichi monogatari*, HZHZ 7:216.

20 *Sekishū onjō ryōjū tōkan*. *Osana monogatari*, HZHZ 7:96–97. For a more detailed discussion of Hakuin's dual "Sound of One Hand" koan, see Yoshizawa's remarks in *Osana monogatari*, HZHZ 7:13, and 34 n 5.

21 T 48:192b–193a. The koan, case 60 of the collection, is read in Japanese *Unmon shujō*. The Zen master Yunmen Wenyan died in 949.

22 See those cards illustrated in Hanazono Daigaku, *Hakuin*, 30 (no. 30), 34 (no. 45), and 72 (no. 135).

23 See, for example, the undated card given to Hakuin's Dharma heir Daijū Zen'nyo (1720–1778), certifying that Zen'nyo has passed (*shōko*) Linji's Three Mysteries together with the "secret Sōtō school transmission (*hiketsu*) of the Five Ranks"—Hakuin having received the last from his own teacher, Shōju. Hakuin's painting on the card depicts Linji giving a shout (*Ho!*; J. *Katsu!*) with a dragon staff rising behind him. Hanazono Daigaku, *Hakuin*, 91 (no. 144), 156. Michel Mohr suggests that the inka cards were distributed by Hakuin to lay disciples in recognition of their initial breakthrough, or kenshō, but given to monks only after completion of koan training. Mohr, "Hakuin," 321.

24 The term *gogo*, as such, appears only in Hakuin's writings after 1757—that is, roughly during the last decade of the master's life.

25 Yoshizawa, *Religious Art*, 63–76.

26 HZHZ 13:17–41. The pairing of a wrinkled crone and a younger woman who embodies good fortune, at least in its broad outline, is reminiscent of a parable in the *Mahaparinirvana Sutra*. In the parable, two women present themselves at the door of a householder, the first woman lovely and bestowing fortune, the other ugly and grotesque and bringing poverty and disaster. The two, however, are sisters and declare themselves to be inseparable, so that much to the householder's dismay, he is forced to dismiss them both. T 12:677a–b. My thanks to Ian Chandler for calling this to my attention.

27 Bankei composed a work song in a similar format, presenting his views on Zen and Buddhism. Reportedly intended for local villagers, the extended poem, dated approximately 1663, is generally known as *Song of Original Mind* (*Honshin no uta*), as well as *Milling Song* (*Usuhiki uta*), a type of song chanted while grinding flour. BZZ, 519–11. Translated in BZ, 125–32.

28 Yoshizawa, *Religious Art*, 77; Yampolsky, *Zen Master Hakuin*, 231.

29 *Nenpu*. Translated in Waddell, *Hakuin's Precious Mirror Cave*, 232; HON, 122. By modern Western reckoning, of course, Hakuin's age would have been eighty-three.

30 *Osana monogatari*, HZHZ 7:113.

31 Bankei dismissed such fixtures of Song Zen as the koan and the great doubt as nothing more than misleading and artficial devices. See *Seppō* (*zenpen*), BZZ, 135. Takuan, too, argued that enlightenment was in no way dependent on koan. "The Zen school has its own special transmission," he wrote in his 1628 letter of protest to the Tokugawa bakufu, or military government. "It doesn't necessarily depend on koan. Precisely because of this, there have

been many in the past who, even after mastering koan, failed to obtain inka."
Kōbensho [Refutation], TOZ 6:70.

32 *Jishō hon'nu* (also read *hon'u*). *Sekishū onjō*, HZHZ 12:39.

33 A still picturesque waterfall, now located in Shimizu City, Shizuoka Prefecture.

34 A biwa is a traditional, generally four-stringed lute-like instrument. It is pear-shaped and curves back at the neck.

35 From the *Takusui kana hōgo*, by the celebrated Rinzai Zen master Takusui Chōmo (d. 1740). Nōnin Kōdō points out that this particular passage does not appear in the *Takusui kana hōgo* as it survives today. Nevertheless, Takusui's popular teachings in the *kana hōgo* lay great stress on the original, intrinsic nature of enlightenment. A woodblock edition appeared in Edo in 1740 and is in the collection of the Waseda University library (01-01586). (The text is available at www.wul.waseda/ac.jp/kotenseki/html/.../index. html.)

36 A mountain near the town of Okitsu (modern Shizuoka Prefecture). It was said to be one of the more hazardous spots along the Tōkaidō.

37 The Chan master Shigong Huizang (n.d.), an heir of the celebrated Mazu. Originally a hunter, Shigong is said to have continued to use his bow and arrow to test students, confronting them with a drawn bow and an arrow aimed at their hearts.

38 Rohatsu is the intensive period of practice traditionally observed at Zen temples from December 1 to dawn of December 8, in commemoration of the Buddha's enlightenment. It is some seventy-five miles from Zuiōji to Hakuin's temple, Shōinji.

39 Referring to a Zen phrase appearing in *Zenrinkushū*: "When chickens are cold they go up into trees / When ducks are cold, they go down to water." See ZS, 351.

40 In premodern Japan, a town south of Kyoto, now part of the city of Kyoto.

41 *Segaki*. The ceremony is a standard part of the liturgy in Japanese Zen temples.

42 Approximately seventy-three miles.

43 A "new" Buddhist name was assigned when one formally became a Myōshinji-line Zen master, and this new name was then placed before one's earlier Buddhist name.

44 July 1764 by Western reckoning.

45 Misshō-an, the pagoda of Myōshinji's founder, Kanzan. Genrō is alluding here to the ceremony in which he received the advanced rank of *dai ichizo* (also read *dai ichiza*) at Myōshinji and paid his respects at Kanzan's pagoda.

46 Gasan Jitō (1727–1797), another of Hakuin's important Dharma heirs.

47 It is unclear what sixteen years refers to here. Suiō formally became a Zen master in 1764, and at Hakuin's death in 1768, he assumed abbacy of Shōinji, reluctantly delivering a sermon at Hakuin's seven-year memorial service in 1778, but none of these dates seem to make sense of the "sixteen years" figure.

48 Ch. *Ho!* The shout frequently employed by Zen masters and associated with Rinzai Zen's Chinese founder, Linji Yixuan.

49 Case 3 of the *Blue Cliff Record,* "*Master Ma Is Unwell*":
"Master Ma was unwell. The temple's treasurer asked, 'Your Reverence, how are you feeling lately?'
"The master replied, 'Sun-faced buddha, moon-faced buddha.'" T48:142c.
Ma is the Tang dynasty master Mazu.

50 Shibata (n.d.) was a well-known children's doctor of the eighteenth century, the author of several early works on pediatrics.

51 A keisaku is the "warning stick" used by the head monk to correct students in the Zen meditation hall.

52 *Ichizuhi no zen.* Referring to a phrase from case 98 of the *Blue Cliff Record,* mocking the false attainment of students. "What a joke! Intellectually, they've mastered a whole bellyful of Zen, but they can't actually *use* it!" T 48:222a.

53 Ryōsai (1706–1786) was born into an Owari samurai household. He entered the temple at age nine and in 1729 went to study with Hakuin and experienced a spiritual breakthrough. Also that year he went to study under the Myōshinji-line master Kogetsu Zenzai, another renowned Zen teacher of the period. One evening during a talk delivered by Kogetsu, in which the master took up the third verse of the Ten Ox-Herding Pictures, "Seeing the Ox," Ryōsai is said to have suddenly experienced enlightenment. (The sequence of Ryōsai's studies given in the text seems to reverse the sequence.)

54 A bodhisattva symbolizing intuitive wisdom, Manjusri, depicted riding a lion and carrying a sword, is often the central image of Japanese Zen meditation halls.

55 Referring to case 40 of the *Blue Cliff Record*, a dialogue between the Zen master Nanquan Puyuan (784–835) and his Dharma heir the government minister Lu Xuan (764–834). Lu remarked, "Dharma Master Chao said, 'Heaven, earth, and I are of the same root; the ten thousand things and I are one substance.' How wonderful!" Nanquan called Lu's attention to a flower in the garden and said, "Men of today see that flower as if in a dream." T 48:178a. Chao is the celebrated early Chinese Buddhist scholar and philosopher Sengzhao (384–414).

56 The Rinzai master Unzan Sotai (1685–1747), a close colleague of Hakuin's.

57 *Zengosaidan.* An expression common in Zen texts, often used as a metaphor for enlightenment. The past and future being mere mental constructs, cutting off both leaves only the present moment. See BGD 2:844b; BJ, 639a.

58 *Shō'netsu jigoku.* Literally, the "hell of scorching heat," one of the eight great Buddhist hells. It is reserved for, among others, those who have indulged in drunkenness, lecherousness, slander, lying, and killing.

59 Case 140 of the medieval Japanese koan collection *Kattōshū.* The somewhat lengthy case is translated in Thomas Y. Kirchner, *Entangling Vines: Zen Koans of the Shūmon Kattōshū* (Kyoto: Tenryu-Ji Institute for Philosophy and Religion, 2004), 69–70. Shushan Guangren (837–909) was an heir of the famous Zen master Dongshan Liangjie (807–869).

60 Case 11 of the *Blue Cliff Record.* Zen Master Huangbo Xiyun (d. 850?) addressed the assembly, saying, "All of you are nothing but drinkers of wine dregs. If you go on wandering on pilgrimage like this, when will today ever come! What's more, did you know that in all the great land of China there are no Zen teachers?" A monk stepped forward and said, "Then what about those all over who are guiding students and directing assemblies of monks?" Huangbo replied, "I didn't say there was no Zen; only that there were no teachers." T 48:151b.

61 Kami are the native Japanese gods, frequently associated with particular geographic areas or features such as rocks, waterfalls, and so forth.

62 Included among the basic Confucian classics, the *Yi jing*, a work of ancient but uncertain origin, has been an important source for Chinese theories of cosmology and prognostication.

63 A volume of Hakuin's works, published in 1758. It is included in vol. 5 of HOZ. (Translation of the title follows Yampolsky, *Zen Master Hakuin*, 227.)

64 Now Ōita Prefecture on Japan's southern island of Kyushu.

65 A shorthand reference to "Doushuai's 'Three Barriers,'" described above.

66 "I" here is presumably Myōki Seiteki, compiler of *Keikyokusōdan.*

67 *Nehandōri no zen.* The Nehandō (literally, "nirvana hall") was the monastery infirmary as well as a kind of hospice for monks in declining health who, faced with the imminence of death, would presumably be driven even more urgently to resolve the question of "birth and death" and realize enlightenment.

68 *Shittsū.* A common metaphor in Zen for ignorance and delusion.

69 The *Hakuin nenpu* gives the date of the poem as Hōei 4 (1707), when Hakuin was twenty-two. In HON, the poem's third line is slightly different: "If Zen mind is like this . . ." HON, 85–86.

70 As noted previously, throughout the Tokugawa period there was antipathy toward Buddhism on the part of many Confucians, who viewed the Buddhist teaching, and Zen in particular, as amoral and worse. The behavior of Zeigan's son toward Suiō seems to reflect this sort of attitude.

71 Grandma Satsu, or Osatsu, as she was commonly known, was a member of Hakuin's father's family, the Nagazawa, daughter of the village head, Yūsai (d. 1750). She married a certain Watabe Ken'eimon (n.d.) and was widowed in her midforties, thereafter devoting herself to Buddhist practice. She is buried at Hakuin's temple Shōinji and is discussed in an article on Hakuin's female followers by Machida Zuihō, "Hakuin monka jōsei zenja no shōsoku," ZB, no. 103 (January 1982): 78–84. A humorous hand-carved portrait sculpture of Osatsu by Hakuin is preserved at Shōinji (photo in Machida, "Hakuin monka jōsei zenga," ZB 103:82).

72 Akeno is in Numazu City (modern Shizuoka Prefecture). Miraculous powers were associated with the shrine in Hakuin's period. The *Tennō Kannon Sutra* is a short scripture extolling the merits of the bodhisattva Kannon. Its formal name is *Kōō Kannon kyō.* T 85:1425b–1426a.

73 The Nagazawa were members of the Lotus sect, which pays special reverence to the *Lotus Sutra,* hence, perhaps, the father's severe alarm at his daughter's sacrilegious behavior. See Dumoulin, *Zen Buddhism,* 2:368.

74 Waka is a traditional thirty-one-syllable Japanese poem.

75 Harajuku is present-day Numazu City, Shizuoka Prefecture. Hara has been referred to earlier as Hakuin's birthplace. *Juku* is a suffix meaning "post station."

76 It is unclear from what source Hakuin appears to be quoting here, although all the expressions he invokes—one's own body is Amida, and so forth—are standard elements of the Zen–Pure Land syncretism widespread in Japanese popular belief and Japanese Zen of the early Tokugawa period. The same syncretism characterized Chan in the Ming and Qing dynasties and remains influential in overseas Chinese Buddhism even today. Elsewhere, by contrast, Hakuin is critical of such Pure Land–Zen teaching. While he thought it unsuitable for Zen monks, it is possible he accepted such practices and beliefs for laypersons. For Hakuin's critical views of Pure Land–Zen syncretism, see Yampolsky, *Zen Master Hakuin*, 25–26, and passages from Hakuin's *Orategama*, translated in Yampolsky, 136–37. For a more benign attitude to such practices, employing expressions similar to those in the present sermon by Hakuin, see the passage in the master's *Yabukōji*, translated in Yampolsky, 161.

RYŌKAN TALES

1 Perhaps the best single source of primary materials for Ryōkan is Tōgō Toyoharu's two-volume *Ryōkan zenshū* (Tokyo: Tokyo Sōgensha, 1959; 9th ed. 1989). Tōgō's *zenshū* (henceforth abbreviated RZ) includes not only Ryōkan's Chinese and Japanese poems, his *kanshi* and waka, annotated by Tōgō, but also important biographical and other materials related to Ryōkan, materials composed during his lifetime and in the decades immediately following his death, the most recent from the close of the nineteenth century (see RZ 2:569–600). Among these is the previously mentioned *Curious Accounts of the Zen Master Ryōkan (Ryōkan zenji kiwa)* composed around 1845–1846 by Kera Yoshishige (1810–1859), whose father, Shukumon (1765–1819), was Ryōkan's close friend and headman (*nanushi*) of the village of Makigahana. Yoshishige, who was nine at Ryōkan's death, was one of the local children who played with the master on his begging rounds, and in adulthood he succeeded his father as village headman. He was thus well placed to compile this intimate memoir of Ryōkan, having been closely acquainted with many of the people and places involved. Also helpful are Tōgō's *Shinshū Ryōkan* (Tokyo: Tokyo Sōgen Shinsha, 1970) and *Ryōkan: Uta to shōgai* (Tokyo: Chikumashobō, 1975) by Yoshino Hideo, a leading scholar of Ryōkan's Japanese poems. A survey of key sources for Ryōkan's poems and biography, beginning in his lifetime, can be found in Ryuichi Abe's "Commemorating Ryōkan: The Origin and Growth of Ryōkan Biographies," GF, 76–87. For a detailed bibliography of Japanese secondary sources for Ryōkan, Abe recommends Watanabe Shūei's "Ryōkan kenkyūshi," in *Ryōkan kenkyū ronshū*, Miya Eiji, ed., (Tokyo: Shōzansha, 1985),

31–72. The material for this abbreviated biography is based on a combination of these and other sources.

2 Ryōkan's contemporary the merchant-literatus Suzuki Bokushi (1770–1842) still cites Izumozaki as a prosperous port in *Hokku'etsu seppu*, a popular account of Echigo life at the beginning of the nineteenth century, translated by Jeffrey Hunter et al. as *Snow Country Tales* (New York: Weatherhill, 1986), 160. Most goods in Edo Japan were transported by water, hence the importance of port towns such as Izumozaki and Amaze.

3 Kitagawa Seīichi, *Teihon Ryōkan yugi* (Tokyo: Shirakawa Shoin, 1983), 28.

4 Quoted in the 1818 biography *Ryōkan zenji den* by Ōzeki Bunchū (d. 1834), a local Confucian scholar and doctor. RZ 1:593. For this period, see also Ishida Yoshisada, *Ryōkan: Sono zenbo to genzo* (Tokyo: Hanawa Shobō, 1975), 21–114.

5 There is some difference among scholars, and even among the biographies of Ryōkan's contemporaries, over the exact age at which Ryōkan entered the Buddhist priesthood. Some maintain it was when Ryōkan entered Koshōji at age seventeen; others claim it was at age twenty-one during Kokusen's visit to the temple. Both may in a sense be correct, Ryōkan entering Koshōji as a novice at seventeen and taking the tonsure and Buddhist vows at twenty-one during Kokusen's visit. Yoshino, *Ryōkan*, 4.

6 Miya Fuyuji, ed., *Ryōkan no sekai* (Tokyo: Bunka shobō hakubunsha, 1985), 165–67; Watanabe Shūei, ed., *Ryōkan shugyō to Tamashima* (Niigata: Kōkodō Shoten, 1975), 118, 190.

7 The name Great Fool may have been conferred by Kokusen along with Ryōkan's inka or perhaps simply assumed at some point by Ryōkan. The master always referred to himself as Ryōkan, and the name Taigu (also read Daigu) is first recorded in autumn 1831 on a mortuary inscription for Ryōkan. RZ 1:596. Tanigawa Toshirō, *Ryōkan no shōgai to itsuwa* (Tokyo: Kōbunsha, 1984), 57–60 and Ishida, *Zengo*, 21. The name itself is not unusual in Zen. It is identical with that of Taigu Sōchiku and perhaps most often recognized as the name of the Tang master Dayu (n.d.), who appears in the *Linji lu* as the Zen teacher instrumental in Linji's sudden enlightenment. T 47:504c. Kokusen's poem confirming Ryōkan's inka refers to him as *anju* (master of the hermitage), probably referring to the subtemple (*an*, or *tatchū*) Kakuju-an on the grounds of Entsūji. The dated poem is included at the end of the *Kiwa*. RZ 2:534.

8 Circumstances described in Ryōkan's extensive Chinese poem "On Reading

the Eihei Record" (*Eihei roku o yomu*), RZ 1:84–86. As Abe notes, Dōgen's writings were only made widely available with the 1815 woodblock edition of his lengthy masterwork *Shōbōgenzō* and till that time as a rule were restricted to qualified members of the Sōtō priesthood. GF, 267n111. *Eihei roku* may refer to Dōgen's short work *Eihei koroku* (see Abe, GF, 280n67) or, in the opinion of Tōgō, may be merely a figurative shorthand for Dōgen's *Shōbōgenzō*. RZ 1:87n1. Ishida Yoshisada observes that there exist many different manuscript copies of the poem, proof Ryōkan revisited it frequently and that it was important to him. Ishida also suggests various possibilities for *Eihei roku*'s identity. *Ryōkan no ayumi* (Tokyo: Bunkashobō hakubusha, 1984), 17–23. *Eihei koroku* is included in *Sōtōshū zensho* (Tokyo: Sōtōshū Zensho Kankokai, 1926–1936), 5:102–3, and was first published in 1673.

9 RZ 2:508–9. Banjō's account is translated in GF, 9–11. Scholars have debated the account's accuracy (see, for example, Tōgō, *Shinshū*, 82–87), but aside from some mistaken homophonic Chinese characters (*ateji*) in Ryōkan's name, it is generally accepted. Yoshino, for example, remarks that "it provides a two-day keyhole through which to view this obscure portion of Ryōkan's life." *Ryōkan*, 14. See also Abe, "Commemorating Ryōkan," GF, 82–83, and Ishida, *Zengo*, 134.

10 See the account by Tachibana Mochiyo in *Hoku'etsu kidan* [Curious tales of Echigo, 1811], RZ, 2:507–8. Tachibana's account is translated in GF, 12–13.

11 In 1810 the merchant house of Tachibana was defeated in a lawsuit that accused it of embezzling public funds. The family property was confiscated by the authorities and Yoshiyuki banished to the nearby ancestral village of Yoita. There he shaved his head and devoted himself to literary pursuits, retiring the following year and leaving family headship to his son. Kurita Isamu, "Ryōkan michi: Tōgō senshin ni makase," in *Geijutsu shinchō* 40, no. 2 (February 1989): 36. Ryōkan remained in close contact with Yoshikyuki, whom he clearly numbered among his friends. Ryōkan's brother was a scholar of Japanese literature and an amateur poet, and Yoshino cites a poem exchange between Yoshiyuki and Ryōkan, in which the latter describes a game of playing stones (*hajiki*) with some prostitutes. *Ryōkan*, 21–23; Tōgō, *Shinshū*, 18.

12 The present hut is a 1914 reconstruction, the mountain road now paved to accommodate busloads of arriving tourists.

13 Following the account in *Kitsu'en shiwa* (Stories of poems and poets told while smoking, 1816) by Ryōkan's friend Suzuki Bundai. RZ 2:489. See also

Abe's remarks in GF, 265n72. The current structure, in the village of Wakemi, is a Meiji-era reconstruction.

14 Perhaps the best known of Chan poetry collections, the Cold Mountain poems (*Hanshan shi*) is actually an assembly of works of three semilegendary eccentrics, Hanshan, Shide, and Fenggan, who reputedly lived at or in the vicinity of the Guoqing temple on Mount Tiantai at some point during the Tang dynasty. The earliest dated edition of the work is from the twelfth century. Hanshan and Shide, in particular, have remained popular as quintessential "Zen lunatics." Burton Watson notes the Hanshan poems' complaints of poverty, despair, and old age, themes shared by Ryōkan in his own Chinese poems, which also make frequent use of Hanshan's five-character-line format. *Cold Mountain Hanshan* (London: Columbia University Press, 1970), 9–12. For a translation of the Cold Mountain poems accompanied by their Chinese characters, see Red Pine (Bill Porter), *The Collected Songs of Cold Mountain* (Port Townsend, WA: Copper Canyon, 2000), and Robert G. Henricks, *The Poetry of Han-shan: A Complete Annotated Translation* (Albany: State University of New York Press, 1999).

15 There was renewed interest in the *Manyoshū* during the Edo period, one aspect of a revival of interest in classical Japanese literature by Kokugaku (National Studies) scholars like Kamo Mabuchi (1697–1769). Under Mabuchi's influence, there developed a group of so-called neo-Manyo poets, among whom Ryōkan is sometimes numbered. Nippon gakujutsu shinkōkai, *The Manyoshū: One Thousand Poems* (New York: Columbia University Press, 1965), xxiii–xxiv.

16 See Abe's remarks in "Commemorating Ryōkan," GF, 85–86. Ryōkan's notes are included in RZ, 2:410–37, 441–45.

17 Saitō Shūhei, *Niigata ken shi* (Niigata: Nojima Shuppan, 1986–88), 4:240ff.

18 *Shinshū*, 90–91.

19 The traditional Japanese children's ball, or *mari*, consists of tightly wound colored threads. Usually the object of the game is to see how many times the mari can be bounced, and special children's songs often accompany the count. *Onigokko*, a sort of combination tag and blindman's bluff, still popular with Japanese children.

20 A Japanese children's game in which players loop two blades of grass and pull to see which will snap the other.

21 *Kitsu'en shiwa*, RZ 2:489.

22 *Ryōkan zenji mokubatsu roku* [Zen Master Ryōkan's wooden bowl record, 1895], RZ 1:591.

23 *Kiwa*, RZ 2:522 and 534n1. Such a list has been preserved in the Suzuki family, descendants of Ryōkan's friend Bundai. Said to have been kept as a family heirloom after it fell from Ryōkan's wallet, the memo contains a list of the master's possessions, plus a reminder (*bibō*) to read the list so as not to leave anything behind. Among the items are foot and hand guards (*kōgake*)—part of a traveling outfit—playing stones (*ohajiki*) and balls for children's games, and a *kara*, a small, informal, square-shaped stole worn by Zen monks. Nakata Yūjiro, ed., *Ryōkan. Shodō geijutsu* 20 (Tokyo: Chuokoron-shinsha, 1982), 153, 224. According to local tradition, Ryōkan lost his pipe and tobacco box so often that someone attached it to the belt of his robe by a six-foot cord. A portrait of the aging Ryōkan by the doctor and painter Sugimoto Shunryō (n.d.) shows Ryōkan's pipe hanging by a string from his monk's staff, lending some credence to the story. Kojima Masaka, "Ningen Ryōkan o saguru roku no wa," *Geijutsu shinchō* 40, no. 2 (February 1989): 66.

24 Ōzeki Bunchū, *Ryōkan zenji den* [Biography of the Zen Master Ryōkan], RZ 1:594.

25 Ryōkan's letters are included in RZ 2:321–92. A selection is translated in GF, 223–29.

26 For a contemporaneous description of the market in Ryōkan fakes, see the 1830 letter of the master's friend and patron Kimura Motouemon in Matsumoto Ichijū, *No no Ryōkan* (Tokyo: Miraisha, 1988), 255n6. See also Abe's comments in "A Poetics of Mendicancy," GF, 24. Most surviving fakes are twentieth century. An exhibition of Ryōkan forgeries from Echigo was even mounted in 1951, with nine different "Ryōkans"—Ryōkan forgers—identified in the province. Komatsu Shigemi, "Ryōkan nisemane shi," *Geijutsu shinchō* 40, no. 2 (February 1989): 60–62. Ryōkan, as he himself attests in the *Kiwa*, was indifferent when it came to technical lapses in his brushwork. He frequently employs wrong or miswritten Chinese characters in his poems, along with omitting or even repeating characters, so that a sure sign of a Ryōkan fake is said to be a total absence of such errors—perhaps the only example of a celebrated calligrapher known for the quantity of his mistakes.

27 RZ 2:490–99. For further background on Teishin, see Yoshino, *Ryōkan*, 29–32.

28 Undated memo from Teishin to the priest Zōun (1813–1869), an early anthologist of Ryōkan's poetry. RZ 1:502. Ryōkan's remains are interred at the

Kimura family temple, Ryūsenji, affiliated with the True Pure Land (Jōdo shinshū) school of Buddhism and located in Shimazaki. Kitagawa, *Yugi*, 62.

29 Saitō Shūhei, *Niigata kenshi, Shiryō hen*, 24:459; Tōgō, *Shinshū*, 20–25.

30 Often as not, the imperial title was issued posthumously. Hakuin, for example, received the title Jinki Dokumyō zenji after his death; although Taigu Sōchiku was awarded the name Shosō Hisō zenji in 1664, during his lifetime.

31 Tōgō, *Shinshū*, 181.

32 See, for example, the official Sōtō lineage chart included in volume 3 of *Zengaku daijiten*, 28, where Ryōkan is the only Dharma heir shown for Kokusen. Nakamura Shūichi attributes this to Ryōkan's posthumous popularity and argues that while Ryōkan had received Kokusen's inka, or sanction of enlightenment, he did not necessarily receive Kokusen's formal Dharma transmission in his Sōtō lineage. *Ryōkan no ge to Shōbōgenzō* (Tokyo: Seishin Shobo, 1984), 7–8. Iriya, however, disagrees. *Shishū*, 35. The rank assigned to Ryōkan at his funeral was that of *shuso*. Though literally meaning "supervisor of the meditation hall," Kitagawa maintains that Sōtō practice since the Middle Ages was to use the term interchangeably with *zenji* for anyone who—unlike Ryōkan—receives it at either of the two great Sōtō headquarters temples, Eiheiji or Sojiji; similarly, the absence of the formal term *oshō*, "teacher," indicates in the Sōtō context that Ryōkan never became abbot of either Sōtō temple. Kitagawa Sōichi, *Ryōkan: Sono daigu no shōgai* (Tokyo: Shirakawa Shoin, 1980), 21–23.

33 *Kiwa*, RZ 2:531.

34 *Hokketen*, RZ 1:435–36; and *Hokkesan*, RZ 1:457–97.

35 T 9:50b–51c. See the related poems in Ryōkan's *Hokkesan*, RZ 1:452–53, 488. (The bodhisattva's name is sometimes also read Jofugyō in Japanese. Skt. Sadaparibhuta.)

36 *Ryōkan shishū* [Ryōkan's collected Chinese poems] (Tokyo: Kōdansha, 1982). Interestingly, as Watson observes, in Japan, where Ryōkan's beloved Hanshan has been revered as the paradigm of a carefree, enlightened Zen layman, modern scholars have similarly sought to "explain away" as symptoms of depression the Cold Mountain poems that deal with distress, loneliness, and doubt, an approach Watson rejects. *Hanshan*, 12.

37 The *Heart Sutra* (T 8:848c), couched as instruction from the Buddha to his disciple Subūthi, is perhaps the shortest of Buddhist sutras. It is often regarded as a crystallization of the Prajnaparamita (Perfection of Wisdom)

teaching of the identity of absolute and phenomenal realms of existence. There survives a handwritten copy of the sutra by Ryōkan. Tōgō, *Shinshū*, 113. *Awakening of Faith* [*in the Mahayana*] (*Qixin lun*, T 32:575a–583b), a scripture of uncertain origin, is among the key texts of Chinese Buddhism. Among its principal themes is the perfect interpenetration of samsara and nirvana, the absolute and phenomenal, in the ultimate reality of thusness, *tathata*. As such, it has been regarded by many as the basis of such Mahayana teachings as Zen, Huayan, and Esoteric Buddhism. The work is translated by Yoshito S. Hakeda as *The Awakening of Faith, Attributed to Asvagosha* (New York: Columbia University Press, 1967). Ryuichi Abe's introduction to the 2006 edition notes how the text "boldly posits as the ultimate reality the minds of sentient beings in their everyday existence. That is, 'Emptiness,' 'Buddha' . . . and all other Buddhist ideals *derive* from sentient beings ordinary state of mind" (17–18), a point stressed in Hakeda's translation and accompanying commentary (see, for example, 39–41).

38 The *Kiwa* is translated in GF, 94–106 (1996). Original text, RZ 2:522–34.

39 ROI, 65.

40 Nagaoka is a castle town in Echigo (Niigata Prefecture). It was ruled from 1618 to 1868 by daimyo of the Makino family. Ryōkan was a member of an Echigo merchant family whose business centered on the port town of Izumozaki, of which his father was headman.

41 Ryōkan's actual family name was Yamamoto, and his childhood name is given as both Eizō and Bunkō.

42 Probably at age seventeen, when Ryōkan abandoned his duties as his father's successor and became a novice at a local Zen temple. The details of Ryōkan's early life are often vague or, as here, often fanciful, but for a more factual account, see GF, 6–13.

43 *Sōsho*. A form of cursive calligraphy used to inscribe Chinese characters.

44 Reference is to *Analects* 6:24: Tsai said, "I take it that a good man, even if told that another good man were at the bottom of a well, would go to join him." "Why should you think so?" Confucius asked. "They say, 'A gentleman can be broken, but cannot be dented, may be deceived, but cannot be led astray.'" Arthur Waley, trans., *The Analects of Confucius* (New York: Vintage, 1938), 121. For the Chinese text, see http//:dsturgeon.net, *Analects* 6, no. 26.

45 An Edo Confucian and a renowned calligrapher of his day, Bōsai (1752–1826)

is said to have traveled to Echigo in 1809. For Ryōkan's influence on Bōsai's calligraphy, see GF, 77.

46 In fact, Ryōkan died in 1831, the era's second year, at age seventy-three.

47 Carrying such funeral money was not unusual for monks in premodern Japan, but here the unstated humor seems to derive from the fact that Ryōkan was known by his friends to be perpetually broke.

48 Noto-ya was the shop name of Kimura's establishment.

49 An important port in what is now Okayama Prefecture. It was the site of Entsūji, the Sōtō Zen temple where Ryōkan trained under his teacher Tainin Kokusen from 1789 till on or around Kokusen's death.

50 The remaining accounts concerning Ryōkan are all oral traditions (*kuden*), assembled by Nōnin Kōdō. Some clearly contradict one another, but taken together they present a colorful spectrum of local beliefs surrounding the eccentric Zen master and poet.

51 *Hiru andon.* An expression used in China and Japan to signify a fool, a simpleton, or something utterly useless, like a lantern in the daytime.

52 Festival of the Dead, or Lantern Festival, generally celebrated from July 13 to July 15 when the spirits of the dead are said to return to their former abodes. Bon is traditionally associated with various dances and songs.

53 The Confucian *Analects* were a staple of childhood education in early modern Japan, with students generally trained to memorize and write out portions of the text.

54 Important shogunal officials, daimyo, and other persons of distinction in Edo-period Japan customarily traveled seated in a *kago*, a kind of closed palanquin with a pair of extended handles at the front and back, which allowed it to be carried by specially designated porters.

55 *Albizzia julibrissin.* A deciduous tree with crimson flowers. Its leaves close and droop in the evening.

56 Mount Koya is in Wakayama Prefecture. The principal monastery and temple complex of the Shingon, or Esoteric, school, founded by Kūkai (774–835), Koya lies some sixty miles south of Kyoto. Ise Shrine is an important Shinto shrine complex dedicated to the sun goddess, Amaterasu. It is located in what is now Mie Prefecture. It was a popular pilgrimage site during the Tokugawa period.

57 Teradomari is a port city facing the Sea of Japan; it lies in present-day Niigata Prefecture. Also in Niigata, Gōmoto is a coastal town lying not far from Ryōkan's native Izumozaki.

58 Saigyō (1118–1190), a former Shingon priest and wandering poet, was a renowned Japanese poet of the Middle Ages. Kisen was a ninth-century Japanese poet-recluse.

59 Ikkyū Sōjun, noted previously. The only medieval Zen master famous for his erotic poetry, Ikkyū is remembered for his flagrant disregard of convention as well as his literary skill.

60 That is, the world of rebirth, after death, when a person will incarnate in one of various realms in accordance with the karma accrued in their lifetime. Ryōkan's waka quoted here are included in RZ 2:101, nos. 598–599.

61 Translation of the final line is tentative. The significance of the adverbial phrase *ukara-ukara to* is unclear and does not appear in any of the dictionaries I have consulted. Taking this as a possible transcription error, I have read it as *unkare*—a stem of *unkareru*, "to make merry, or frolic."

62 Miso, or soybean paste, a staple of Japanese cooking. Although more commonly produced in factories today, in the countryside in Ryōkan's period, farmers would often prepare their own miso by soaking and boiling soybeans till they could be processed into a paste that was then mixed with salt and wheat or rice malt. The pounding and grinding process can be messy and smelly, and the humor of the anecdote lies in Ryōkan's nonchalant use of the same bowl to then wash his face and hands.

63 A town northeast of Ryōkan's native Izumozaki, lying inland near the Seba River.

64 Apparently a beach hut used to produce salt—a valuable commodity in premodern Japan—by boiling salt water.

65 The following story, according to oral tradition, describes the period when Ryōkan was a training monk at Entsūji under Tainin Kokusen. The story appears in Soma Gyōfu's *Taigu Ryōkan* (1918). An accompanying note states, "This story is a legend passed on and still current at Entsūji. It was related to me by the temple's present abbot Ishikawa Kaizen (n.d.)." ROI, 96, 98. In premodern Japan, the local officials, *mura yakunin*, were village-level representatives of the shogunal government.

66 The verse's humor depends largely on a pun: Rosewood (*Cassia siamea*; J. *tagayasan*) is a rare wood imported from South Asia, and Ryōkan contrasts

Chūmin's connoisseurship with the doctor's reportedly neglectful attitude toward his medical practice. It is to the latter, Ryōkan says, that Chūmin should be "applying himself"—in Japanese also read *tagayasan*, a form of the verb *tagayasu*, literally "to plow, till, work the soil," and here, by extension, keep one's nose to the grindstone. The verse is included in RZ 2:106; see also, for comparison, poem 1381 in RZ 2:276.

67 *Kusha ron*, Skt. *Abhidharma-kosa-bhyasya* [Discourse on the repository of Abidharma discussions], T 29, no. 1558, is a celebrated treatise on Buddhist doctrine. Man'inji is a True Pure Land temple in Izumozaki.

68 As indicated in Bundai's account, Ryōkan's calligraphy was highly valued, and already during the master's lifetime, fakes had begun to appear on the market (see GF, 261n6). Ryōkan himself tended to resist requests for samples of his distinctive brushwork but was always anxious to please the local children, and a common ruse was for a collector to use a child as a pretext to obtain pieces of the master's calligraphy. The episode described here by Bundai may well be such an instance, according to Tōgō Toyoharu. See *Shinshū Ryōkan*, 295. A close-up photo of the piece of calligraphy, among Ryōkan's most famous, forms the cover art of GF.

69 N.d. Ryōkan was actually born in Izumozaki, a neighboring port town to Amaze.

70 Kōshōji was the first Sōtō school Zen temple, founded by Dōgen Kigen in 1233 at Uji, a town south of Kyoto but within the present-day Kyoto municipal district.

71 That is, *renga*, a Japanese form of linked verse based on waka, in which poets meet to link verses in often long sequences. It was highly popular in literary society during the Edo period.

72 Various versions of the story exist. In the *Kiwa*, for example, Ryōkan deliberately allows the thief to slip his quilt out from under him (RZ 2:530; GF, 104), while elsewhere, as we have seen, the master compliantly hands over his robe.

73 *Hachi no ko*. The iron bowl carried by Buddhist monks on their begging rounds. At times Ryōkan substituted a wooden bowl. Several waka on the subject by Ryōkan survive, among them: "I left behind my begging bowl / but no one would take it / My pitiful begging bowl!" ROI, 108; RZ 2:10. See also GF, 111–17.

74 Yamada Tokō (1775–1844), Ryōkan's friend and cousin. He was a haiku poet and sake brewer resident in Yoita.

75 Makiri is unidentified. Niigata is an important city facing the island of Sado, some thirty miles up the coast from Ryōkan's native town of Izumozaki. It is now the capital of Niigata Prefecture.

76 Ugan (d. 1808) was a close friend of Ryōkan's who became a monk as a young man and apparently returned later to lay life, as indicated by Ryōkan's Chinese poem (kanshi) "Visiting the Layman Ugan." RZ 1:383–84; GF, 179, 282n85. Tsubame is now a city in Ryōkan's area of Niigata Prefecture.

77 The Kano school of painting was one of the leading schools of painting in early modern Japan. Its roots go back to the fifteenth century, and it has continued into modern times.

78 Hizen is an old province in Japan's south, now Nagasaki Prefecture, and thus a considerable distance from the snow country of Ryōkan's native Echigo.

79 See RZ 2, no. 1238, 195. Several similar waka are included in RZ. See RZ 2, nos. 1238–1240, 195.

80 Around three hundred yards. A chō is an old unit of measurement, one chō equivalent to sixty ken, or "intervals," a ken measuring about six feet.

BIBLIOGRAPHY

Abe Ryūichi and Peter Haskel. *Great Fool: Zen Master Ryōkan*. Honolulu: University of Hawaii Press, 2001.

Adamek, Wendi. "The Lidai fabaoji [Record of the Jewel through the Ages]." In *The Zen Canon: Understanding the Classic Texts*, ed. Steven Heine and Dale S. Wright, 81–106. New York: Oxford University Press, 2004.

Akamatsu Shinmei. *Ōbakushū kōyō*. Tokyo: Bukkyō Nenkansha, 1934.

Akao Ryūji. *Bankei zenji zenshū*. Tokyo: Daizōshuppan, 1970.

Amakuki Setsu'nan. *Myōshinji roppyakunenshi*. Tokyo: Daihōekyoku, 1930.

App, Urs. *Master Yunmen*. New York: Kodansha International, 1994.

Atsuo Masamune, ed. *Banzan zenshū*. 6 vols. Tokyo: Meicho Shuppan, 1940.

Baroni, Helen. *Ōbaku Zen*. Honolulu: Univeristy of Hawaii Press, 2000.

Bowers, Faubian. *Japanese Theater*. New York: Hermitage House, 1952.

Braverman, Arthur. *Warrior of Zen*. New York: Kodansha International, 1994.

Broughton, Jeffrey R. *The Chan Whip Anthology*. New York: Oxford University Press, 2015.

———. *The Record of Linji: A New Translation of the Linjilu in the Light of Ten Japanese Commentaries*. New York: Oxford University Press, 2012.

———. *Zongmi on Chan*. New York: Columbia University Press, 2009.

Brown, David Douglas. "From Tempo to Meiji: Fukuoka Han in Late Tokugawa Japan." PhD diss., University of Hawaii at Manoa, 1981.

Buswell, Robert E., Jr. "The Short-Cut Approach of K'an-hua Meditation: The Evolution of a Practical Subitism in Chinese Ch'an Buddhism." In *Sudden and Gradual Approaches to Enlightenment in Chinese Thought*, edited by Peter N. Gregory, 321–77. Honolulu: University of Hawaii Press, 1987.

Cuellar, Eduardo. "Tokugawa Zen Master Shidō Mu'nan." Master's thesis, University of Arizona, 2016.

Dumoulin, Heinrich. *Zen Buddhism: A History.* 2 vols. New York: Macmillan Publishing, 1990.

Fontein, Jan, and Money Hickman. *Zen Painting and Calligraphy.* Boston: Museum of Fine Arts, 1970. Exhibition catalog.

Foulk, T. Griffith. "Form and Function in Koan Literature." In *The Koan,* ed. Steven Heine and Dale S. Wright, 15–45. New York: Oxford University Press, 2000.

Friday, Karl F. "Off the Warpath: Military Science and Budō in the Evolution of Ryūha Bugei." In *Budō Perspectives,* ed. Alexander Bennet, 249–68. Auckland: Kendo World Publications, 2005.

Fujimoto Tsuchishige. *Bankei kokushi no kenkyū.* Tokyo: Shunjūsha, 1987.

Fujita Takushi. "Shi ni tomonai: Sengai Gibon." *Zen bunka,* no. 224 (2012): 46–56.

Fukuoka shi, ed. *Shōfukuji shi.* Fukuoka: Shōfukuji Bunko Kankōkai, 1964.

Furuta Shōkin. *Gudō, Mu'nan, Shōju.* Tokyo: Kōdansha, 1944.

———. *Sengai.* Sydney: Trustees Art Gallery of New South Wales, 1985.

———. *Sengai: Master Zen Painter.* Tokyo: Kōdansha, 2000.

———. "Shidō Mu'nan no anshū zen." *Zen bunka* 77 (June 1975): 58–64.

Gernet, Jacques. *A History of Chinese Civilization.* Cambridge: Cambridge University Press, 1982.

Goto Mitsumura, ed. *Hakuin oshō zenshū.* Tokyo: Tokyo Ryūginsha, 1967.

Hakeda, Yoshito S. *The Awakening of Faith, Attributed to Asvagosha.* New York: Columbia University Press, 1967, 2006.

Hanazono Daigaku Hakubutsukan. *Hakuin zenji nihyaku gojunen onkinen.* Kyoto: Hanazono Daigaku Rekishi Hakubutsukan, 2017. Exhibition catalog.

Haskel, Peter. "Bankei and His World." PhD diss., Columbia University, New York, 1988.

———. *Bankei Zen.* Edited by Yoshito Hakeda. New York: Grove Atlantic, 1984.

———. *Letting Go: The Story of Zen Master Tōsui.* Honolulu: University of Hawaii Press, 2001.

———. *Sword of Zen.* Honolulu: University of Hawaii Press, 2013.

Hori, Victor. *Zen Sand*. Honolulu: University of Hawaii Press, 2003.

Hōseki Genjō. "Shidō Mu'nan." *Zen bunka* 77 (June 1975): 48–53.

Hunter, Jeffrey et al. *Snow Country Tales*. New York: Weatherhill, 1986.

Imaeda Aishin. *Zenshū no rekishi*. Tokyo: Shibundō, 1966.

Inagaki Hisao. *Glossary of Zen Terms*. Kyoto: Nagata Bunshōdō, 1991.

Iriya Yoshitaka. *Baso no goroku*. Kyoto: Zen Bunka Kenkyōjo, 1984.

———. *Ryōkan shishū*. Tokyo: Kōdansha, 1982.

Ishida Yoshisada. *Ryōkan no ayumi*. Tokyo: Bunkashobō Hakunbusha, 1983.

———. *Ryōkan: Sono zengo to genzo*. Tokyo: Bunkashobō Hakunbusha, 1975.

Ishii Shūdō. "Kung-an Ch'an and the Tsung-men t'ung-yao chi." Translated by Albert Welter. In *The Koan*, ed. Steven Heine and Dale S. Wright, 110–36. New York: Oxford University Press, 2000.

Itō Kazuo. "Hakuyūshi no hito to shi." *Zen bunka*, no. 6 (November 1956): 48–68.

———. *Hakuyūshi: Shijitsu no shintankyū*. Kyoto: Yamaguchi Shoten, 1960.

Itō Kokan. "Gudō." *Zen bunka*, nos. 15–16 (April 1959): 98–107.

———. "Gudō kokushi no zen." *Zengaku kenkyū*, no. 49 (February 1959): 1–22.

Jansen, Marius B. *The Making of Modern Japan*. Cambridge, MA: Harvard University Press, 2000.

Kamata Shigeo. *Chūgoku no zen*. Tokyo: Kōdansha, 1980.

Katō Shōshun, ed. *Hakuin oshō nenpu*. Kyoto: Shibunkaku, 1985.

Kawakami Kōzan. *Myōshinji shi*. 2 vols. Kyoto: Myōshinjiha Kyōmu Honjo, 1917.

———. *Zōho Myōshinji shi*. Kyoto: Shibunkaku, 1975.

Kimura Seiyū. "Ungo Kiyō: Sono daigo to nenbutsu zen." *Zen bunka*, no. 70 (September 1973): 112–17.

Kirchner, Thomas Y. *Entangling Vines: Zen Koans of the Shūmon kattōshū*. Kyoto: Tenryu-ji Institute for Philosophy and Religion, 2004.

Kitagawa Seiichi. *Ryōkan: Sono daigu no shōgai*. Tokyo: Shirakawa Shoin, 1980.

———. *Teihon Ryōkan yugi*. Tokyo: Shirakawa Shoin, 1983.

Kobori Sōhaku and Norman Waddell. "Sokushinki." *Eastern Buddhist* 3, no. 2 (October 1970): 89–118.

———. "Sokushinki." *Eastern Buddhist* 4, no. 1 (May 1971): 116–23.

Koda Rentarō, ed. *Shidō Mu'nan zenji shū*. Tokyo: Shunjūsha, 1956.

Kojima Masaka. "Ningen Ryōkan o saguru roku no wa." *Geijutsu shinchō* 40, no. 2 (February 89): 64–69.

Komatsu Shigemi. "Ryōkan nisemane shi." *Geijutsu shinchō* 40, no. 2 (February 1989): 57–62.

Kurita Isamu. "Ryōkan michi: Tōgō senshin ni makase." *Geijutsu shinchō* 40, no. 2 (February 1989): 19–24.

Machida Zuihō. "Hakuin monka jōsei zenga no shōsoku." *Zen bunka*, no. 103 (January 1982): 77–89.

Mangen Shipan. *Honchō kosōden*. (See DNBZ, v. 63.)

Matsukura Zentei. "Taigu Sōchiku zenji no gyōjō." *Zengaku kenkyū* 52 (1963): 40–82.

Matsumoto Ichijū. *No no Ryōkan*. Tokyo: Miraisha, 1988.

McRae, John R. *Seeing through Zen: Encounter, Transformation, and Geneology in Chinese Chan Buddhism*. Berkeley: University of California Press, 2003.

Miya Fuyuji, ed. *Ryōkan no sekai*. Tokyo: Bunka shobō hakubunsha, 1985.

Miyake Shukudō. *Hakata to Sengai*. Tokyo: Bunken Shuppan, 1978.

———. *Sengai goroku*. Tokyo: Bunken Shuppan, 1979.

Mohr, Michel. "Hakuin." In *Buddhist Spirituality*, ed. Takeuchi Yoshinori, 307–28. New York: Crossroad, 1999.

———. "Sengai's Multifaceted Legacy." In *Zen Master Sengai*, ed. Katharina Eppreck, 16–25. Zurich: Scheidegger and Spiess, 2014.

Mujaku Dōchū. *Shōbōzanshi*. Kyoto: Shibunkaku, 1975.

Nakamura Hajime, ed. *Bukkyō daijiten*. 3 vols. Tokyo: Tokyo Shoseki, 1976.

———. et al. *Ajia Bukkyōshi: Nihon ben*. Tokyo: Tokyo Shoseki, 1972.

Nakamura Sōichi. *Ryōkan no ge to Shōbōgenzō*. Tokyo: Seishin Shobō, 1984.

Nakane Chie. *Tokugawa Japan: The Social and Economic Antecedents of Modern Japan*. Tokyo: Univeristy of Tokyo Press, 1990.

Nakata Yūjiro, ed. *Ryōkan. Shodō geijutsu* 20. Tokyo: Chuokoron-shinsha, 1982.

Nakayama Kiichiro. *Sengai: Sono shōgai to geijutsu.* Fukuoka: Fukuoka shi Bijut-sukan Kyōkai, 1992.

Nippon gakujutsu shinkōkai. *The Manyoshū: One Thousand Poems.* New York: Columbia University Press, 1965.

Nishimura Eishin and Satō Giei. *Unsui.* Honolulu: University of Hawaii Press, 1973.

Nōnin Keidō. "Edo zenki no daizensho." Pts. 1–4. *Zen bunka,* no. 225 (2012): 25–28; no. 226 (2012): 132–37; no. 229 (2013): 136–41; no. 230 (2013): 70–72.

———. *Hakuin monka itsuwasen.* Kyoto: Zen Bunka Kenkyūjo, 2000.

———. *Ryōkan oshō itsuwasen.* Kyoto: Zen Bunka Kenkyūjo, 1999

———. *Sengai oshō itsuwasen.* Kyoto: Zen Bunka Kenkyūjo, 1999.

———. *Taigu oshō goroku, shūi, gyōjitsu.* Kyoto: Zen Bunka Kenkyūjo, 2012.

———. *Ungo oshō goroku.* Matsushima: Zuigonji, 2009.

Ogisu Jundō. "Ingen zenji no Ōbaku zen." *Zen bunka* 18 (June 1960): 9–21.

———. *Kinsei zenrin sōbōden.* Edited by Ogisu Jundō. 3 vols. Tokyo: Shibunkaku, 1973.

———. *Shōbōzan rokusoden kunchū.* Kyoto: Shibunkaku, 1979.

Okayama Sōtōshū seinenkai, ed. *Ryōkan no shi: Tainin Kokusen zenji den.* Kurashiki: Okayama-ken Sōtōshū Seinenkai, 1982.

Ōmori Sōgen. "Shidō Mu'nan no zen." *Zen bunka* 77 (June 1975): 38–45.

Pedersen, Priscilla. "Jishōki." *Eastern Buddhist,* n.s., 8, no. 1 (May 1975): 96–132.

Poceski, Mario. *The Records of Mazu and the Making of Classical Chan Literature.* New York: Oxford University Press, 2015.

Red Pine [Bill Porter]. *The Collected Songs of Cold Mountain.* Port Townsend, WA: Copper Canyon Press, 2000.

———. *The Platform Sutra.* Berkeley: Counterpoint, 2006.

Rikugawa Taiun. *Kōshō Hakuin oshō shōden.* Tokyo: Sankibō Busshorin, 1963.

Saitō Shūhei. *Niigata-ken shi.* 5 vols. Niigata: Nojima Shuppan, 1961–1964.

Sasaki, Ruth F., and Thomas Y. Kirchner. *The Record of Linji.* Honolulu: University of Hawaii Press, 2009.

Sasaki Shigetsu [Sokei-an]. *Original Nature: Zen Comments on the Sixth Patriarch's Platform Sutra.* Bloomington, IN: iUniverse, 2010.

Sasao Tetsuō. *Kinsei ni okeru Myōshinji kyōdan no kenkyū.* Akita: Daihi Zenji, 1977.

Schlutter, Morten. *How Zen Became Zen.* Honolulu: University of Hawaii Press, 2008.

Seo, Audrey, and Stephan Addiss. *The Sound of One Hand: Paintings and Calligraphy of Zen Master Hakuin.* Boulder: Shambhala Publications, 2010.

Shinano kyōkai, ed. *Shōju rojinshū.* Tokyo: Shigensha, 1975 (originally published in 1937).

Shōfukuji Bunko Kankōkai. *Sengai oshō.* Fukuoka: Shōfukuji Bunko Kankōkai, 1963.

Shore, Jeff. "Great Doubt." Unpublished article. Kyoto, 2010.

Suzuki Daisetsu, ed. *Bankei zenji goroku.* Tokyo: Iwanami Shoten, 1942.

———. *Sengai, the Zen Master.* Greenwich, CT: New York Graphic Society, 1971.

———. *Zen shisōshi kenkyū.* Vol. 1. Tokyo: Iwanami Shoten, 1969.

Suzuki Gakujutsu Zaidan, ed. *Dai Nihon Bukkyō zensho.* 94 vols. Tokyo: Kōdansha Hatsubai, 1970–73.

Suzuki Masaya. *Katana to kubitori: Sengoku kassen issetsu.* Tokyo: Heibonsha, 2000.

Suzuki Taizan. *Zenshū no chihō hatten.* Tokyo: Yoshikawa Kōbunkan, 1942.

Suzuki Tesshin, ed. *Suzuki Shōsan dōnin zenshū.* Tokyo: Sankibō Busshorin, 1962.

Takakusu Junjirō et al., eds. *Taishō shinshū daizōkyō.* 100 vols. Tokyo: Taisho shinshu daizokyo kanko kai, 1924–34.

Takuan Oshō zenshū kankokai, ed. *Takuan oshō zenshū.* 6 vols. Tokyo: Kōgeisha, 1928–30.

Tamamura Takeji. "Go Nara Tennō to Myōshinji." *Nihon zenshūshi.* 3 vols. Kyoto: Daizō Shuppan, 1976–1981. Vol. 1:317–31.

Tanigawa Toshirō. *Ryōkan no shōgai to itsuwa.* Tokyo: Kōbunsha, 1984.

Tōgō Toyoharu, ed. *Ryōkan zenshū.* 2 vols. Tokyo: Tokyo Sōgensha, 1959.

———. *Shinshū Ryōkan.* Tokyo: Tokyo Sōgensha, 1970.

Tsuji Zennosuke. *Nihon Bukkyōshi,* 7th ed. Tokyo: Iwanami Shoten, 1992.

Tyler, Royall. *Selected Writings of Suzuki Shōsan.* Cornell East Asian Papers. Ithaca, NY: China-Japan Program, Cornell University, 1977.

——. "Suzuki Shōsan: A Fighting Man of Zen." PhD diss., Columbia University, New York, 1972.

Ueda Makoto. *Matsuo Bashō*. New York: Twayne, 1970.

Ui Hakuju, ed. *Bukkyō jiten*. Tokyo: Daitō shuppansha, 1978.

Uratsuji Kendō. *Hakata Sengai*. Fukuoka: Nishi Nihon Shinbunsha, 1990.

Waddell, Norman. *Essential Teachings of the Zen Master Hakuin: A Translation of the Kaien Fusetsu*. Boulder: Shambhala Publications, 1994.

——. *Hakuin's Precious Mirror Cave*. Berkeley: Counterpoint, 2009.

——. *The Unborn: The Life and Teaching of the Zen Master Bankei*. San Francisco: North Point, 1984.

——. *Wild Ivy*. Boulder: Shambhala Publications, 1999.

Watanabe Shūei, ed. *Ryōkan shugyō to Tamashima*. Niigata: Niigata kōkodō shoten, 1975.

Watson, Burton. *Cold Mountain Hanshan*. London: Columbia University Press, 1970.

Welter, Albert. *The Linji lu and the Creation of Chan Orthodoxy*. New York: Oxford University Press, 2008.

——. "Mahakashyapa's Smile: Silent Transmission and the Kung-an (Koan) Tradition." In *The Koan*, ed. Steven Heine and Dale S. Wright, 75–109. New York: Oxford University Press, 2000.

——. *Monks, Rulers, and Literati: The Political Ascendancy of Chan Buddhism*. New York: Oxford University Press, 2006.

Yampolsky, Phillip B. *The Platform Sutra of the Sixth Patriarch*. New York: Columbia University Press, 1967.

——. *The Zen Master Hakuin*. New York: Columbia University Press, 1972.

Yanagida Seizan. *Rinzai roku*. Tokyo: Daizō Shuppansha, 1973.

Yoshino Hideo. *Ryōkan: Uta to shōgai*. Tokyo: Chikumashobō, 1975.

Yoshizawa Katsuhiro, ed. *Hakuin zenji hōgo zenshū*. 15 vols. Kyoto: Zen Bunka kenkyūjo, 1999–2003.

Yoshizawa Katsuhiro, with Norman Waddell. *The Religious Art of the Zen Master Hakuin*. Berkeley: Counterpoint, 2009.

Zengaku Daijiten Hensanjo, ed. *Zengaku daijiten*. 3 vols. Tokyo: Taishūkan Shoten, 1978.

INDEX

Praise for *The Parrot and the Igloo*

"David Lipsky spins top-flight climate literature into cliffhanger entertainment . . . Lipsky's book is a project of maximum ambition. He retells the entire climate story, from the dawn of electricity to the dire straits of our present day [and] makes it page turning and appropriately infuriating. He says it up front: He wants this to be like a Netflix series, bingeable. . . . *The Parrot* is a thriller of deceptions, side deals and close calls. . . . What are the magic words? We have the facts and the wildfires to prove them. But climate communication—how to make those facts penetrate hearts and minds—seems always a losing battle. The denialists have always had sexier language, and they pay handsomely for it. Lipsky, with his cinematic account, has a good chance to grab back some of that ground."

—Zoë Schlager, *New York Times Book Review*

"One of the best books I've read in a decade. . . . This is an extraordinary work. . . . The book is so important, I want so many people to read it. Not just because it's important, but because it's so damned entertaining. Because this book is written with love. With love for the reader, with love for humanity, with a huge understanding gaze, a huge nod to the fact that we are in this together. . . . I promise you this book is worth it. David Lipsky has delivered on the promise of his brilliance in this book."—Brian Koppelman, *Moment*

"Lipsky, award-winning author of books about West Point and a road trip with David Foster Wallace, brings his wide-angle lens to bear on global warming in *The Parrot and the Igloo*. It's about not just the science of climate change but also the self-interested deniers constantly working to undermine it—'more research is needed' is a central strategy—and inflicting long-term damage in the process. Lipsky strives to make the book as readable as possible [and] his deep research and outrage continually shine through."

—Stuart Miller, *Los Angeles Times*

"David Lipsky's topic in *The Parrot and the Igloo*—his preoccupation, his obsession—is climate change. On page after page, in chapter after chapter, he sets out how the warming world came to know, and actually has known for decades, that the planet is on fire, that the implications are dire, that the timetable to fight climate change is finite. . . . An excellent, approachable primer on the science of global warming [and] a dizzying account of how long we have known so much about an issue that means so much."

—David Shribman, *Boston Globe*

"There may be no such thing as a definitive look at the climate crisis, but Lipsky tries to cover what 'a reasonably well-informed person might have been expected to know.' . . . Lipsky masterfully recounts it with tempered outrage and a winking, wry wit."
—Eric Roston, *Bloomberg News*

"The best nonfiction book I've read in decades. And the best book of its kind I've ever read."
—Darin Strauss, National Book Critics Circle Award–winning author of *Half a Life*

"A comprehensive history of climate denialism."
—ABC News

"This is not a book lacking in ambition. Lipsky wants to tell the whole, sprawling, messy tale of climate change: how modern technology made it all happen, how scientists figured it out, and how a network of hustlers and hucksters distracted the public from the threat before our eyes. In the end he pulls it off, delivering a propulsive read that has the snap of a screenplay. Lipsky's a major talent. . . . It's the velvety texture of well-tailored prose that makes this book a climate must-read. . . . Lipsky marries a novelist's stylishness to a journalist's rigor to create a cinematic refashioning of the climate change story. . . . My only quibble with this fantastic book [is] that it ends too soon."
—Jason Mark, *Sierra*

"Essential. . . . A history of how we got from there to here."
—*Rolling Stone*

"[A] history of the idea that human actions are warming the world to cataclysmic effect. . . . The awareness of human-induced warming dawns in 1896 and resurfaces periodically throughout the twentieth century—in 1956, the *Times* imagined an Arctic so hot that it was home to tropical birds, a landscape that gives Lipsky's book its title. . . . A consensus finally arrives with the release of the fourth I.P.C.C. assessment, in 2007, but this triumph becomes an anticlimax when governments prove unwilling to regulate fossil fuels."
—*The New Yorker*

"An important book that will leave your head shaking."
—*Kirkus Reviews*, starred review

"It is a book that should be read by just about everyone. . . . Sure, many of us have been angry about the collective failure to act on the facts of climate change for years, even for decades, but in *The Parrot and the Igloo* Lipsky lays bare the inner workings of the long-running countercurrent to common sense. Here a talented writer has painstakingly brought together facts, timelines, and personalities to portray a greater whole. And he has done so in a way that can only leave readers seething, wrathful, and ready for action." —Bill Streever, *E—The Environmental Magazine*

"Humor accompanies horrific truths in this vital look at the rise of climate change denial. With dry wit and novelistic flair, National Magazine Award winner Lipsky chronicles how harnessing electricity changed the world. . . . [R]evelatory. . . . [S]obering and incisive. Buoyed by thorough historical research, this is a first-rate entry." —*Publishers Weekly*, starred review

"It can be hard, sometimes, to keep in mind the distinction between weather—what's it doing outside today?—and climate: What do statistical models suggest it's likely to be doing decades from now? That confusion plays into the hands of oil companies and others who have long used pleasant days (weather) to downplay the threat of global warming (climate), as if a diseased patient can't feel perfectly good some of the time. So David Lipsky's new book, *The Parrot and the Igloo*, is a useful corrective; all the more so since Lipsky is a journalist rather than a climate scientist, whose aim is to gather the known facts about climate change and denialism into a compelling narrative that's easy to grasp." —Gregory Cowles, *New York Times*

"David Lipsky tells the story of how climate-change denial went mainstream. . . . Lipsky makes thinking about the planet's impending doom not just palatable but entertaining." —Jensen Davis, *Air Mail*

"Award-winning author Lipsky takes the reader on a journey through the evolution of climate change denial. . . . [T]his can be considered the historical record to date." —*Booklist*

"I've got to thank bestselling author David Lipsky for pulling off a nifty trick in his latest book—making me laugh while reading about the potential end of human life on this planet. . . . *The Parrot and the Igloo* gives readers the confidence that we can get through this treatise on such a somber subject as climate change. . . . [T]here's so much more to this book than a focus on the hideous history of climate-change denialism and the vile people who still traffic in it today. . . . Lipsky connects all the dashes and dots [and] makes it easier to understand. . . . [A]s fascinating as the destination of denialism is, the author's stops along the way are equally enthralling." —Christopher Lancette, *Washington Independent Review of Books*

"Enticing and eminently readable. . . . An offbeat history of climate science and politics." —Michael Svoboda, *Yale Climate Connections*

"A National Magazine Award-winning, *New York Times* best-selling author, Lipsky explains how antiscience sentiment became so strong in the United States by focusing on climate change denial. He lays bare the science of climate change, understood decades ago, then shows how fake news about products like aspirin created the tools for denier ideas to take hold." —*Library Journal*

"Well-researched and captivatingly written, it's a must-read." —Sandy Dominy, *Prime Women*

"Lipsky offers a history of climate science—and with it, climate denial—starring a large cast of swindlers, zealots, politicians and hucksters to get to the heart of virulent anti-science ideologies in America." —Barbara VanDenburgh, *USA Today*

"[An] unflinching look at this vital topic. . . . It's a whirlwind tour, and Lipsky pulls it off. . . . The beauty of this book is that it could expose a new audience to the crimes committed in the name of continued profit; so many climate books are preaching to the choir." —John Schwartz, *Undark*

"Deep and detailed. . . . Lipsky's energetic, often irreverent narrative makes it all intensely readable, although infuriating. . . . *The Parrot and the Igloo* arrives in a world on fire and perhaps, just perhaps, finally waking up to its peril." —Steve Donoghue, *Open Letters Review*

"What is the lure of anti-science rhetoric and climate change denial? That's the question at the heart of David Lipsky's *The Parrot and the Igloo*. . . . Lipsky profiles not only the experts who sounded the alarm on the climate crisis but also those who lied about the science and misled the public. The book explores themes of ecological disinformation and greed through the stories of an incredible cast of characters." —*Toronto Life*

"Climate change and climate denial . . . have shared the stage in a gripping tragicomic drama for nearly four decades. In *The Parrot and the Igloo* David Lipsky brings that drama irresistibly to life in a narrative guaranteed to have readers alternately laughing at the headlong rush of human stupidity and cupidity and screaming helplessly

into the void. . . . Lipsky's dizzying no-brakes account of the progression to climate consensus—and of the dogged deniers-for-hire who have attacked it with relentless, reckless abandon—proves engaging and enraging in equal measure. . . . Ingeniou[s] and hilariou[s]."
　　　　　　　　　　　　　　　　　—Steve Nathans-Kelly, *New York Journal of Books*

"A story of facts versus falsehoods and the climate-change deniers who have benefitted from both the hired guns and playbook of Big Tobacco. These are the folks who still pit themselves against the scientists who reveal the unyielding truths of melting glaciers, warming temperatures, and catastrophic weather events, including wildfires. In a painstakingly researched yet witty text, Lipsky bags the culprits." 　—*AudioFile*

"Riveting."
　　　　　　　　　　　　　　　　　—Alessandra Stanley, *Air Mail*

"David Lipsky's *The Parrot and the Igloo* is so playful and sharp—one of my favorites of the year."
　　　　　　　　　　　　　　　　　—Jeva Lange, *Heatmap*

"A huge accomplishment."
　　　　　　　　　　　　　　　　　—Matt Bucher, *Concavity Show*

"Where can a person living on a melting planet turn—at least before the spaceship fleet is ready—for enlightenment? I'd start, and finish, with David Lipsky's brilliant epic *The Parrot and the Igloo,* which I devoured in a single, feverish, page-turning sitting, a perspective-altering dream, a story told in language as sharp and clear as the spring air we knew before all the carbon was released. . . . You will stare out the same windows when you've finished, but nothing will look the same."
—Rich Cohen, *New York Times* best-selling author of *Sweet and Low* and *Monsters*

"Exposing climate science deniers took its toll on Lipsky. . . . 'There's something about reading people who are lying that makes you suspicious and argumentative company.' You'll have a similar reaction reading Lipsky's book. In selling their souls for fame and fortune, deniers have sowed doubt, eroded trust in science and cost us time we don't have in the fight to keep our only home from baking, burning and flooding."
　　　　　　　　　　　　　　　　　—Jay Robb, *Hamilton Spectator*

ALSO BY DAVID LIPSKY

Although Of Course You End Up Becoming Yourself

Absolutely American

The Art Fair

Three Thousand Dollars